MAX NUSSBAUM:
FROM BERLIN TO HOLLYWOOD

*

A Mid-Century Vision
of Jewish Life

Rabbi Max Nussbaum in his study

MAX NUSSBAUM: FROM BERLIN TO HOLLYWOOD

*

A Mid-Century Vision of Jewish Life

EDITED BY LEWIS M. BARTH
WITH RUTH NUSSBAUM

Joseph Simon / Pangloss Press
MALIBU, CALIFORNIA

Contents

vi

---⟨⟨⟨⟨---

ILLUSTRATIONS

Acknowledgments

Many people have helped to bring this volume into being, including members of Temple Israel and friends who provided financial support for publication. Special thanks go to the following members of the "Rabbi Max Nussbaum Honor Roll":

Dr. Morris and Mrs. Lillian Abber
Florence Altura
Rita H. Altura
Sydney and Florence Becker
Pearl Berg (in loving memory of Mark F. Berg *z"l*)
Alan and Sigrid Belinkoff
Irene Benaron (In loving memory of Joseph Benaron *z"l*)
Bernard and Judy Briskin
Irwin Buchalter (in loving memory of Ethel Buchalter *z"l*)
Paul and Isabel Cohen
Bruce and Toni Corwin
Dorothy Corwin
Everett and Helen Daniels
The Finegood Family
Ruben (*z"l*) and Minnie Finkelstein
Sam and Sylvia Good
Ron and Shelli Goodman
Dr. Norman and Mrs. Nell Gottlieb
Joseph and Dorothy Gould and Family
Esther Grifkin
George and Janet Hecker
Joe and Heni Herman
Hillside Memorial Park
Norman Hirschfield (*z"l*) and Sylvia Weisz Hirschfield
Dr. Ralph Kaplan
Charles and Audrey Kenis
Walter (*z"l*) and Gertrude Maier
Frieda Meltzer
Marvin and Florene Mirisch
Hal and Gita Moskowitz
The Mund Family
Conrad and Adele Morse Platt
Jeanne N. Polesky and Fred A. Polesky, M.D.
Senior Rabbi's Discretionary Fund

Irv (*z"l*) and Joyce Sepkowitz
Eryk and Mira Spektor (Spektor Family Foundation)
Herman and Bernice Sperling
Jack and Lenore Wax/Sylvia Kahanowitz (*z"l*)/Eva Wax
The Ziffren Family

All the material in this volume is from the Nussbaum legacy in the possession of Ruth Nussbaum. Some of the publications in which Nussbaum's sermons, speeches or articles first appeared no longer exist. The full reference to the printed source of each selection is found in the Select Bibliography. The following are specially noted:

"Zionism Under Hitler," reprinted with permission from *CONGRESS WEEKLY,* Volume 9, No. 27. Copyright 1942 American Jewish Congress; "'Israel'-The Career of a Name," reprinted with permission from *CONGRESS WEEKLY,* Volume 19, No. 18. Copyright 1952 American Jewish Congress.

"Nachman Krochmal: The Philosopher of Jewish Eternity," reprinted with permission from the *American Jewish Year Book,* 44 (1942-43), published by the American Jewish Committee and the Jewish Publication Society of America.

"Ministry Under Stress: A Rabbi's Recollections of Nazi Berlin," reprinted with permission from *Gegenwart im Rückblick,* published by the Lothar Stiehm Verlag, Heidelberg.

The sermon "Chosen and Called: A Sermon for Shavuot" originally appeared in *A Set of Holiday Sermons: 5702-1941,* and the essay "Integration Without Assimilation" in *American Judaism,* both publications of the Union of American Hebrew Congregations. The articles "Can Conservative and Reform Judaism Merge: A Symposium" and "Jews in the Motion Picture Industry: How Jewish Are They?" were printed in *The Reconstructionist,* a publication of the Jewish Reconstructionist Foundation.

In the essay, "The Jewish Community Today and Tomorrow," the reference to Trude Weiss-Rosmarin refers to her report on the work of Professor Abraham I. Katsh in an article entitled "Hebrew's Academic Prestige," originally published in *The Jewish Chronicle.*

The article "Reform Judaism Appraises the Relationship of American Jewry to the State" which appeared in the *CCAR Journal* (June, 1971)—a publication of the Central Conference of American Rabbis—is based upon an address delivered at the

50th General Assembly of the Union of American Hebrew Congregations in Miami.

All selections found in the chapter "Observations" are taken from the *Observer,* the weekly and later monthly bulletin of Temple Israel of Hollywood. Several articles were originally published in *The American Zionist,* a magazine of the Zionist Organization of America.

Many of the photographs found in this volume appeared in the press or Temple Israel publications of the time. Some were recently reprinted in "Rabbi Max Nussbaum of Hollywood and the World," *Western States Jewish History,* XXV:2 (January 1993), edited by William M. Kramer. Several were originally taken by Leo Wainschel who was the photographer at Temple Israel for many years. Edith Pelz took photographs for some of the personal portraits.

Unless otherwise noted, all translations from German are by Ruth Nussbaum. Belle Hess translated "The Path to a Zionist Mass-Movement" from Yiddish.

Special thanks are due to a number of individuals: David Ellenson shared two forthcoming articles, "The Rabbiner-Seminar Codicil: An Instrument of Boundary Maintenance" and "Zion in the Mind of the American Rabbinate: A Survey of Sermons and Pamphlets of the 1940's," which provided additional information on seminary training in Breslau, the wording of the Breslau Seminary's *s'micha* (ordination certificate), and early rabbinic Zionist activity in the United States; Abraham Peck of the American Jewish Archives at Hebrew Union College–Cincinnati, found references to reports and discussions of the Central Conference of American Rabbis from the early 1940's; Harvey Horowitz and his staff at the Frances–Henry Library of Hebrew Union College–Los Angeles and Phillip Miller of the Library of Hebrew Union College–New York made available special bibliographic resources; Walter Jens and the staff of the Akademie der Künste, Berlin, kindly sent a copy of *Geschlossene Vorstellung: Der Jüdische Kulturbund in Deutschland 1933-1941,* which contained several references to Nussbaum's activities with the *Kulturbund;* Rabbi William Kramer over the years published the results of his own research on some of the Nussbaum materials; and Rebecca Meyer devoted countless hours to entering the original texts of sermons, speeches and essays into the now indispensable computer format.

My gratitude to John L. Rosove, rabbi of Temple Israel of Hollywood, for asking me to undertake the task of editing the sermons, speeches and writings of Max Nussbaum—and to him and Dean Lee Bycel, of Hebrew Union College-Los Angeles, for inviting me to deliver the 1994 Max Nussbaum Memorial Lecture.

Finally, Ruth Nussbaum has been a full partner in this project. Without her efforts, the book could not have been completed. Every page of this volume reflects her careful review and is filled with her excellent editorial suggestions. I am especially grateful for the opportunity I have had to spend wonderful hours of discussion, research and conversation with her.

Lewis M. Barth

It has been a joy and a privilege to assist in the compilation of this book. I have had the constant encouragement and support of my rabbi, John Rosove, and am deeply grateful to the members of Temple Israel and friends who have made its publication possible. Special thanks go to Joseph Simon, of Pangloss Press, for his knowledgeable advice, understanding and patience.

To say thank-you to Lewis Barth is almost impossible. For him, the work turned out to be an all-encompassing task, occupying an enormous amount of time—on top of his normal work schedule.

For me, the two years of collaboration with him have been years of delight and fulfillment, of creation and re-creation, of living and re-living. For months on end he selected, discarded, probed and researched. With unfailing instinct he knew what to include and what to put aside. He guided us both with gentle strength through a maze of material, always applying his high academic standards with thoroughness and integrity, coupled with an emotional affinity for his subject. He approached it not only with the gifts of his mind, but also with the gifts of his heart: intuition, imagination, and great empathy. To me he has been the kindest of teachers, rewarding me for my modest part in this work with constant recognition, with deep understanding, and with a true friendship.

It is in this spirit that I thank Lew Barth for two of the best years of my life.

Ruth Nussbaum

xi

As a Rabbi in Berlin, c. 1936

Foreword

By John L. Rosove

It is rare that a person as historically and Jewishly significant as Rabbi Max Nussbaum comes to occupy the pulpit of an American synagogue. Temple Israel of Hollywood was blessed for thirty-two years, during a period in American Jewish life when strong rabbinic leadership was critical in determining the nature of the American Jewish community itself. Max Nussbaum bridged the chasm between an American Jewish experience lacking in historical rootedness and the historically rich religious experience of European Jewry. He brought with him to Los Angeles not only an urbane gentility, but also the age-old Jewish prophetic zeal. He was a scholar whose intellect was revered by his academic peers, an international Zionist leader whose counsel Israeli prime ministers and American presidents sought, a community activist passionately committed to justice for all peoples and races in America, and a gifted congregational rabbi.

Long-time Temple Israel members remember the eloquent power of his oratorical voice from the pulpit, his dogged commitment to the ethical principles of Reform Judaism, and the timeliness of his message. Max Nussbaum anticipated many of the great events of his day which confronted the Jewish world, and he was a frequent participant in the unfolding of those events.

The selections, chosen by Lewis M. Barth, Professor of Midrash and Related Literature at the Hebrew Union College-Jewish Institute of Religion in Los Angeles, together with Ruth Nussbaum, represent some of the most stirring and probing of Max Nussbaum's writings and sermons. As the reader will discover, Max Nussbaum's expansive knowledge and keen grasp of contemporary issues and his eloquent expression of the timeless values of prophetic and liberal Judaism represent a personal diary of the internal and external forces which shaped his soul. Throughout we glimpse the mid-century vision of Jewish life from a leader whose sojournings crossed continents and who was personally touched by the most significant and transformational Jewish events of modern Jewish history.

His was a soul singed by the suffering of European Jewry, inspired by the Zionist dream, and ennobled by the American democratic and pluralistic experience. A rabbi in Berlin under the tutelage of Germany's leading Jewish figure, Rabbi Leo Baeck, saved with his wife, Ruth, and daughter, Hannah, from the fires of the Holocaust by the American Zionist leader, Rabbi Stephen S. Wise, Max Nussbaum eventually became rabbi to the stars of Hollywood in its golden age. He was ubiquitous in place and spirit. He was prolific with the pen, and eloquent in several languages. His voice bridged worlds and spoke directly to the Jewish heart even as he inspired respect from the interfaith community. Max Nussbaum enjoyed not only a strong local following, but a national and international position of influence as well.

Unfortunately, Max Nussbaum's death not only took him prematurely from his family and community, but he was denied also the opportunity to witness the fulfillment of so many of his own life-long dreams. He would have felt enormous joy to watch as hundreds of thousands of Russian Jews achieved their freedom before and after the crumbling of the Soviet Union. He would have been exhilarated to have lived to witness President Anwar Sadat's trip to Jerusalem and the Israeli-Egyptian Camp David Peace Accords. He would have been hopeful that at last Israel now stands on the verge of entering into peace treaties with the Palestinians, Jordan, and the other nations of the Middle East.

Yet, Max Nussbaum most likely would be grieved also to witness the violence that has become so pervasive in American society. He would continue to rail against the disparity that still exists between the rich and the poor. And he would mourn the demise of those traditional societal institutions which once stood for moral and ethical principles. Were he here to preach and write, I suspect that Max Nussbaum would be challenging us to remember our ethical mission as Jews and our moral responsibility to build and rebuild our society founded upon the prophetic principles of justice and peace.

This Foreword would be incomplete without acknowledging Max's devoted life-partner, Ruth. Gracious and refined, Ruth occupies a treasured place within Temple Israel of Hollywood.

This volume grew out of the occasion of the naming of the Rabbi Max and Ruth Nussbaum Sanctuary at Temple Israel of Hollywood on March 27, 1992. To my knowledge, no other Sanctuary of any synagogue in the world is named or has ever been named for an esteemed former rabbi *and* rebbetzin.

Temple Israel's Board of Trustees determined that the naming ceremony would coincide with the annual Rabbi Max Nussbaum Memorial Lecture, co-sponsored by Temple Israel with the Hebrew Union College—Jewish Institute of Religion in Los Angeles. Rabbi Alexander Schindler, President of the Union of American Hebrew Congregations, a landsman and close personal friend of Max's and Ruth's, was invited to be the 1992 Nussbaum Scholar. In addition, a special fundraising effort was undertaken to produce a volume of selections from Max Nussbaum's writings. Dr. Lewis M. Barth, who grew up at Temple Israel and was inspired by Max Nussbaum to pursue a rabbinic-academic career, was invited to oversee this project as editor and to write Max's biographical introduction. He has done so with appreciation for the depth and breadth of Max Nussbaum's achievements, and, also, as a labor of love for Max and Ruth. As he indicates in the Acknowledgements, he worked very closely with Ruth in selecting representative pieces from the enormous archive of material that spanned Max Nussbaum's entire career.

I regret that I never personally met Max Nussbaum, although as a child growing up in Los Angeles I was aware of his leadership and stature. I feel privileged to occupy the same pulpit from which he taught and preached. I am especially grateful for the enduring legacy of his remarkable spirit which is still felt within the halls of Temple Israel.

May this volume serve as a living memorial to one of American Jewry's most esteemed religious leaders, and also as a challenge to each of us to seek our tradition's ethical principles and ancient wisdom continually, to identify with Israel's cause, and to be passionate pursuers of peace and lovers of humankind.

Parents Josef and Rachel Nussbaum and Sister Hannah Spasser and son, c. 1930

Introduction

By Lewis M. Barth

My initial recollection of Rabbi Max Nussbaum: it must have been during the High Holidays, 1943. I sat with my mother, father and brother in the Temple. In what I—a five-year-old—experienced as a massive cavernous hall, there appeared way off in the distance a grand white-robed figure high up on the bima. I began to get fidgety and to talk when my mother said, "Be quiet, the rabbi is saying something very important."

That is what I remember of him—though less tall a figure than in my childhood imagination—powerful, imposing, and always saying something very important. In late August 1953, my confirmation class, for a now long forgotten scheduling reason, met with him every morning for a week of study so that we could be confirmed at Hanukkah time rather than Shavuot. He took us through a survey of Jewish history, the structure of the prayerbook, the values of Judaism which he most cherished. This was the context in which the names Maimonides, Judah ha-Levi, Herzl, first took on meaning for me. When I became an undergraduate, I passed my "Subject A" exam at UCLA by writing an essay which simply restated in my own words the perfectly organized, lucid and cogently argued sermon I heard Max Nussbaum preach the previous Friday evening. Later, when the Hebrew Union College opened its Los Angeles campus, he taught as a visiting professor. He introduced those of us who were then rabbinic students to selections from *Sefer ha-Aggada*—Bialik and Ravnitsky's anthology of rabbinic legends—and to the use of classical sources in preaching. Over many years, whoever heard his sermons or listened to him teach always knew that he was saying something very important.

* * *

1

Max Nussbaum was an extraordinarily productive preacher, lecturer and writer. The material included in this volume represents a selection of a much vaster literary oeuvre. The original manuscripts and printed sources come from the large personal archive of Ruth Nussbaum. This archive contains copies of the *Observer*, typescripts of his sermons and speeches, and newspaper and journal articles. The largest part of what I have included reflects the period Nussbaum served as rabbi at Temple Israel. He also had, however, a full professional life as a young rabbi before coming to Hollywood, first in Berlin and then briefly in Muskogee and Norman, Oklahoma. Some selections from these earlier periods have been included as well. In addition, Nussbaum, together with his wife, wrote a draft of an autobiography, only a few sections of which have been published. One of these, "Ministry Under Stress," is also included here.

* * *

Nussbaum's greatest talent was in oral presentation. He employed a stenographer to take down his sermons from the tapes on which they were recorded. These "first drafts" were edited, often by Ruth Nussbaum, and then typed in final form by Thelma Cohen, Nussbaum's devoted secretary of many years. They appeared either in the *Observer* or other publications.

Because of an exceptionally heavy speaking schedule, Nussbaum often utilized the same material for different settings. In cases of repetition, Ruth Nussbaum and I chose together what we considered the best literary representation of his ideas. If the same material appeared in more than one piece we decided to use, it will be found here only once, in what we considered to be the most appropriate or cogent context. There is, of necessity, some repetition in this volume, but where it appears, the repeated passage is consciously included to demonstrate a certain constancy of vision and values.

This volume is designed to be representative of Nussbaum's thinking and not a critical or scholarly edition of his works. I have felt it appropriate to clarify occasional sentences or passages, correct some grammatical constructions, and delete passages which might be a suitable aside for an oral presentation but not essential for the flow of written argument. Some published materials also appear in a slightly abridged form. This process was aided considerably by the excellent editorial sense of Ruth Nussbaum, who also had exercised the same good judgment on her husband's writings during his lifetime.

* * *

A few technical comments. Nussbaum was competent in German, French, Yiddish and Hebrew. Within a short time after his arrival in the United States in 1940, he devoted himself to mastering English which he quickly came to use with extraordinary force. Some language patterns of German are evident throughout his work. This is especially noticeable in his frequent capitalization of the first letter of nouns; it was also the practice of some writers in English in the 1940's and 1950's to capitalize words representing religious or philosophical concepts. In this volume such nouns—with the exception of references to the deity—appear in lower case. He also capitalized entire words or phrases for emphasis in several of the original printed versions of his writings. Depending on context and significance, these words or phrases are either italicized or presented here in regular font.

A further reflection of Nussbaum's European and Rabbinic education is the large number of German, French and especially Hebrew words and phrases with which he embellished his sermons, speeches and writings. Many of these "foreign" words have now entered English usage and they are not italicized. For example: "leitmotif," "noblesse oblige" and "fait accomplis"—to cite some of his favorite expressions. Numerous Hebrew and Jewish religious terms which he employed regularly are now considered part of American English as well. These include: "kaddish," "galut," "matzah," "mikva," "shul" and a host of other terms. These words will only be italicized if they are used with special emphasis, or where the special meaning of the term is discussed.

As a devoted Zionist, Nussbaum was committed from an early period to the use of the Sephardic pronunciation of Hebrew, and this naturally continued after the establishment of the State of Israel. However, many of his earlier published essays reflect Ashkenazic and occasionally specifically Ger-

3

man Jewish pronunciation. All transliterations of Hebrew in this volume have been modified to reflect Sephardic or Modern Hebrew usage.

Regarding the use of gender in language, Nussbaum's writings are typical of his time. No attempt has been made to change masculine references to the deity or similar designations referring to human beings generally.

Nussbaum generally quoted the *Holy Scriptures* published by the Jewish Publication Society (Philadelphia, 1917[1]) as his source for biblical quotations. However, he often translated a biblical passage himself—sometimes quite freely in order to support the point he was making. This is typical of a long tradition of rabbinic and midrashic use of scripture and perfectly appropriate for preaching purposes. In general I have let these translations stand; however, where the stenographer did not catch a reasonable version of the translation from a tape, the text generally will follow the JPS version. Translations from rabbinic literature are generally his own, except in a few instances in which I felt revision was necessary.

Biblical references appearing originally in footnotes have been placed in the text itself, at the end of the citation. In addition, where the biblical reference was not cited in the original it has now been included. Often a footnote introducing or accompanying an article was not from Nussbaum himself, but from a later editor, who provided the context in which the sermon was first preached. Original or editorial footnotes have not been included in this volume. For further detail, see the Note on Transliteration and Citation at the end of this volume.

Each selection is presented without an extensive introductory comment. My approach was to let each piece stand on its own. For purposes of identification, the date of a sermon, speech or article as well as brief reference to publication of articles appear after the title, except in the chapter "Observations" in which all the material comes from the *Observer*. The complete reference to the publication source appears in the Select Bibliography. In a few cases where an indication of context might be helpful, a brief explanatory phrase follows the title of the selection. Because so much of what Nussbaum said or wrote transcends the initial occasion for the statement, it seemed to me that this limited information would allow his writings to speak for themselves. An example of this broader scope or quality of timelessness is found in the first selection in Beginnings, *"Den Musischen Freunden*—1936." This material is taken from a privately printed memento written on the occasion of Ruth Nussbaum's leaving Berlin for Amsterdam. Yet it represents the pain and sadness of so many German Jews seeing their friends or loved ones flee Germany.

* * *

Finally, some explanation is necessary regarding categories of material or specific writings not included. In consultation with Ruth Nussbaum, I made a decision early on not to include celebrity wedding sermons or eulogies. Some of this material was already published in the newspapers of the time or, in the case of Al Jolson and Fanny Brice, in *Temple Israel Pulpit: A Selection of Published Sermons, Speeches and Articles* [of Rabbis Max Nussbaum and William M. Kramer] (College of Jewish Studies: Los Angeles, 1957).

A large collection of Nussbaum's sermons continues to be preserved on magnetic tape at Temple Israel. These tapes were not consulted because of special technical problems of transcription and because of necessary limitations of size for this book. It is my hope that at some point they will be utilized for a complete edition of his writings.

* * *

Selecting and editing the sermons, speeches, and writings found in this volume was an opportunity for me to revisit the lessons Max Nussbaum taught not so very long ago, and to realize again how important—even prophetic—were many of his words.

Ordination Picture, Breslau, Germany, 1933
(Nussbaum fourth from right)

Biographical Sketch

By LEWIS M. BARTH *with* RUTH NUSSBAUM

Suceava, Bukovina—a small town, though also a regional capital, in the north-east corner of what became Romania after World War I. In 1908—the year Max (Moshe) Nussbaum was born—Bukovina was still part of the Austro-Hungarian Empire. That fact is important for understanding the cultural orientation of Jews of this area and the direction Nussbaum was to go—geographically and spiritually—for his education and career.

The majority of Bukovina's Jews considered themselves to be more "European" than other Jewish communities in Eastern Europe. They were active in business, industry, and agriculture. Jewish life in the entire region was open to the currents of the modern world. Secularist tendencies dominated in education and politics. Zionism and the Jewish Bundist (Socialist) Movement vied for the loyalties of a Jewish community that was growing in size and influence. Some people considered Suceava itself to be a last outpost of European culture—and then Asia began. For many people, including the majority of Jews in this area, German was the language of culture and politics.

In 1914 there were approximately eight thousand Jews in Suceava. Jewish community life flourished with Orthodox synagogues, a Reform temple, a Talmud Torah, a Bible School or kindergarten and a Jewish lyceum or high school. Hebraists and Zionists were active; there was an early "Theodor Herzl Society" and later representative organizations of every Zionist viewpoint, from the leftist *ha-Shomer ha-Tza-ir* to the Revisionists on the right. The town was also known as a center for wonder-workers and a focal point for thousands of Hasidic Jews in the entire surrounding area.

Nussbaum spent his childhood in this religiously and culturally intense Jewish environment. His own home life was

7

one of extreme Orthodoxy. A family photograph showing the father in traditional garb and a later description that young Moshe was required to dress in a caftan, suggest that the Nussbaums were part of the large local Hasidic community. In any case, his father, Josef, was a devoutly religious man. Nussbaum recalled that his father rose each morning at 3:00 A.M. to study Talmud and never failed to attend synagogue. As was typical in traditionalist communities, his parents enrolled Moshe in a heder when he was three years old, then in the elementary Jewish school.

Yet in spite of the strict Orthodoxy in his home, he remembered his father as being a worldly person. Typical of the area, the family spoke a dialect of German as well as Yiddish, but not Romanian. Books of Goethe and Schiller were found on the same shelves as Torah and Talmud. The home in which Moshe—the youngest of the three children—grew up, along with his sisters Malka Rosa (later called Shoshana) and Channah, was among the first in Suceava to have electric lights and a pump for sanitation. The father was employed by the Jewish community as a *shochet,* a ritual slaughterer. Daily life was a constant struggle and the family was very poor.

By his early teens Nussbaum began to break away from Orthodoxy and to demonstrate an independence of thought and tenacity that were among his lifelong qualities. The first step was symbolic: he clandestinely arranged with his mother to purchase a Western style suit so that he could attend the social affairs of various Jewish youth organizations. Later he had a major conflict with his father over his desire to go to public high school. Josef feared that secular learning would lead to the alienation of his son from religion. Moshe climbed up on the roof of the house, wrote a long poem of lamentation, and went on a hunger strike. With the help of his mother, Rachel—whom he viewed as gentleness personified and a balance to a strict and sometimes difficult father—the young rebel prevailed.

At fifteen Nussbaum began high school in Suceava. He is already mentioned as a member of "Ziona," a high-school Zionist youth group, in a list of names published in a history of the Jews of Bukovina. Two years later he left Suceava to go to the nearby town of Stroginetz to finish high school at the *Jüdi-*

sche Ober-Realgymnasium. This educational institution was well known and highly regarded; its curriculum included Latin, German and French, in addition to Jewish subjects. The student-body contained Catholic and Greek Orthodox students as well—a further reflection of the school's openness. To support himself away from home—a need he had to face throughout his education—Nussbaum taught Hebrew privately and at school. It was also at this point that he took the name Max.

At nineteen he returned to Suceava to take his first *Abitur* (high school completion examination) at the local *Realgymnasium.* He remained at home for a brief period before he left for his first university experience. In a letter to his sister from December 1927—a letter filled with adolescent irony and sarcasm—he depicts Suceava as a religiously stifling and culturally boring town. He expressed great disappointment that the one exciting event he had looked forward to—a visit to the community by Chaim Weizmann—was canceled at the last minute. It was already clear that Nussbaum was moving in new directions, and that he was beginning to identify with a world quite different from that of his parents.

He spent his first winter semester (1927-1928) as a student at the University of Cernauti (Czernowitz), where he began to study philosophy. It is likely that he was exposed for the first time to Marxist thought, a subject to which he later returned in his doctoral dissertation. In addition, he joined a local amateur theater company and began to write for the periodical *Moledet.* It also appears that at this juncture he decided—after serious family discussions and with his father's approval—to leave Cernauti for Germany to begin his rabbinic studies.

In the fall of 1928 he enrolled at the *Jüdisch-Theologisches Seminar* (Jewish Theological Seminary) and, as was required by the *Seminar,* also at the University of Breslau. The *Seminar* in Breslau, founded by Zacharia Frankel in 1854, was the first modern seminary for the training of rabbis. It had an outstanding faculty, exceptionally rich library, and published the first comprehensive scholarly journal devoted to the exploration of Jewish life.

Breslau was a perfect place for Nussbaum's own religious and cultural development. He knew from an early age that he could not be Orthodox; at the same time he was not attracted to the extreme wing of German Reform. The Breslau Seminary educated rabbis for the Orthodox *and* Liberal branches of German and European Jewry. In the framework of German Judaism prior to World War II, Nussbaum prepared himself to be a "Liberal Rabbi." His *s'micha* (ordination diploma) is typical of those received by the majority of Breslau rabbinic students. It authorized the bearer to serve as rabbi and religious teacher. However, it does not contain permission to issue halakhic rulings—a distinction reserved specifically for students who displayed superior mastery of Jewish law.

Because his basic schooling had been in Romania, he was required to take a second German *Abitur* in order to be accepted at the university in Breslau. He passed this examination, entered the university and used this opportunity to deepen his grasp of Western Culture. He read modern German, Russian and general European literature and studied French. It was also in Breslau that Nussbaum became an expert in European and Jewish theater, worked as a theater critic on radio, and began his lifelong career of lecturing. He continued as well to tutor students in Hebrew as he had done previously.

Though he had gravitated toward Zionism earlier in Suceava, it is in Breslau that he was exposed to major Zionist thinkers and became active in Zionist organizations. In Breslau, Nussbaum first heard Vladimir Jabotinsky (1880-1940), who, along with Joseph Trumpeldor, developed the idea for a Jewish Legion to fight with the Allies in World War I, founded the World Union of Zionist Revisionists in 1925, and later—in 1937—became the supreme commander of the Irgun. He was a brilliant orator, intellectual and linguist. Nussbaum appreciated Jabotinsky's talents and accomplishments but remained opposed to his rightist ideology throughout his life. (Years later he viewed positively the decision of the Israeli government to permit Jabotinsky's reburial in Israel.) It was during the Breslau period that Nussbaum also began to frame for himself a new model of rabbinic service. His student sermon, "Modern Zionist Rabbis," reflects his conception of the need for a new generation of Zionist rabbis capable of reaching young people and of sharing the dream of a Jewish homeland.

In order to fulfill the regular requirements of the *Seminar* for rabbinic ordination Nussbaum also needed a doctoral degree. To achieve this he spent the academic year 1931 at the University of Würzburg, completed his graduate exams in 1932, and wrote his doctoral dissertation, *Kantianismus und Marxismus in der Socialphilosophie Max Adlers*. Max Adler (1873-1937) was at that time an influential Austrian Marxist social theorist and professor of sociology at the University of Vienna. The decision to write on a contemporary thinker whose own work was grounded in German philosophical Idealism and Marxism is significant. It required Nussbaum to confront directly the major currents of European intellectual and political thought of the day. Adler developed the concept that there were ethical dimensions, not just materialistic forces, in the social movements that shaped society. This idea closely conformed to Nussbaum's own thinking—increasingly informed by the message of the biblical prophets—regarding the never-ending human struggle to establish a just society and the need for liberation of oppressed peoples.

Toward the end of 1933 he completed his examinations at the *Seminar* and received ordination.

In the early 1930's—the final years Nussbaum spent as a student in Breslau and in Würzburg—political life in Germany became increasingly chaotic and threatening. Daily existence was progressively more difficult for Germany's Jews, and the consciousness of the degenerating situation was nowhere clearer than in the nation's capital. Nussbaum arrived in Berlin to serve as rabbi in 1934, more than a year after Hitler had become Chancellor (January 30, 1933). As the power of the Nazi movement developed, Nussbaum clarified and sharpened his own political views. In addition, because of the historical context, his liberalism—religious and political—merged with his now complete identification with the plight of the people he served and whose fate he shared. He later published several essays describing Jewish life under the Nazis ("How Jews Live in Germany Today"), his rabbinic role in Berlin ("Ministry Under Stress"), and the anomalous position of the Zionist movement in Germany during this period ("Zionism Under Hitler"). He was employed by the Jewish community as a rabbi, from 1934 through 1936 at the rank of *Lehrer* (Teacher), then as *Prediger* (Preacher) and finally, from 1936 until he left in 1940, as *Gemeinde Rabbiner* (Community Rabbi).

11

His role in the Jewish community of Berlin was somewhat unique. He was the youngest, and the only *Ostjude*—Eastern European Jew—of the young rabbinic generation. In spite of the misgivings of some of the *bal ha-batim* (leadership), these qualities seemed to add to the attractiveness of the handsome, fiery, and scholarly newcomer whose sermons created sensations on the pulpits of Berlin.

Along with the few other rabbis who still remained in Berlin, the Jewish Community kept him extremely busy with a heavy schedule of preaching and teaching. Because of his earlier interest in theater, he also became involved with the *Jüdische Kulturbund in Deutschland.* This organization offered theater and musical presentations from 1933-1942 to the Jewish community. It became especially important after the Nazis no longer permitted Jews to frequent public cultural events. He lectured and wrote theater critiques. Together with Rabbi Joachim Prinz, he provided information for Jewish actors and audiences so that they could appreciate the Jewish elements in the plays in which they performed or which they viewed.

In 1935 the Nazis still permitted Jews to go to public theater and opera. One evening at the *Städtische Oper* mutual friends introduced Nussbaum to Ruth Offenstadt-Toby, who was to become his wife. Ruth was born in Berlin to a traditional German Jewish family. She received her education at the Universities of Geneva and Berlin, and studied English and Romance Languages until the Nazis made it impossible for Jews to attend university. She then began a career as a writer and translator. They met on several other occasions, fell in love, and eventually were married on July 6, 1938, by the civil authority in Amsterdam where Ruth was then living. Almost immediately after the wedding they returned to Berlin, traveling on Nussbaum's Romanian passport. (Despite his early admiration for Western culture, Nussbaum kept his Romanian passport. He did not apply for German citizenship during his student years—a decision that was to have profoundly positive consequences as it later enabled the couple to emigrate from Germany.) On July 14, 1938, Rabbi Leo Baeck married them in a religious ceremony in Berlin. In his wedding sermon, Rabbi Baeck stressed the symbolism of the meeting of East and West in the personalities of the young couple.

Now and then the Nazis did permit Nussbaum to travel abroad. On at least two occasions he went to London for Zionist activities. There he met with Chaim Weizmann and reported to him about the deteriorating situation of the Jews in Germany. It was on one of these trips that Weizmann introduced him to Rabbi Stephen S. Wise, who was to become his mentor. Wise arranged for the invitation that allowed him to come to the United States, eventually recommended him for the pulpit of Temple Israel of Hollywood and continued to encourage his Zionist activities.

* * *

Max and Ruth Nussbaum left Berlin on July 31, 1940, and arrived one month later in New York via Lisbon. The departure from Berlin was painfully difficult. For bureaucratic reasons, the American Embassy refused to grant Ruth's daughter Hannah a visa and she and Ruth's parents remained behind. The couple knew they had to leave. Nevertheless, they shared an extraordinary confidence that they would succeed and eventually bring out the rest of Ruth's family.

Tragically, Nussbaum did not succeed in rescuing his own parents whom he never saw again. On October 9, 1941, they—together with the entire Jewish community of Suceava—were deported to Transnistria. After unbelievable hardships suffered on that trip, they arrived at Sargorod where—early in 1942—they died of cold, hunger and typhoid fever. Only later did Nussbaum learn of their fate from a Red Cross announcement.

The harrowing adventures and terrible frustrations Max and Ruth Nussbaum met on the way to Lisbon are something of a life and death tale not unlike the stories of others who escaped Nazi Germany. Some people never looked back—Nussbaum, however, did. He preserved an intense sense of responsibility toward the community he had just left and continued his connection to Berlin and Germany for the rest of his life. The first indication: before departing Lisbon, he sent a letter to the leaders of the Berlin community. In it he detailed the route he and Ruth had taken, the transportation problems they encountered and the costs they had to bear. Always the teacher and leader, his purpose was to provide those who were to follow with some guidance to prepare for the journey.

The couple was welcomed in New York by friends, but also besieged by reporters who apparently knew of his coming. People were desperately interested in direct news of the situation in Germany. Two weeks after their arrival, through Rabbi Wise's contact with Arthur Sulzberger of the *New York Times,* the Nussbaums found themselves in Washington, DC. They went to the capital to report to Henry Morgenthau, Roosevelt's Secretary of the Treasury, on the situation in Germany. Nussbaum used this opportunity to urge the US Government to ease procedures for Jews who were trying to get out and could not because of bureaucratic restrictions—the most poignant example being his and Ruth's own experience. The Washington visit was a brief side trip before the couple left New York for Nussbaum's first American pulpit—Beth Ahaba Temple in Muskogee, Oklahoma.

* * *

In Muskogee, Nussbaum devoted himself to mastering English and jumped headlong into the organizational activities of the American Jewish community. Even in his first year he traveled extensively—primarily to report on the situation of the Jews in Germany, but also to share his view that the conflict with Nazism was a religious war. In his second year, 1941-42, he received an invitation from the School of Religion at the State University of Oklahoma at Norman to become a member of the faculty. He also served as director of the Department of Hebrew Language and Literature. He lectured on Western and German philosophy. With some excitement about his language progress he noted to Ruth that it was easier for him to teach Kant in English than in German. In Norman he went out of his way to enter the life of the university as a typical faculty member. He recalled going to baseball games and faculty picnics— but he also devoted himself to serving the needs of the Jewish students on campus. While at Norman, he founded the Jewish Students' Center at the State University. This was a forerunner of the Hillel organization; Abram Sachar, then national director of the Hillel Foundations, came to speak and install Nussbaum as the first local director.

Nussbaum liked to lecture, but did not want a full time academic career. He and Ruth had found a genuine welcome in Muskogee. Between Muskogee and Norman they received a unique exposure to American life—very different from the experience of many German Jewish refugees who remained in New York City. Professionally, Muskogee was a springboard for the rest of his rabbinic and organizational career. Personally, it was the community that had given the guarantees which saved their lives. The confidence the couple shared on leaving Germany was fulfilled. Hannah arrived, and then Ruth's parents came after a detour to Cuba. Finally, the Nussbaums' son Jeremy was born in Muskogee.

* * *

The September 4, 1942 issue of *The Observer*, the bulletin of Temple Israel of Hollywood, contained the following headline: "Dr. Nussbaum Assumes Duties." A week earlier, on his arrival in Los Angeles, Nussbaum wrote to Ruth who was soon to bring the family from Muskogee:

> I had lunch with a member of the Board, who afterwards took me on a ride through Hollywood. I have to confess that I am simply drunk with this beauty. It must be one of the spots on earth which God designed and created during one of his most inspired dreams. You can only compare it to Italy and Switzerland, and if the palm trees of Southern Italy aroused Goethe's poetic enthusiasm, what would he have said about these here. You drive through the streets with your mouth open: exotic trees, luscious lawns and flowers, beautiful homes—you just cannot believe it!

The Temple needed a war-time replacement for Rabbi Morton Bauman, who was then serving as a military chaplain. Abram Sachar and Stephen S. Wise recommended Nussbaum. Just a few years earlier in Berlin he had been teased because he did not exactly fit the image of the traditional rabbi. People had said to him: "You should be Rabbi of Hollywood, that's where you belong, Charles Boyer-Kosher Style." Now it was happening and Nussbaum immediately plunged into a full round of rabbinic and organizational responsibilities.

A word about Nussbaum in Hollywood and the background of the congregation in this community. In 1988, Neal Gabler published a study on the Jewish moguls of the film industry, their shaping of a new American image and re-creation of themselves into Americans—as they imagined Americans to be. He called his book *An Empire of their Own: How the Jews Invented Hollywood.* He mentions the two leading rabbis in Los Angeles in the early post-war period—Edgar Magnin and Max Nussbaum—but focuses primarily on the former. Magnin was a colorful California personality. Several of the subjects in Gabler's book—those few Jews who "invented Hollywood"—belonged in the main to "Magnin's Temple."

There was another group of Jews, however, who actually lived in Hollywood. Many worked in the film industry; most were in production. In 1927 this group organized their own Reform congregation. Their initial self-image during the late 1920's and throughout the 1930's was best symbolized by the slogan in the masthead of the congregational bulletin: *Temple Israel of Hollywood, Filmland's House of Worship.*

Within a decade—for the world and for the Jews—the rise of Nazi Germany, the historical processes that led to World War II, and then the post-war struggle against anti-Semitism all overshadowed the surface glamour and glitz of Hollywood. In 1942, the leaders of the still young Temple Israel brought Max Nussbaum to this community to be their rabbi. They consciously chose a person whose Jewish religious orientation was formed in the extreme Orthodoxy of Bukovina and the traditional yet "scientific" study of Judaism in Breslau, whose Western political liberalism and cultural imagination had been shaped by the excitement of pre-Nazi Germany in the late 1920's, but whose Jewish consciousness was seared by what he later was to call—over and over again—"the tragedy."

For the next thirty-two years as rabbi of Temple Israel of Hollywood, Max Nussbaum did have significant contact with "the industry." He performed the marriages of several "stars"—the best known: the wedding of Elizabeth Taylor and Eddie Fischer—and he officiated at nearly a dozen celebrity funerals, including those of Fanny Brice, Samuel Goldwyn, Al Jolson, Edward G. Robinson, and a memorial service for Michael Todd. He also socialized periodically with the elite German and German Jewish writers and musicians "in exile" in Los Angeles, including Thomas Mann and Lion Feuchtwanger. Yet the focus of his local public life was his pulpit and his people. To paraphrase Gabler's title and with a very differ-

16

ent focus: the sermons Nussbaum preached, the speeches he gave, and essays he wrote tell the story of how Jews were created—as Jews—in Hollywood from the early 1940's through the early 1970's.

* * *

Nussbaum's rabbinic task was the shaping of a new American Jewish identity, for himself and for his people. The elements in that identity were a passionate appreciation of the American democracy which saved his own and his family's lives, an intense connection to the concept of a unified Jewish People, a profound commitment to Zionism and later the newborn State of Israel, and a deep rootedness in the grand traditions of Western and Rabbinic Jewish cultures—understood from a liberal or Reform perspective. He defended Jews internationally, worked for and then rejoiced in the establishment of the State of Israel, and all the while brought his message of Judaism to his congregation at home. He knew "the tragedy," but he also preached and proclaimed "the triumph."

Several other themes appear in Nussbaum's writings. He understood the war against Germany to be a battle of Judaism and Christianity against "the Brown religion"—a reference to the brown shirts of the Nazis. He felt that the basic structures and values of Western Civilization were at risk. In Muskogee he had first experienced racial segregation—American style— and determined to fight it from the pulpit and in the life of the community. Years later in Hollywood he spoke of the civil rights movement and the work of Martin Luther King as "Zionism in Black." This metaphor reflected his view that both Zionism *and* the movement for black equality aspired to the same goal of human liberation. He argued that both drew inspiration from commonly shared biblical imperatives, and pressed for Jews to understand and identify with the black struggle. In response to growing ethnic and racial tensions within American society, he risked urging American Jews to reconceptualize their own identity. He appealed to them to view themselves as an ethnic-religious group—using the emerging consciousness of the Black and Chicano communities for a model. On the subject of Jewish life in America, the phrases "integration without assimilation" and "commitment and identification" recur with great frequency in his sermons and writings.

17

In regard to Zionism, he worked for and publicly defended the young State of Israel. In a constant stream of sermons and speeches he spoke of the courage of the Israeli population and its need for material and political support. He lashed out, when he deemed it necessary, at the US State Department's dealings in the Middle East, and at what he considered false steps in American policy. At the same time, he did not hold back from criticizing the actions of Israel's political leaders from the pulpit and from conference platforms. He deeply resented the denigration of the World Zionist movement and the dismissive attitude of some Israeli government officials toward American Zionist leadership soon after the establishment of the State. In addition, he felt that Ben-Gurion was unnecessarily creating divisions between Israelis and American Jews. He also focused attention on emerging social concerns in the new State and on the problem of religious coercion by the religious parties in the government. As a research project and a reflection of his interests in Zionism and inter-faith dialogue, he devoted years—beginning in Germany and continuing in the United States—to the study of Christian advocates of Zionism. He published two of his articles on this subject.

Nussbaum had a strong commitment to Reform Judaism and spoke again and again at local, regional and national conferences and biennials of the Union of American Hebrew Congregations. He served on the Administrative Board, later the Board of Overseers, which was responsible for establishing the Hebrew Union College campus in Los Angeles. But he was also very interested in Reconstructionism. He invited Mordecai Kaplan, the founder of the Reconstructionist Movement, to speak at Temple Israel, established a Reconstructionist group within the congregation, and wrote several articles for the national publication, the *Reconstructionist.*

* * *

Within a few years of his arrival in Los Angeles, Nussbaum began to take on major organizational leadership roles outside the congregation. From a historical perspective, throughout Nussbaum's organizational life, bridging the mid-1940's through the early 1970's, the center of Jewish institutional life in the United States was clearly New York City and the East Coast gen-

18

erally. Nevertheless, he did not allow geographic distance to keep him from being a player on the larger scene of Jewish organizational activity. Already in 1946 he was elected as a national vice-president of the American Jewish Congress. Just prior to the establishment of the State of Israel he served as a member of the first United Jewish Appeal delegation to Palestine. He was one of the first persons in the Los Angeles Jewish community to head a national Jewish organization and became president of the Zionist Organization of America in 1962.

He did feel fenced in occasionally by being in Los Angeles and not in the geographic center of the action. In addition, he had periodic conflicts with the Board of Trustees of Temple Israel over his frequent trips for the organizations in which he held leadership positions nationally and internationally. These included the Zionist Organization of America, the American Jewish Congress and the World Jewish Congress. The congregation was very appreciative of his rising reputation, but not always happy with his being away. On several occasions after he came to Hollywood, he received offers for organizational positions on the East Coast. He was pursued for pulpit positions as well. Louis Finkelstein, President of the Jewish Theological Seminary of New York, and a foremost leader of Conservative Judaism, contacted him regarding a congregation in New York City. Nussbaum, however, did not want to be a Jewish organizational executive and he was too independent in thought and practice to leave the Reform Movement for a Conservative pulpit. Nor did Ruth want to leave the many friends they had made or be uprooted again. Hollywood was home now for both of them.

There was an extraordinary range to his public activities. The following list of ten selected items provides some sense of what his commitments, travels and awards were at the height of his career—in the decade of the 1960's. It does not, of course, reflect either his Temple responsibilities or include even a fraction of his local organizational involvements. It is, however, typical of the lists provided each month of "Rabbis' Activities" that appeared in the *Observer*:

> 1958-1962—Chair, National Executive Committee, Zionist Organization of America; National Vice-President, American Jewish Congress.

19

December 1960—delegate to the 25th World Zionist Congress, Jerusalem; elected a member of the Actions Committee, (governing body of the World Zionist Organization which met between Congresses.).

In April 1961—received a Doctor of Literature Degree, honoris causa, conferred by Dropsie College for Hebrew and Cognate Learning, Philadelphia.

1962-1965—President, Zionist Organization of America.

1964-1966—Chairman, American Zionist Council.

October 1964-September 1968—Chairman, American Section, World Jewish Congress.

July 1965— visited West Germany on the invitation of the Federal Republic of Germany following the establishment of diplomatic relations by the Federal Republic of Germany with Israel; participated in meetings of the World Executive of the World Jewish Congress, Strasbourg, France.

January-February 1968—during his only sabbatical, visited Japan, Hong Kong, Bangkok, New Delhi, Bombay, Iran, as representative of the World Jewish Congress, the Union of American Hebrew Congregations and the World Union for Progressive Judaism, meeting with the members of the Jewish communities and lecturing.

December 1968—honored by the State of Israel Bond Organization, and presented with the Eleanor Roosevelt Humanities Award, in recognition of long and devoted service to Judaism and Israel. (The first time the award was presented in the West.)

February 1969—shared with Ruth Nussbaum the Brandeis Award of the Zionist Organization of America. (The first time the award was presented in the West.)

* * *

Though committed to his various organizational roles, the pulpit and daily rabbinic responsibilities at Temple Israel were very important to him. It is true that some members of the congregation viewed him as "detached." He also developed a reputation as a strict rabbinic figure. Periodically he would stop in the middle of a sermon to stare someone down who was talking during services. Yet as a congregational rabbi he was deeply involved in lives of member families, especially when there were difficulties with children or teenagers. He sensed when people were in trouble and was surprisingly good in moments of personal crises which he handled very well—often being on the phone with congregants day and night. The Temple archives contain hundreds of personal letters he wrote to members of the congregation for every occasion. He was gifted with a memory for personal detail and never overlooked an event in the life of a congregant or forgot an act of generosity. At the Temple itself he created a nursery school and an intensive adult education program at which he lectured. Nussbaum joined with others in the Reform movement in the late 1960's to argue for the establishment of congregational day schools. American Reform Judaism, however, required another decade before this was to happen. Long before it became the practice in other congregations, he led a study minyan prior to the regular Shabbat morning bar mitzvah or bat mitzvah service. Finally, he gave book reviews and critiques of Broadway play he had recently seen, from the pulpit and in the context of Temple Sisterhood meetings.

Nussbaum invited to the pulpit of Temple Israel several leading figures in American and Jewish life—Rabbi Mordecai Kaplan, as previously mentioned, as well as Rabbis Stephen S. Wise, Leo Baeck and others. Later Nussbaum recalled two powerful pulpit experiences, each reflecting a historical context laden with significance. The first was the Friday evening service on February 26, 1965, during which the Reverend Martin Luther King spoke. The second was Friday evening October 5, 1973. Gregor Piatigorsky, the world renown cellist, played the Kol Nidre melody. At that same moment half way around the world it was already October 6. Egypt and Syria had just launched their attacks against Israel and the Yom Kippur War began.

Because of the pressures of his speaking schedule he was constantly preparing for future presentations. He was a voracious reader, constantly clipping articles which he placed in well organized files, marking books and magazines and collecting material for subjects he intended to discuss. He complained periodically that he had no time to study Torah *lishma,* for its own sake, because all his reading was connected with his work. He lived something of a crazy and hectic life. He was busy at the Temple all day and had meetings at night. He would often come home, read for an hour to relax before he and Ruth shared late night tea and talked through the day's events or family matters.

* * *

On Monday, May 18, 1964, a simple white envelope arrived at Temple Israel. It bore the return address in gold lettering: The White House. Inside the invitation read, "The President and Mrs. Johnson request the pleasure of the company of Rabbi and Mrs. Nussbaum at dinner on Monday, June 1, 1964 at eight o'clock." An enclosure stated simply, "On the occasion of the visit of His Excellency The Prime Minister of Israel and Mrs. Eshkol."

During the plane trip to Washington with Ruth, Max Nussbaum recalled the first visit they had nearly twenty-four years earlier to the capital. Though he was not a self-reflective person, one question haunted him through all the years he had been in the United States. He spoke of it publicly when he first came to Hollywood. It came back now with great inner emotional force: "how did it happen that I escaped Hitler's hell" when so many of his loved ones, friends, millions of other Jews did not?

He had given his answer by devoting himself to telling the story of what happened, by working for the establishment and security of the State of Israel, and by developing a meaningful Jewish life for his congregation and community in an America that he loved. At the end of the White House dinner he felt that,

> For one brief moment it seemed as if everything was well with the world. For once, after centuries of suffering, we finally seemed to be on the right side of history—in harmony with ourselves and with the outside world. This was truly a time of fulfillment: my country, the great United States, my President, my Israel and its Prime Minister—standing together. There was nothing to do but silently thank God, *she-*

hecheyanu, who had kept us alive, sustained us and brought us to this moment.

* * *

Friday, July 19, 1974, was a warm summer day in Hollywood. Nussbaum was working in his study preparing his notes for that evening's talk. He planned to report to the congregation—as he had done so many times—on his recent trip to Israel and the ZOA Conference there. His young granddaughter Margaret was playing with a hose in the garden, watering the flowers and splashing herself to keep cool. Nussbaum came down for iced tea and went out on the patio to watch. It was a beautiful scene—grandfather and granddaughter in a moment of pleasure. Ruth quickly found her camera and took a snapshot.

That evening at Shabbat dinner Max Nussbaum was stricken with a heart attack. The next morning he died.

* * *

Some say that only true *zaddikim* die on the Sabbath; others say that he ascended to report to the *yeshiva shel ma'ala,* the Heavenly Academy.

* * *

"In this spirit"—one of Rabbi Max Nussbaum's favorite phrases—I would add that he left us his words. Now go, study.

Ruth and Max Nussbaum, 1971

Beginnings

DEN MUSISCHEN FREUNDEN/
TO OUR FRIENDS, 1936

I

Unser Leben gleicht einem feinen Gewebe aus schwarz und weiß getönten Fäden. In unserer Gegenwart bedeckt die schwarze Abtönung eine viel größere Fläche unseres Seins als die weiße, und somit stehen alle unsere Veranstaltungen und gesellschaftlichen Zusammenkünfte privater und offizieller Natur unter dem Motto zweier Begriffe; des Gedenkens und des Abschieds.

II

Weil die Mauern rings um uns immer höher werden und uns den freien Blick nach außen nehmen, verlieren unsere Menschen mit der Zeit das Bewußtsein ihrer inneren Qualität und Leistung. Um ihnen den Blick in die Zukunft nicht zu nehmen, richten wir den Scheinwerfer der Geschichte auf die Vergangenheit und zeigen ihnen, was sie gewesen sind. Weil wir trotz allem von unseren Menschen noch eine Zukunft fordern, gedenken wir unwillkürlich unserer Leistungen in der Vergangenheit. So wird jede jüdische Kundgebung zu einer Gedenkstunde.

Und das andere: der Abschied. Die Tragödie unserer Tage ist eine doppelte. Die hohen Mauern, die um uns wachsen, nehmen uns die Weite. Das Weggehen von Freunden und lieben Menschen höhlt unsere Welt von innen aus. Sie wird nicht nur kleiner, sie wird leerer. Sie wird nicht nur enger, sie wird inhaltsloser. Sie mindert nicht lediglich die Zahl von Individuen, sondern die von Menschen und Persönlichkeiten.

TO OUR FRIENDS, 1936/
DEN MUSISCHEN FREUNDEN

I

Our life is like a fine cloth, woven from white and black threads. In these days the black occupies a much larger area than the white, and so all our gatherings—be they private or official—stand under the shadow of two ideas: the one of remembering and the one of farewell.

II

With the walls around us rising higher and higher, depriving us of a view to the outside world, our people are also gradually losing the perspective of their inner world, of their own abilities and qualities. In order not to take away their outlook into the future, we aim the spotlight of history to the past—to show them what we once were. Thus every Jewish gathering is an act of remembering.

And the other: the farewell. The tragedy of our days is two-fold: we are losing the outside world—and the departure of friends and loved ones hollows out our inside world. It not only becomes smaller—it becomes empty, narrow, and meaningless.

Zwischen diesen beiden Begriffen, Gedenken und Abschied, bewegt sich unsere Welt pendelartig hin und her. Wird sie zusammenbrechen wegen der Mauern von außen oder wegen des Verlustes von innen?

III

Auf die Trostlosigkeit unseres Seins hat man schon viele Antworten gegeben. Nur *die* Antwort steht noch aus. Der Trost ist noch nicht vorhanden. Und wenn es einen solchen in der Welt unserer Tage gibt, so befindet er sich innerhalb der Sphäre, die seit Anbeginn des Lebens letzter Zufluchtsort gewesen ist und selbst der Tröstung ihren Ursprung verdankt: die Musik.

IV

Wie ist sie eigentlich entstanden? Wann hat sie zum ersten Mal das Licht der Welt erblickt?

Ich glaube: Musik entstand in der Minute, in welcher der erste Mensch gezwungen wurde, Liebe in Sehnsucht umzuwandeln. Als das Gefühl—schicksalsbefohlen—sich anschikken mußte, zeitunbedingt und raumlos fortzuleben.

V

Wie im Privaten, so ist es im Nationalen. Das Judentum hat als Volk getan, was wir Menschen als Individuen in großen Stunden unseres Gefühlslebens tun. Eines Tages hat es seine Heimat verloren und wurde räumlich von ihr getrennt. Es stand vor der Entscheidung, ob es sie aufgibt, oder sie von einer anderen Ebene aus bejaht. In zweitausendjähriger Sehnsucht verwandelte das jüdische Volk seine Liebe in den Messianismus.

VI

So ist es immer: man lebt mit Menschen lange Zeit zusammen. Oft hat man gemeinsam Musik gehört. Irgendwo in der Welt sitzt man in einem kleinen blauen Zimmer mit Kerzenbeleuchtung. Ein Grammophon spielt. Mendelssohns Sommernachtstraum. Das Schicksal kommt. Räumlich trennt es uns von diesen Menschen. Dann sprechen wir: hörst Du irgendwo in der Welt, in Berlin oder in Amsterdam, dieselben Klänge, so weißt Du, wir sind bei Dir.

Und Du hast uns nie verlassen.

Between these two poles of remembering and of farewell our life swings like a pendulum. Will it break down because of the walls outside and the loss inside?

III

Where do we turn for consolation? Many answers to this question have been given: hope—religion—or other spheres of our spiritual reservoir. Tonight I want to suggest one of them: music .

IV

When was music born?

There are many theories, but I believe: music was born when the first human being was forced to transform love into longing; when love was forced by destiny to exist beyond time and space.

V

Judaism did for our people what we as individuals are doing at crucial moments of our emotional life. One day the people had lost its home and was geographically separated from it. It had to make a decision: give it up, or affirm it on a different plane. In two thousand years of longing the Jewish people transformed its love into messianism. But its sounds, its melodies, its music remained the same.

VI

It is always like this: you have been together for a long time, you have listened to music together. Sometimes, like tonight, sitting in a small, blue room, by candlelight, you have listened to a recording: maybe Mendelssohn's Midsummernight's Dream. Fate steps in, separates us geographically from each other. Then we say: if you hear these same sounds anywhere in the world, in Berlin or in Amsterdam, then you know we are with you.

And you have never left us.

DER SINN DER WELT/
THE MEANING OF THE WORLD

From *Jüdische Rundschau*, Berlin 1938

Noch atemberaubender als der Gedanke der Schöfung der Welt aus dem Nichts ist wohl der, dass dem Anfang der Welt ihre kosmische Sinngebung voranging. Es gehört zu den aufregendsten Darlegungen der Tradition, dass die Thora vor der Schöpfung existierte, und dass der Thora wiederum die praesumptive Idee "Israel" voranging. Die Thora spielte hiernach bei der Ershaffung der Welt die Rolle der Lehrmeisterin, des künstlerischen Vorwurfs. Architekten bauen ihre Paläste nach einem bestimmten, aus den Quellen der Kunst geschöpften Plan; so studierte der Schöpfer den Plan der Thora und schuf danach seine Welt. — Er warf einen Blick auf Israel und wusste, dass es viele Generationen später zum Träger des Gebäudes auserkoren sein werde. Also baute er seine Welt im Rückblick auf den sinnvollen Plan der Thora und im Hinblick auf den künftigen Träger dieses Sinnes, Israel.

So hat die Welt ihren Himmel und ihre Erde, ihren Plan und seinen Verwirklicher, ihren Sinn und seinen Träger. Es ist dies die praestabilisierte Harmonie der Welt, und es liegt ihr ob, in diesem Gleichgewicht zu bleiben. Deshalb führt Gott den ersten Menschen durch die Welt und zeigt ihm ihre Konturen und ihre friedliche Ausgeglichenheit. "Sieh, wie schön sie ist, —und alles nur für Dich! Gib acht, dass Du nicht ausgleitest; Du würdest sie zerstören, und es gibt keinen nach Dir, der sie wieder herstellen könnte..." —Als sich aber eine Generation erdreistete, das Gleichgewicht der Welt zu stören, da schickte Gott die Sintflut, vernichtete die Welt und schuf einen neuen Anfang mit einer reineren Menschheit. Durch Noah gab er der Welt ihr Gleichgewicht, ihre alte Bestimmung, ihren Sinn wieder. Seit dieser Zeit warten wir, dass auch der andere Teil der Verheissung sich erfülle: dass der Sinn der Welt durch seinen Träger Israel verwirklicht werde!

THE MEANING OF THE WORLD/
DER SINN DER WELT

Even more breathtaking than the concept of creation from nothingness is the thought that prior to the beginning of the world there was a cosmic predestination for it. One of the most exciting claims of our tradition is that the Torah existed prior to creation, and preceding the Torah there was the presumptive idea of "Israel."

At the creation of the world, Torah thus played the role of the teacher, the designer. Architects build their palaces after a certain plan, based on the sources of their art. So God studied the blueprint of Torah, and from it created his world. He turned his eyes on Israel and knew that many generations later it would be chosen to be the bearer of that building. So he constructed his world looking back to the meaningful plan of Torah and looking forward to the future bearer of that meaning, Israel.

So the world has its heaven and its earth, its meaning and its bearer. This is the preestablished harmony of the world, and its task it is to keep its balance. That is why God led the first human through the world, showed him its contours and its peaceful serenity. "Look, how beautiful it is—and all this only for you! Take care that you do not stumble; you might destroy it, and there is no one after you able to repair it."

But when a generation dared to upset the equilibrium of the world, God sent the flood, destroyed the world, and made a new beginning with a purer humanity. Through Noah, he restored to the world its balance, its countenance, its meaning. Since then we have been waiting for the other part of the promise to be fulfilled: that the destiny of the world be realized through its bearer: Israel.

THE PATH TO A ZIONIST MASS-MOVEMENT/
DER VEG TZU A TZIONISTISHER MASEN—BAVEGUNG

From *Dos Yiddishe Folk,* May, 1942

I believe that the best solution for the Jewish youth in America would be the Zionist idea, provided it is properly introduced and followed by education. Zionism alone would give them confidence when they see that assimilation puts them in a peculiar inexplicable predicament where their self-esteem is bound to suffer. We should explain that the surest way to assimilate in America is to be or become a normal national minority group in this country, true to its tradition and its culture. The best way for a Jewish youth to be considered a full-fledged American is to identify with his own ethnic group, to be true to his religion, to study Hebrew, help build *eretz yisrael* as a Jewish homeland, and to be like all other nations. This type of Zionism they will understand. From my experience with Jewish youth and many circles of Jewish intelligentsia, I know that this is the way to make Zionism a mass movement.

DER VEG TZU A TZIONISTISHER MASEN—BAVEGUNG/
THE PATH TO A ZIONIST MASS-MOVEMENT

From *Dos Yiddishe Folk,* May, 1942

דער וועג צו אַ ציוניסטישער מאַסען=באַוועגונג

איך גלויב, אז די ציוניסטישע אידעע אין אמעריקא וואָלט געווען די
גליקליכסטע לייזונג פאַר דער אידישער יוגענד, ווען מען זאָל נאָר קומען
צו איהר מיט דער געהעריגער אויפקלעהרונג און ערציהונג. דער ציוניזם
אליין קען זיי געבען זיכערקייט בעת זיי פיהלען און זעהען אז די
אסימילאציע ברענגט זיי אין א קוריאָזער, אומפאַרשטענדליכער לאַגע
וואו זייער זעלבסטרעספעקט מוז שטאַק ליידען. מיר קענען זיי
אויפקלעהרען און געבען זיי צו פארשטעהן, אז דער איינציגער און
זיכרסטער וועג, ווי אזוי זיך צו אַסימילירען אין אמעריקא, איז צו זיין
און צו ווערען א נאָרמאלע פאָלקס-גרופע, גענוי ווי אלע אנדערע
פעלקער-גרופען דאָ אין לאַנד, וואָס זיינען טריי זיײערע טראַדיציעס און
זייער קולטור. דער בעסטער וועג פאר א אידישען יונגענמאַן,
אנערקענט צו ווערען אלס א פולשטענדיגער אמעריקאנער איז זיך צו
אינדענטיפיצירען מיט זיין אייגענעם פאָלק. טריי צו זיין זיין רעליגיע,
צו לערנען העברעאיש, אויפצובויען ארץ ישראל אלס א אידישע
היימלאנד און צו זיין גלייך מיט אלע אנדערע פעלקער. אזא ציוניזם
וועלען זיי פארשטעהן. און פון מיין ערפאהרונג וואָס איך האָב געהאָט
מיט דער אידישער יוגענד און מיט מעהרערע קריזען פון דער אידישער
אינטעליגענץ וויים איך, אז דאס איז דער וועג וואס וועט מאַכען פון
ציוניזם אן אמת׳ע מאַסען-באַוועגונג.

Observations

With Martin Luther King, February 26, 1965

WE ARE NOT ALONE

September 11, 1942

At the beginning of this New Year, 5703, it is fitting to let pass in review not only the horrifying pictures in Jewish life, of which we know, but the advantages and merits of the concluding year, which seldom enter our mind. The characteristic feature of many centuries of Jewish history was not so much persecution as loneliness. In days of tribulation we usually stood completely alone, without friends, and what is more, without neighbors.

The passing year, 5702, changed a very important item in our life among the nations. For the first time in our history, the nations, united in democratic gospel, stand with us and we are a part of them. They and we know that our fate is interdependent. It is this togetherness of a spiritual neighborhood that marks the outstanding symbol of the year 5702 in our Jewish calendar—indeed an unusual result of a war-torn time.

It is, also, this war that brought us together, you the congregation, and me the rabbi. I want both of us, you and me, to live up to that unparalleled gift that fate has brought to us as a result of this war. I do not want to stand alone, and do not want you to stay aloof. I want you, members of our congregation, to be neighbors to each other and individually to me. It is because of the togetherness of the United Nations that we will win this war. It is because of the togetherness of congregation and rabbi, of you and me, that we will create an atmosphere of close friendship that will enable our generation to be capable of winning the peace.

We are fervently praying that the year to come may bring the spirit of neighborliness, friendship to our congregation, liberation and equality to Israel, and peace and happiness to the world.

FLAMES OVER GERMANY: AN EYE-WITNESS ACCOUNT

November 27, 1942

When those three days—of the tenth, eleventh, and twelfth of November, 1938—were over, we took stock of our tragedy and

35

counted our curses: more than five hundred synagogues in Germany, Austria, Czechoslovakia and Danzig burnt, scores of charity institutions destroyed, hundreds of homes devastated, thousands of stores pillaged, and one hundred thousand Jews in the concentration camps of Oranienburg, Dachau and Sachsenhausen, beside those who had been ruthlessly slaughtered in their homes during those three nights. The destruction was complete. It surpassed the blackest pages of our tearful history, including the Inquisition of the Middle Ages. So thoroughly organized was this new barbarism that there was no shade of hope of resuming our life anew—life which was aggravated enough before.

Why do we devote a Friday evening, which is supposed to be imbued with a character of Sabbath calm and Sabbath peace, to the commemoration of such an anniversary? It is being done not only because of a special request of the Synagogue Council of America and the National Refugee Service— although this is important enough—but because of a lesson in history to American Jewry.

The question which arises is this. What does it mean to you here that in 1942, four years after the great destruction, our Jewish institutions are untouched, our homes intact, our synagogues open and all of us alive? Tragedies in history do not happen by coincidence. They have a deep meaning. They convey a message. Some of us died over there in the shadow of the Gestapo so that others may live in the light of security. Some of us survived, surely not because we were better or deserved it. We survived in order to hammer home to the free parts of world Jewry the weight of that tragedy, and to tell the story "of the exodus from Egypt." Some of American Jewry have neither gone through that experience of death, nor survived it—it was completely untouched by that process of destruction. This, however, has a meaning too. Such a privilege does not occur by coincidence. The nobility of freedom obliges one to responsibility. Each time the law of Jewish history allows one part of our people to stay outside the ghetto walls, it lends them liberty under the express condition of rendering its service to the other part which is deprived of it.

A Jewry which lives in liberty, enjoys the freedom of religion, and does not fill its synagogues and temples to capacity, destroys them from within as those gangsters have done from without. A Jewry which enjoys freedom of speech and does not utilize it to fill houses of Jewish learning, to speak our language, to know our tradition and to be acquainted with our heritage—burns the Torah Scrolls from within as did the modern barbarians from without. A Jewry which enjoys the freedom from want and the freedom from fear, and that does not feel its responsibility for all of Israel and does not prepare to take over the leadership in this time of crisis, forfeits the unusual privilege of its unparalleled position. This is the meaning of that tragedy for all three participants: the victims, the survivors, and the untouched.

There is a legend in Jewish lore. When the Temple in Jerusalem burst into flames, sparks spread all over the globe in twos seeking refuge for a long time. One spark of such a couplet entered a synagogue, the other one the soul of a Jew. Out of the first came the "perpetual light" of our Temple. Out of the second, the "Jewish heart of our people." These two sparks being separated are yearning for each other, since they belong together. Thus, every time a Jew enters a synagogue, praying or learning from the depths of his heart, the pair of sparks come together, a piece of the old Temple is built anew, and the spirit of Israel celebrates its revival.

Sparks are neutral in character. They can be a part of flames over Germany or a part of fires over North Africa. They can be either flames of destruction or fires of hope. Thus, to reunite the Jewish heart of our people with the perpetual light of our temples is the message of tonight. To convert flames of destruction into fires of hope is the mission of American Israel.

THE CRISIS OF OUR GENERATION

September 15, 1944

The New Jewish Year which will commence Sunday, September 17, will usher in a new epic for American Israel. It will be a year of dedication to the principles of Liberal Judaism, spiritu-

37

al values and American Democracy—in short a year of dedication to the ideals for which this horrible war is being fought.

The crisis of our generation is, in its deepest sense, of a religious nature. It is only because Christians remain Gentiles, and Jews Israelites, both united more in lip service than in practical deeds to religious ideals, that the world finds itself in the catastrophe that envelops us all.

There will be no peace even after victory is won unless our generation learns the redemptive skill of dedication—in thought as in deed—to the religious values hallowed by centuries of Jewish traditions.

We are accusing the world, and justifiably so, of having developed political systems with complete disregard of the ethical system of Western Civilization. Only those whose hands are clean have the right to accuse others. Modern Judaism has to be the vanguard in this plan of spiritual reconversion. It seems that destiny has chosen American Israel to fall heir to European Jewry and to take the lead. It is upon us to fulfill the promise given to a generation whose sons and daughters are dying on every battlefield of our global war

It is the synagogue, that bastion of old and modern Judaism, that has to become again the center of our life. Assimilated Jews and Yahrzeit-Israelites who do the Lord the favor of meeting him once a year will have no place in our post-war history, neither on the American nor on the Jewish scene. They will become the unwept, unsung and unhonored caricatures of our modern age. Only true dedication to Liberal Judaism and its central institution, the temple, will provide our adult and young generation with a philosophy of life, a psychology of dignity, an attitude of normalcy and the gift of happiness.

To those who have suffered bereavement, we extend our heart-felt sympathy. With all of you, I pray that the day of final victory and total peace may come speedily and return our sons and daughters from the four corners of the earth to their families and their homes. "May all of us be inscribed into the book of life."

CHARGE TO THE CONFIRMATION CLASS

June 16, 1950

What is Torah? A book. The Five Books of Moses. The Prophets. The Law. It is a "way of life" and—formulated in terms meaningful to our young generation—it centers around three words: knowledge, faith and belongingness.

As to knowledge—do not, I beg of you, allow yourself to fall into the trap of ignorance. Do not join the host of empty minds. They are not an asset to any community. Professor Hutchins' words to his students should be a guide on your way. Said he: "If we are not going to substitute knowledge for fun in our schools, we will have a generation of morons within a quarter of a century."

Ignorant people are not only a liability to society, they are also very bad ambassadors of goodwill. Millions of Marshall Plan money will not wash away the ridicule to which our country was exposed in the European press the other day, when some of our senators, on their recent trip to Europe, could not distinguish between Bucharest and Budapest, between the Louvre and a Paris night club. Multiply the effect of such ignorance tenfold and you will understand what a pitiful human being an ignorant Jew is in our own ranks, and the type of ambassador of good will he can be for us to others.

Our Rabbis, in their wisdom, said long ago that ignorant people cannot be pious. But it is actually piety and faith that are necessary for our generation. In the script of an unreleased motion picture entitled, "The Next Voice You Hear," there is a scene in which God speaks to mankind through radio transmission. One hears God's voice saying: "I have performed many miracles: the raindrops and the snowflakes, the valleys and the hills, the mountains and the rivers, the sun and the moon and the stars; why shouldn't you, men of this earth, perform your miracles of love and mercy, of justice and freedom, of fairness and decency, of peace and goodwill?" It is this type of faith that is necessary in our harassed world. Even if we have to stand alone in it, you and we have to be the advance guard of this militant faith.

There is the last word, "belongingness." The crisis of our generation consists of the loneliness of individuals and isolationism of whole groups. One can never derive happiness from life unless one accepts one's self fully as a member of the family, of the community, of the people from which one comes, of the nation to which one belongs, and as a member of society at large. In a recent play, "Member of the Wedding," Julie Harris, playing a half-sophisticated, half-naive girl, insists on accompanying her brother on his honeymoon. When Ethel Waters, who portrays the maid, tries to elicit from her the reason for this strange decision, she replies: "When you say 'we', you mean the Church; when my brother says 'we', he means the Marine Corps; when my sister-in-law says 'we', she means the two of them; when I say 'we', it is completely empty, it means nothing."

When you say "we," it should mean the knowledge of, the faith in, and the belongingness to the Jewish People and Israel, America and the United Nations.

REFORM CONGREGATIONS IN EUROPE

August 28, 1958

It is good to be back again in your midst. This was a strenuous, but most exciting journey through France, Italy, Israel, Berlin, Holland, Belgium and England. I made it a point to see at close range all the Reform congregations of the European capitals which we visited: the small, but beautiful synagogue on the Rue Copernic in Paris; the simple, but very modern chapel of the Liberal Congregation in Amsterdam, the institutions and offices of the World Union for Progressive Judaism (which is the international organization of the Reform Movement) in London; and I also met with the Liberal groups which are just commencing modest activities in Israel, principally in Tel Aviv and Jerusalem.

In each instance, they are struggling for their very existence, and, with the exception of England, almost completely dependent upon American aid, be it in books and programming, or be it actually in financial subsidies. In each instance there is an uphill battle against the established synagogue of

Orthodox Jewry which does not recognize them, refuses to give them any official status, and in most places, makes their existence even more complicated than it already is.

When, against this background, you begin to contemplate our fortunate position on these shores—both in freedom of expression and in the financial capability of American Jewry— there swells up a prayer of thankfulness in your heart for the "goodly heritage" that is ours as Jews in these United States.

There is much which is attractive and impressive, yes, even overpowering and overwhelming in what Europe has to offer—in art and literature, music and drama, museums and historical sights. Still, apart from Israel, America is the only place in which you would choose, anytime anew, to live and spend your days. As I said at the outset—it is very good to be home again.

CONSCIOUSNESS OF HISTORY

September 11, 1958

The day I am dictating this article has brought about a sharpening of racial tensions in Arkansas; the immediate possibility of an open conflict between Communist China and the United States in the Far East; a highly dangerous encirclement of Israel by Nasser's Pan-Arabic Empire, with accompanying symptoms of such explosiveness that it may set the whole of the Middle East afire. Never since the end of the Second World War have so many clouds of war been darkening our horizon in such proximity.

When, against the background of these events, a Jew enters the synagogue for the High Holyday Service, he may attempt to come as a detached individual, pray for his own happiness and the welfare of his family. But how long will he be able to worship exclusively on this level? How can he pray for the passing away from this earth of "the dominion of arrogance" and "the smoke-like vanishing of wickedness" without thinking of Little Rock? How can one ask the Lord of the Universe that the nations of the world "should form themselves into one single entity to do according to Thy will with perfect

41

heart" without reflecting on Formosa? How can one, as a Jew, beseech the God of Israel "to grant great peace for Israel Thy people for all the years to come, for Thou art the King and Master of peace and it is pleasant in Thine eyes to bless Thy people Israel with Thy peace at all times and in each hour"— without considering the desperate situation of Israel now entirely surrounded by forces of hostility? How could any one of us dare ask to be inscribed in the Book of Life, on a personal level, without identifying himself with the causes of Israel, peace, and human brotherhood? One cannot any more travel through life—more than that, one cannot even enter a synagogue—without consciousness of history.

On the other hand, those who have given of time and energy, of substance and devotion to these causes will exult in the knowledge of a good conscience and will, in a mood of serenity, yes, with perfect ease, ask for the blessing of life for themselves and those they love, as it has become traditional with the ancient heritage of our people. To the others, Rosh Hashanah and Yom Kippur are a stirring admonition to join the ranks of those who battle for a more secure Israel, for a better approach to peace, and for the speedy emergence of human brotherhood.

It is a serious time in which we live. The challenges come, simultaneously, from all sides. But we, as Jews—tested in the fire of experience and masters in the art of survival because of a deeply rooted faith in God and man—will know the answer that can only flow from a religious soul and believing heart.

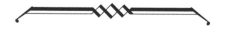

CLARIFYING A CONFUSION

December 24, 1959

There are personal, Jewish, American, and universal holidays which a Jew can legitimately celebrate; and there are others, basically Christian or Moslem holidays, which belong to the sacred repository of other religions and have, therefore, to be left alone by a conscientious Jew.

There is a simple criterion by which to test the legitimacy of holiday celebrations: whenever you can put a holiday into the synagogue, weave it into the tapestry of a service, and watch it fit harmoniously into the mosaic of Judaism—then, and then only, can a holiday be celebrated in good conscience.

Birthdays and wedding anniversaries, all Jewish holidays in the rhythm of the Jewish calendar, all American holidays— Thanksgiving, the Fourth of July, Memorial Day, Washington's and Lincoln's birthdays—which stem from the very historical experience of the nation, and all universal holidays—Brotherhood Week, United Nations Month, the secular New Year— can, therefore, and have actually been made a part of the religious service of the synagogue in perfect blending with the idealism of our ancient tradition.

Imagine for a single moment to do the same with Christmas, and you will discover at first glance that it does not belong to you and you do not belong to it, because it stands as a sacred symbol of basic Christianity. It is as immoral to trespass upon the theological tradition of another religion as it is to help one's self to the accumulated bank account of a neighbor in your block.

To sum it up: in observances and customs, in ceremonies and holiday celebrations, you are on safe ground only when you, personally, can identify yourself unreservedly and without qualifications with the leitmotif of each one of them.

It is quite puzzling that there should be any confusion in this matter. It is rather clear and quite simple. A Jew worthy of the honored name of our people will easily be guided by these noble principles.

Let us, then, in this spirit, celebrate this year the Festival of Hanukkah, which is our very own holiday, by kindling the lights and singing the songs, by decorating our homes and playing the games, by performing the music and telling the story, by attending the services and by exchanging the gifts.

RESPONSE TO HANNAH ARENDT'S
EICHMANN IN JERUSALEM

May 2, 1963

It is apparently easy for Professor Arendt to write such articles, rather detached, two decades after the occurrence of the events and then seek scapegoats in devoted and courageous Jews, all of whom ended in concentration camps.

Dr. Arendt was not in Berlin at the time, but I was. I knew Rabbi Leo Baeck, Paul Epstein and several others personally— the most faithful sons of our people, who reflected in their own lives the qualities of Judaism at its very best. Rabbi Baeck was probably the saintliest figure that has ever walked on this earth. To characterize him as a "Jewish Fuehrer" is the most vicious character assassination I have seen in a very long time. As I can speak of personal experiences, I can state frankly that rarely in modern literature has a historic period been described with more brilliance of language and more viciousness of content. If what the author has to say about the other Jewish communities in Europe is as "true" as her remarks about the leadership of German Jewry, then you must begin to question the utter integrity of her research.

The superficiality of Professor Arendt's interpretation is nowhere as disturbing as in her glib and invidious comments on the submission to death of our helpless brothers and sisters, and in her effrontery of depicting Eichmann as the small cog in the large wheel of the Nazi machine. Those of us who had the doubtful privilege of knowing him and his activities in Berlin did not have to wait for the Eichmann trial—and the careful research made as a result of it—to disclose the primary responsibility of Eichmann for saturating a whole continent with the blood of our people.

Our prophets warned us once that some of the greatest enemies we will encounter will come from the inside. I am afraid Professor Arendt has done a great disservice to the Jewish people and most of all to the cause of truth.

THE ECUMENICAL COUNCIL ON THE JEWS

December 17, 1964

The decision of the Ecumenical Council on the Jews is an event of historic proportion—not because the Jewish people needed an exoneration from deicide—but because the Church has long been in dire need of atoning for the guilt of its own past.

Anti-Semitism has its main roots in some of the teachings of the Church, and there is a direct link between the auto-da-fé of the Inquisition and the vilification of the Jew throughout the centuries of church history to the concentration camps and burning ovens of Hitler's crematoria. This has, in recent years, been acknowledged, over and over again, by the highest leaders of the Church both at home and abroad. These statements of individual Princes of the Church have now received the official stamp of the Vatican. Under the impact of our people's catastrophe in this generation, the Church searched its soul, found it wanting, and admitted the error of its ways. This is an act of repentance long overdue—but we welcome it as heralding a new chapter in Catholic-Jewish relations and, possibly, a new era in human relations.

Now that the main millennia-old obstacle has been removed, we hope that the Vatican will instruct its churches throughout the world—especially those in South America—not only to desist from overt and covert assistance to Nazism, but to live up to the expectations of the newly proclaimed doctrine. This is the historic significance of the declaration: conscience asserted itself and justice triumphed over expediency.

It is a day which the Lord has made, and we may be glad and rejoice in it.

THE FREEDOM STORY OF PASSOVER

April 8, 1965

Our Jewish tradition has always looked upon the Exodus from Egypt as an historic event of gigantic proportions. With it there came into the world all the ingredients that go into the making of a just society: the dignity of the human being, the sacredness of personality, the freedom of the individual and the liberty of the group. Because of this, Judaism has always considered the birth of freedom a drama of greater import than even the creation of the universe. This is why the divine voice on

45

Sinai does not introduce the Decalogue with the words "I am the Lord who created heaven and earth," but with the proclamation "I am the Lord thy God who brought thee out of the land of Egypt."

The amazing insight of our classic tradition has been validated by the test of history. No other story in the annals of human events has exerted so deep an influence upon generations of men as has the Freedom Story of Passover. Every revolution in human history drew its inspiration from it. Every quest for freedom was motivated by it. It was the ideal behind the French Revolution. It was the very text book of the American Revolution. In the latter case, the identification with the Passover Story is such that one cannot understand the vocabulary of the Pilgrims and Puritans in early American history unless one knows the language which the Bible employs in telling the Story of the Exodus. When James Russell Lowell desired to pay a special compliment to "The little shipload of outcasts who landed at Plymouth," he said of them that "They are destined to influence the future of mankind...next to the fugitives whom Moses led out of Egypt." Such has been the influence of the Passover Story upon men and nations.

It is fascinating to behold that our Passover Haggadah is the spiritual motivation of the Negro Revolution of our own days. Those of us who had the privilege of listening to Dr. Martin Luther King in our own temple, will undoubtedly remember his remarkable sermon which was entirely based upon the Freedom Story of Passover. Only this week, prior to the March on Montgomery, he again drew a parallel between the experiences of American Negroes and our forefathers led out of Egypt by Moses. He said, "Like the Negroes, the Children of Israel were exploited economically, dominated politically, and humiliated by the power structure of Egypt. Like the Israelites, American Negroes fall into three classes: those who would return to Egypt, those who do not want to turn back but fear to move ahead, and a third group that will not be turned around. I believe by your very presence, you represent the third group." Thus the impact of the Passover Story is still with us in our own generation. This is why our Rabbis always spoke of a *pesach l'atid*, "A Passover of the Future," meaning that no society can ever grow into wholesomeness unless it imple-

46

ments the ideals that were projected into the universe by the Story of Passover.

This is the meaning of our holiday, this year, and this is its formidable challenge. The Negro Revolution still draws its inspiration from this chapter of our biblical history. The Negro Revolution is "Zionism-in-Black." We, more than any other group, ought to have the fullest understanding for it and evolve a complete identification with it. One can best fulfill the commandment of the seder in 1965 by drinking one of the four cups to the Negro Revolution and say *l'chayim* to Martin Luther King.

A MESSAGE FROM TEL AVIV

March 14, 1968

After many weeks of journey through the Far East, Ruth and I have finally arrived in Israel which, in turn, means being at home. I use the word "home" for two reasons: Israel is the old-new home of our ancient people, and I am dictating this article at the ZOA House, which is a veritable piece of America within the Jewish State.

Our trip through the Far Eastern part of the world was one of the most fascinating experiences in the whole of our lives—both as tourists looking upon an unknown and completely strange continent, and as Jews looking with Jewish eyes upon small Jewish communities dispersed throughout the area and held together by an inner longing to be part and parcel of the Jewish people.

The highlights of our trip will forever be the ancient and colorful cultures of Japan and India, Cambodia and Iran, enhanced by incredible artistic achievements in sculptured monuments going back to the tenth and even to the seventh centuries. Without any apparent contact with Western Civilization and preceding the Italian Renaissance by many centuries, the Eastern mind conceived architectural miracles of temples, shrines, and palaces which defy description, and in front of which you stand with utter awe before the magnitude of the creativity of the human spirit.

It is already good to visit that part of the world in order to acquire a sense of proportion. All of us in the West are so taken in by our own civilization and by the dominant factors of Judaism and Christianity, that we often equate the part with the whole; and suddenly you are confronted with a world which, though it has accepted the outer trappings of the West, has retained the strange peculiarity of its innermost soul, with a philosophy which is as different from ours as is day from night and a mentality which has never heard of Judaism nor of Christianity, but is nurtured by Shintoism, Buddhism, Hinduism and Zoroastrianism. The people who belong to these Eastern philosophies and religions are many times our numbers, and if our world would tomorrow sink into nothingness, it would—on the spiritual level—create hardly a ripple in the vast oceans comprising the world of the Orient. Yes, a visit to these places is a "must" from the viewpoint of proportion—you begin to look upon the universe in a larger vista, from a different focus, and gain a more balanced insight into the immense variety of human existence.

There are the small Jewish communities: we visited the ones in Tokyo and Kobe of Japan; the one of Bangkok in Thailand; the small Jewish community of Hong Kong as well as the large Jewish communities of Bombay and Teheran. What cements Jewish life in these areas and what is holding them together as Jews, are two elements, and two elements only: the Synagogue and the State of Israel. In one form or another, all of them have a kind of Jewish Community Center which includes a small synagogue. Very few of them have full-time rabbis, but they skillfully take advantage of young American rabbis stationed as chaplains throughout the areas. These rabbis usually conduct services, deliver sermons and give lectures, and thus contribute much to the spiritual life of these Jewish centers. But beyond that, and in some places even with greater strength, it is the love of Zion, the yearning to be part of the upbuilding of the Jewish state, which motivates their daily lives. Possibly because of a bad conscience that they live in such far away places and outside the stream of Jewish life, they breathe and speak and live Israel amidst a Babel of foreign tongues, maintain their Jewishness via this identification, and usually send their children to Israel either for study or for real aliyah. One has to speak with the leadership of these small Jewish communities to understand the meaning of the two words "Synagogue" and "Israel," with all the implications emanating from them. Things which we in the States take so easily for granted have to be fought for here in a daily struggle in order to maintain the synagogue as a symbol of Jewish identification, or to succeed in getting a teacher from a far away place to teach some Hebrew or Jewish history to the children of Jewish families.

We attended services in Hong Kong, in Bangkok and in Teheran. Receptions were given in our honor by all these Jewish communities with whom we made contact, because they knew of our visit though the offices of the World Jewish Congress. In Hong Kong I addressed the congregation during the Friday evening services, and in Bombay I spoke at a mass meeting of the Jewish community, attended a reception the following day, and at the Institute of Oriental Research I lectured on "The Moral Values of Judaism and Zoroastrianism."

All in all, it was a most enriching experience, both from a general human as well as from a specific Jewish viewpoint.

Looking back upon these weeks, I come again and again to the same conclusion; how happy is our generation, which, living in the United States, has all these facilities so matter of factly that we take them for granted—the synagogues, the rabbis, religious schools, Jewish education, and freedom of communication. How terribly difficult is all this in the Oriental part of the universe! Let us cherish what we have—other Jewish communities would sell their last possession to have even part of what is our portion in our beloved America.

THE REMARKABLE FINALE OF 1968

January 9, 1969

The Festival of Hanukkah which we just concluded will not be easily forgotten. The year 1968, which reached its nadir in August (by the Russian invasion of Czechoslovakia), lifted itself to the zenith the older it grew—and all these spectacular events took place during the Hanukkah week.

It commenced December 16, the first day of Hanukkah, with a formal declaration by the Spanish Government which rescinded the decree of 1492 ordering the expulsion of the Jewish Community from its borders. Four hundred and seventy-six years, then, after the edict of King Ferdinand and Queen Isabella, the Ministry of Justice handed this document to one of the leaders of the Madrid Jewish Community, Samuel Toledano, himself a direct descendent of Rabbi Daniel Toledano, the Rabbi of Toledo at the time of the expulsion.

To dramatize this unique event, the government declaration was read from the pulpit on the occasion of the dedication of Madrid's new synagogue, the first Jewish temple to be built on Spanish soil since the fourteenth century.

Seldom have the lights of the Hanukkah menorah radiated such a miracle in Jewish history.

On December 17, the second day of Hanukkah, the Social, Humanitarian and Cultural Committee of the UN General Assembly adopted a resolution which "once again resolutely condemns racism, Nazism, apartheid and all similar ideologies and practices which are based on racial intolerance and terror, as a gross violation of human rights and fundamental freedoms and of the principles of the Charter of the United Nations, and which may jeopardize world peace." The UN Resolution warns that "such ideologies have in the past led to barbarous acts which outraged the conscience of mankind and to other heinous violations of human rights and, eventually, to a war which brought indescribable suffering to mankind." It is only a resolution of the Third Committee, and has to be voted on by the full Assembly—but as a first step in the direction of building a better and more just society, the draft resolution is of historic importance.

Seldom have the lights of Hanukkah ever had the opportunity of bringing us such a message of hope from the international community.

On the sixth day of the festival, namely on the Sabbath of Hanukkah, three American astronauts were launched on Apollo 8 toward an orbit on the moon, so as to look at our nearest neighbor as it has never been seen before, and they reached their goal of entering the moon's orbit on the twenty-third of this month, meaning the last day of Hanukkah. These times will live in our and in our children's memory for all the years to come, because our generation has apparently been singled out for the privilege of organizing man's greatest voyage of discovery—the landing on the moon.

Living in these days of the most ambitious and most difficult mission ever undertaken by man, one remembers nostalgically what Shakespeare thought about this idea three hundred and fifty years ago when, in *King Henry IV,* he puts into the mouth of one of his actors the words:

> By heaven, methinks it were an easy leap
> To pluck bright honour from the pale fac'ed moon.

The journey of the astronauts was not an easy undertaking. But Shakespeare was right in predicting the honor that would come to a generation which can reach that high point in scientific achievements as to master the contact between human beings and celestial bodies.

The reaction of the American people to this spectacular event was a fascinating lesson in human relations. The hundreds that were interviewed said that if human cooperation can achieve such success in outer space, why not build bridges between ethnic groups, religions, nations and states in the inner space of Earth itself?

On Christmas Eve, Commander Frank Borman offered a prayer for mankind from Apollo 8, in which he said:

> Give us, O God, the vision which can see Thy love in the world in spite of human failure.

> Give us the faith to trust the goodness in spite of our ignorance and weakness.

> Give us the knowledge that we may continue to pray with understanding hearts, and show us what each of us can do to set forward the coming of the day of universal peace. Amen.

Isn't this message from outer space flowing from the ideal of the Maccabean festival, so challengingly phrased by the prophet of old, "Not by might and not by power but by My spirit, sayeth the Lord (Zechariah 4:6)"?

Indeed, rarely in the history of mankind could the Hanukkah lights tell of such miraculous tales.

A MEASURE OF HOPE

February 12, 1971

There is a silver lining on the dark horizon of Russian Jewry. It is not the commutation of the death sentences to long prison terms—which is only a change from the instant firing squad to a slow death. It is not the reduction of some prison terms from fifteen to twelve years—most of them are too old to survive the harassment of these years anyway. A measure of hope, however, still exists in the lesson we have learned as a result of the experiences: the Soviet Union is very sensitive to world public opinion. The fact that twenty-four governments, including our own, the Pope, the Secretary General of the United Nations, international Leftist organizations, and Western Communist parties protested against the injustices of the Russian system, shows that the cry of an aroused world conscience can still accomplish miracles, even within a violent, dehumanized society. It is a lesson never to be forgotten.

This, coupled with the miracle of Jewish resistance to Soviet oppression, the incredible identification with Israel and the Jewish people of Soviet Jewry after fifty-three years of Communist Revolution, the heroic defiance, at the risk of their very lives, of the younger generation—all this is, historically speaking, the great miracle of our generation.

If the international community will remain alert to the dangerous situation, and Russian Jewry will continue to manifest its militant spirit, the day will come in which we will live to see the dawn of liberation for three million Jews imprisoned behind the walls of an anti-Semitic government.

Let us keep Russian Jewry on the top of our agenda for 1971, and let us pray and work for the hour of redemption.

RECAPTURING SHAVUOT

May 21, 1971

The way in which a generation relates itself to the festivals of its group is always indicative of its own system of values. The holiday season now upon us is a good case in point.

In our tradition, Passover is the birthday of the Jewish People and Shavuot is the birthday of the Jewish religion. Whereas Passover has been increasing in popularity and is now a huge success—Shavuot has been on the losing side of American Jewish life and is now an utter failure.

Nothing points more dramatically to the despiritualization of Jewish life in the United States than the negative attitude to the Feast of Weeks. The identification with Jewish Peoplehood is, undoubtedly, the positive ingredient for Jewish survival. But is it enough? What type of people will we be without the Book, without spiritual undergirding, without religious anchorage, in short without Judaism? To what will six million American Jews amount without our biblical heritage?

Shavuot is, next to Rosh Hashanah and Yom Kippur, the most spiritual of Jewish holidays. Yet the Reform Movement had to "save" the festival by introducing the Confirmation Service, through which our young graduates pledge their loyalty and commitment to the majestic tradition of Judaism. It is a beautiful custom, has been copied by the Conservative and Orthodox Synagogues alike, and has given Shavuot its raison d'être. But if our members do not happen to be parents of confirmands—where and how do they celebrate "the season of the giving of our Torah"? The depreciation of the festival is a serious symptom of the spiritual erosion of American Jewry. The time has come to proclaim Shavuot as "Torah Day" in our synagogues, set aside for an Institute of Adult Jewish Learning, and thus recapture the spirit of the Holiday and manifest to our children that we are serious about the synagogue as the sanctuary of our people's spirit.

A REDEFINITION OF THE
AMERICAN JEWISH COMMUNITY

November 12, 1971

One of the fascinating elements in the drama of Jewish survival has always been our stubbornness to hold on to the substance of Judaism and the flexibility to change our method of interpretation. It was the same Judaism which the eleventh century interpreted as a road to inwardness (Bachya in *Duties of the Heart*) and the twelfth century as the intellectual way to the cognition of God (Maimonides in *Guide to the Perplexed*). It was the same Jewish group which Abraham Geiger, the founder of the Reform Movement, defined, in the first half of the nineteenth century, as a strictly religious community—and Theodor Herzl, the founder of the Zionist Movement, in the second half of the same century, as an historic people or a nation.

Dozens of similar examples could be given. The reason for this constant change in interpretation is to be found in the fact that Judaism is not a church, meaning an institution for a particular doctrine, but the evolving religious civilization of a living people and the result of its historic experiences. Because of it one can find within Jewish thought rationalism and mysticism, nationalism and universalism. Depending upon the spiritual atmosphere of a particular era, the one or the other ingredient will by necessity come to the fore: Bachya wrote his works in a century of mysticism; Maimonides in an atmosphere of rationalism; Geiger emphasized universalism because this was the prevailing mood of the period; and Herzl wrote his *Judenstaat* because nationalism was the dominating idea of his time. Each one of these interpretations is completely legitimate because they are all elements to be found within Judaism. But it is the shifting of the ingredients which has served as a potent instrument for our capacity to survive the hostile environment.

There is a need for such fresh interpretation in the decade of the seventies. As long as America was the "melting pot of the world," where the "huddled masses" were welcomed, accepted and integrated into the larger society of the nation of immigrants, our definition of ourselves as a religious community was in keeping with the spirit of the time. But America has changed radically. The melting pot idea is as good as dead, and what is emerging before our eyes is an America of cultural pluralism, meaning a country which makes allowances for identity with, and rootage and anchorage of, each group in its own historic moorings. This being the case, there is no reason any more to cling to an outmoded definition but, on the contrary, to find the courage to proclaim ourselves openly as an ethnic community—to be exact, an ethnic-religious community—meaning that we are part and parcel of the transglobal Jewish People and identify ourselves with the religious-cultural heritage it has produced.

In an age in which "black," "brown" and "red" (Negro, Mexican and Indian) are "beautiful," why should Jewishness not echo the same vocabulary of beauty and dignity, of identity and rootage? It is honest. It is straight. Most of all, it is the historic truth. It will easily be understood by our own children as well as by our neighbors, and will allow for the growth of the American Jewish Community within the evolving pluralism of contemporary society.

MIRROR OF A PEOPLE'S SOUL

December 10, 1971

Holidays are the mirror of a people's soul, for one celebrates only what one cherishes. Hanukkah is a good case in point. It tells the story of the military victory of the Maccabeans over the Greco-Syrians. What was the reason for this war? Was it territorial aggrandizement or physical security? The answer is, neither. But—so states the First Book of the Maccabees—"on the fifteenth day of the month of Kislev" the messengers of King Antiochus set up an idol on the altar of God, and they gave orders that the people of Judea should forsake the law and the covenant, and profane the Sabbath, and pollute the sanctuary (I Maccabees 1:41-54). It was then a purely religious war—of a people going to battle in defense of their spiritual heritage. It is actually the first recorded war in history for religious liberty, for freedom of conscience, and for the right to be different, though a minority.

This is why we have never celebrated Hanukkah with military parades or war-like games but rather in the manner our forefathers did: "On the twenty-fifth day of Kislev...the sanctu-

55

ary of God was dedicated anew with song and music...and they celebrated the dedication of the altar for eight days...and there was great rejoicing among the people.... Moreover, Judah and his brethren with the whole congregation of Israel ordained that the days of the dedication of the altar should be celebrated from year to year in gladness and thanksgiving (I Maccabees 4:52-59)." As the reason for the uprising was religious in nature, so was the goal. Once this was achieved, the war was over, as far as the people were concerned. It was from beginning to end a spiritual undertaking.

We have retained this tradition for two millennia now. The celebration takes place in the synagogue and the home, featuring the kindling of the lights which tell the Hanukkah story silently but penetratingly, accompanied by songs which interpret the event. In modern times we have extended the concept of *Hanukkah Gelt* to include the giving of gifts to family, to friends, and to those in need; and we decorate our homes with Jewish symbols—all in the atmosphere of peaceful tranquillity and warmth of family life.

Nowhere in the history of man has a military victory been celebrated in such a strange way. But this is the Hebrew genius of our people. We hate wars, we cherish peace, and we only celebrate what we cherish. Our sages wisely selected as Haftarah reading for the Sabbath of Hanukkah Zechariah's profound observation: "Not by might and not by power, but by my spirit, sayeth the Lord (Zechariah 4:6)."

WELCOMING THE SECULAR NEW YEAR

January 21, 1972

On Friday last, we welcomed the secular New Year. Looking back upon 1971, one comes to the conclusion that the year was one of base violence, on the one hand, and of challenging liberation, on the other. The terror and the killings were executed by established governments; and the acts of freedom by ethnic and religious groups.

The first aspect reflects power structures going mad: the

West Pakistani military junta committing genocide against its own people in the eastern half of the country; India, the apostle of non-violence, crushing its neighbor with tanks and bombers—undoubtedly in the spirit of Gandhi; the Protestant Establishment of Northern Ireland depriving its Catholic minority of its basic human rights—undoubtedly in the spirit of Jesus; and the Communist Regime of the Soviet Union harassing and imprisoning its Jewish citizens, because of their desire to emigrate to Israel.

Can any society sink to a lower morality? The answer is yes—when the United Nations, the community of nations, reaches the point of such impotence that it cannot even agree on a cease-fire, let alone the prevention of wars. Yet, all this happened in 1971!

Fortunately, there is also the other side: Bangladesh was born, and millions of people are learning, for the first time, the meaning of freedom; the Irish Catholics are fighting magnificently, and the unification of Ireland appears, by now, to be inevitable; and Russian Jews have been defying the authorities, staging demonstrations, identifying themselves openly as Jews, and are now coming to Israel in unprecedented numbers.

Suppressed minorities, motivated by indomitable faith in their just cause, can change history—in spite of terror, brutality and murder. Thus, 1971 was not only a year of moral degradation, but also one of national liberation.

And Israel? How wonderful to behold its strength of character! It stood, last year, like a rock—against the pressure of enemies and friends alike. It is because of this that the situation now looks more hopeful.

Sadat threatened to make 1971 "a year of decision." He failed. The year 1972 may well be it. Not necessarily a year of decision, but surely one of negotiations.

There is some hope in these historic developments. In the long run, ruthlessness and terror of the mighty are not the decisive elements in history—but the spirit and determination of the oppressed are.

ISRAEL'S SILVER ANNIVERSARY

September 21, 1973

With the arrival of the High Holidays of 5734, we are bringing Israel's Silver Anniversary year to its glorious conclusion. The historic event was celebrated with editorials and columns, supplements and special editions by all major newspapers and important magazines and, literally, through thousands of festive assemblies in the United States and all over the free world. Yet, the old year, about to enter history, may not finish on a note of triumph.

The Arabs, having failed in all their maneuvers of recent months to dislodge Israel from the occupied territories—and thus eliminate direct negotiations with Israel—have decided to play the last trump card available to them, namely, oil.

The Saudi Arabians, some weeks ago, notified Washington that oil was a political weapon that can and will be employed, if the United States did not change its Middle East policy. The oil companies were warned by King Faisal that they better "use their good offices" to influence their governments—specifically the United States—in the right direction, if they wished the oil to continue flowing through the pipelines. Needless to repeat here, that the Mobil and Standard Oil companies listened and followed suit.

There have, also, been signs, in recent weeks, that the United States—afraid that the shortage of oil may soon become acute—has commenced to give expression to greater "even-handedness," prodding Israel to come up with some fresh initiatives, more palatable to the Arabs, so as to open new possibilities for peace in the Middle East. Thus, the Arabs, in the Middle East, and the oil companies, here at home, have combined their forces in order to change the character of the American foreign policy—and Washington is beginning to react accordingly.

At the approach of the New Jewish Year, we hope and pray that our government will not bow to the blackmail of "oil diplomacy," and will retain its former position of refusing to impose a settlement at Israel's expense, and of insisting that only through direct negotiations between the contending parties can peace be established in that troubled area.

58

The man whom the president has nominated for the office of Secretary of State, has always stressed his convictions that only a direct agreement of the parties of the region could resolve this difficult regional conflict. He will, undoubtedly, continue to carry out this policy established by the White House long ago. The question arises whether Dr. Kissinger will succeed where all others failed.

His nomination for this high office, which will in all likelihood be soon confirmed by the Senate, fills me with great pride as an American. He will be the first Jewish secretary of state in the almost two hundred year old history of our country. He will be the first immigrant—he fled Hitler and arrived in the United States in 1938—to come to such high estate, with only thirty-five years on American soil. He comes from a thoroughly Jewish home, received a good Jewish education, and became bar mitzvah in Nazi Germany. He is a Jew, without any inferiority complex, who has never shunned his Judaism, but, on the contrary, always asserted his Jewish identification. He is as matter-of-factly Jewish as Kennedy was Catholic and Johnson was Protestant. He will, also, continue the unique historic line of the American Jewish Community which shows that all our Jewish leaders in American public life, including our senators and congressmen, are conscientious and committed Jews. In this deplorable Watergate decade of our country, I am proud that the United States can make such a phenomenon as Dr. Kissinger possible—and acceptable.

Yet, as a Jew, I wish he would have become secretary of state after the peace settlement between Israel and the Arabs had been accomplished.

The parallel examples in our modern Jewish history are not too encouraging: Lord Herbert Samuel, the high commissioner of Palestine, (1920-1925), was a tragedy for the Jewish Community—though he was a proud and professing Jew—because he thought it necessary to show leniency, beyond the call of duty, toward the most militant Arabs of that period; Walther Rathenau, the first and only Jewish foreign minister of the Weimar Republic, (in 1922), was constantly forced to lean over backwards, in order to show his "Germanism"—and even this did not prevent his assassination by German anti-Semites; Leon Blum, the premier of France in the crucial years between

59

1936 and 1938, was forced to show an incredible restraint against the Nazis, not to be accused of dragging France into a "Jewish" war.

I am afraid that Henry Kissinger, able, capable and brilliant, will have to counteract Arab hostility which is already filling the airways, mass media and the press of the Arab world—calling his appointment "a victory for the Zionists comparable to the defeat of the Arabs in the Six Day War"—and may be compelled by historic circumstances beyond his control to placate Arab demands at the expense of Israel, in order to show that his Jewishness did not make him a partisan to the conflict.

At the beginning of this holy season of the new Jewish Year, I pray to the Father Above that I should be proven wrong in this analysis; that Dr. Kissinger may escape the fate of the other great political Jewish figures; and that he may be as successful with Cairo, as he was with Moscow and Peking, and that he may, thus, continue to make his formidable contributions to world peace in the years that lie ahead, as he has so nobly done in the years gone by.

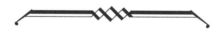

ONLY IN AMERICA

March 22, 1974

The other day something happened in my rabbinical work which can occur only in the United States.

On January 30, Minerva Burr, the mother of Raymond Burr, of stage and screen fame, died at the age of eighty-one, and was buried by an Episcopal minister. But to her sons Raymond and Edmond this was not sufficient. They felt the inner need for an Ecumenical memorial service for their mother. So motivated, they contacted our neighbor, Canon Noble L. Owings of the St. Thomas Episcopal Church, Father Hugh Noonan, a friend of the Burr Family—and my office here at Temple Israel, requesting that the Protestant minister, the Catholic father, and I as rabbi participate in this service.

Is there any Jewish blood in the Burr family? The answer

is no. Why then this very beautiful and moving, but strange desire for an Ecumenical service involving a rabbi? The explanation is quite simple: Mrs. Burr was a professional organist and a deeply religious person who found her life's fulfillment in playing and teaching music. She often played the organ in churches and synagogues—and this was the motivation for the family to have a memorial service in the Protestant church to which she belonged, but, in the genuine spirit of Ecumenism, with Catholic and Jewish participation.

This was a new experience for me and a "first" in my ministry.

I read selections from the Hebrew Bible, eulogized Mrs. Burr, stressing the beauty of her character and the religiosity of her soul. At the special request of the family, I recited the kaddish, after explaining to the Christian audience the meaning and message of this unique prayer in the religious literature of Judaism.

The Burr family was deeply moved by the spirit of brotherhood manifested in this interfaith service, conducted by Christian and Jewish clergy in mutual harmony. Indeed to the three of us, it was an enriching lesson in ecumenical cooperation.

It can only happen in the United States.

Wedding in Berlin, July 14, 1938

Sermons

SHEHECHEYANU—HAPPINESS

First delivered in Berlin: *Erev Rosh Hashanah,* 1937

Shehecheyanu, v'kiymanu, v'higianu lazeman ha-zeh, "Praised be Thou who hast kept us in life, sustained us, and brought us to this day."

At all corners and ends of the Jewish world this sentence is being read on Rosh Hashanah—a song of thanksgiving goes around the world. In the small shul of the ghetto congregations in the East, in the great synagogues of the West and in the Reform temples overseas, Jews are saying *shehecheyanu,* and thank God that they were permitted to live to see these times. Looking at this world, these days, and at our people, I ask myself: "Truly *shehecheyanu?* Or is an entire people lying? Do we say it out of piety, knowing that it is a lie? Or is there perhaps some reason why this sentence is being said today everywhere?"

Even when I was a child, I could not understand why the tradition legally prescribed to a people of eighteen million to say, at certain hours each year, a fixed, standardized prayer of thanksgiving. The only explanation for the *shehecheyanu* is that formerly Judaism's attitude toward life was different from ours today. It makes one feel sad to think how many inner treasures of the old Judaism we must have lost if we today could doubt the appropriateness of the *shehecheyanu* prayer. For in these few Hebrew words a certain Jewish philosophy of life is expressed. We have apparently lost it.

I shall explain what I mean. There is, in our Jewish tradition, a discussion, naive, but extremely interesting, on the question: does the Jewish people have *mazal* or does it not? Do we Jews have a star called Happiness, or do we not? The answer is: we do! Ours is a star of happiness. On the question: "How is it possible?" follows the reply: We are standing above that star called Happiness. Our happiness is not dependent on possession or loss, not determined by the facts of being well off or badly off. Happiness is a quality, independent of what you possess or what has been taken away from you. To stand above *mazal;* to be able to live knowing that this star has its whims, has light and shadow, but that it is nourished by sources beyond light and shadow—this is how our old Jewish tradition defines happiness.

64

In the German Romantic period—far away from everything Jewish—Hoelderlin said in his *Commandment and Fulfillment:* "As with the seasons of life, so it is with the days. None seems satisfying to us, none is completely beautiful, and each has—if not its trouble—so at least its imperfection. But if you add them up, you will get a sum total of a happy life."

This means: we still consider the minutes of happiness as the normal thing, and hardly notice them, yet overrate and resent as abnormal everything that does not quite correspond to our conception of happiness. If we would only add up the happy minutes of our life and distribute them proportionally, we would see that we have had a good life and much happiness. If we—and now I am speaking of our generation in these days—had the capacity of charting the statistics of our happiness not vertically, but horizontally; if we were able to add up; if we would count the highs instead of the lows, the mountain tops instead of the valleys; if we would not forget so quickly how good it was once, and not feel so strongly how bad it is now; if we would distribute according to proportion—maybe we would have become less unhappy in the last years.

Sometimes we are facing a riddle. In the years past our people have become very unhappy. It cannot be only for the reason that one has taken this and that from us; it cannot be only for the reason that this or that existence has been broken, though this is tragic enough. But as in ancient Judaism every song of lament ended up with a prayer of thanks to the Creator, there must have been a level from which life was viewed differently. Therefore, I believe that the reasons for our unhappiness in these days are to be found not only in the events of the outside world, but also in ourselves—lacking as we are some Jewish-historical and religious values.

I believe, our people has forgotten one thing. They have lost the ability to have an unforced, natural, inner feeling of joy. To put it pointedly: we have lost the ability to laugh. I hear already the voices telling me that the time is not fit for laughter. But I think of an episode of the time of the Russian pogroms. A small Jewish village was penalized with a collective fine. The chief of the Cossacks, using stronger methods every day, asks his soldiers how the Jews are reacting. "They are crying," is the answer. "Good. Use fiercer methods!" The second day the

65

answer is the same "The Jews are crying."—"Use fiercer methods!" But by the end of the week, his men came and said: "Captain, the Jews are laughing." The next day one could read in the order-of-the-day of the chief: "Measures are to be stopped."

There is one kind of suffering in this our life which is being expressed by tears and a broken back. And there is one degree for which there are no more tears, a degree that puts one above the situation. Once upon a time Jews were able to stand above the stars and to laugh, because life had taught them a different kind of happiness—one that was independent from the thrills of possession or the tortures of martyrdom. Even when their suffering had reached the highest degree, they proved their unshakable ability to stand above the star *mazal.* Thus very often in the history of our Diaspora have the measures of our adversaries stifled themselves.

Something else: in these last years our Jews have come closer to each other, but this closer contact has been caused by a condition called fear. This, however, is a rather primitive feeling; all the animals react this way; if lightning strikes, the flock is crowding together, because no living being can stand fear alone. Solitude is a luxurious quality of a safe person in a secure position. In insecure periods we need the armchair of the community. But when the Jewish masses moved from the periphery to the center of Jewishness, we expected more; we expected from them the heart-warming ability to love each other; and in this we have been quite disappointed. These years should have made Jews feel neighborly about each other, because your son may be working with his son at the same stonewall in Africa, or be tilling Palestinian soil in the same kibbutz—because the only meaning of these times may be to forge together an entire people like a single block of granite. Yes, maybe the recent historical events have only happened in order to create anew: love among Jews.

If we want to stop the process toward isolation and despair that is well under way already, we must start to do justice to life, and in spite of all tragedies find some measure of happiness. We must understand what the time wants from us, and therefore be able to love one another again. We must try, like any other normal people, even to laugh again.

I know that the lips that are being moved tonight all over

the world to say *shehecheyanu* belong to a tortured face with a sad mouth and painfully melancholy eyes looking shyly into the gray distance. But I wish for our Jews this year to obtain again that quality that was once given us as a gift: to stand above the star of *mazal.* I wish our people to regain the ability to love and even to laugh, and thus to say in full sincerity "that Thou hast kept us in life, sustained us, and brought us to this day."

CHOSEN AND CALLED: A SERMON FOR SHAVUOT

Delivered in Berlin, May 1940
Printed in *A Set of Holiday Sermons:* 5702-1941

I

Shavuot in these days—what a discrepancy between the inner atmosphere of this holiday and the mood of our hearts. The radiance of calm and peace, the ideals and the spirit of this festival seem entirely out of place amid our world, tossed up, warlike, and brutal. I often feel that this would be the adequate time to celebrate Rosh Hashanah or Yom Kippur—the *yamim nora-im*—the Formidable Days—rather than Shavuot. Perhaps that is why for days I have had in my mind a prayer that we used to say on Rosh Hashanah after sounding the shofar; I have it in my mind and on my heart, though according to the letter of the prayerbook, it certainly has nothing to do with Shavuot; yet in its inmost sense it belongs to our Shavuot this year. All of us remember the words of this prayer. We have uttered them dozens of times, and their secret beauty has deeply impressed us. But suddenly the outer world has changed and we find, while saying these words of old, that they reveal surprisingly the newly drawn picture of the present situation. Moreover, this is a characteristic of many of the ancient and eternal prayers of our Jewish tradition.

Do you remember the words the congregation used to repeat on Rosh Hashanah after sounding the shofar? They said that Rosh Hashanah is the day of the creation of the world, on which all creatures stand before the tribunal of God, "as children or as servants." Do you remember the sublime conclusion: "If as children, have pity upon us as a father pitieth his children; and if as servants, our eyes wait on thee until thou be gracious unto us and bring forth our judgment as the light"? Thousands and thousands of times we have read those words, seen them, translated them, explained them to our children, and have been shaken by their meaning. Yet, it is overwhelming to read them over today, on Shavuot, word by word, as you would read an old source, and to find within them the newly created picture of the world in these days. The translation, paraphrased in our own words, would then be: "These are days that bear in their womb a new world. In these days all the peoples of the earth are standing in judgment. Will they be considered as equal children of one Father in Heaven or as servants of many masters on earth? If we shall be there as children, then have pity upon us as a father pitieth his children; if as slaves, O Lord, then our eyes will wait on thee until thou be gracious unto us and maketh our right radiate as the light." Nothing can better outline the most important question of our time than these few short and dramatic sentences. In fact, the thoughts stated therein present the problem of the world of today and the problem of the World-Spirit of tomorrow.

I say "World-Spirit." You know that Hegel created this concept in philosophy. But it is, at the same time, an old idea of religion. Shavuot is its birthday; the Ten Commandments its testament; the Bible its code. "World-Spirit" means that nations may live together on a basis of justice, without oppressor and oppressed, without persecutor and persecuted. This was the Sinai proclamation more than three thousand years ago, putting the "Spirit" into the World, creating the "World-Spirit." Today, in the epoch of the twentieth century, we have to ask: how then could the world have fallen into its present condition? Who has failed? Whose fault has it been? Have the peoples failed or has it been the World-Spirit itself that has hindered the realization of the ideas of Mount Sinai? To answer these questions we must go back to the psychological process of the first entrance into history of the World-Spirit. Its appearance was performed by a spontaneous act of revelation on the one side and a spontaneous though not voluntary act of choosing on the other side. This means that in the hour of birth of the World-Spirit, its voice—or the voice of God—sounded from the top of the mountain, and that below, at the foot of the mountain, there were standing those few who perceived the voice and carried it forth into reality. Those were the chosen ones; for not everybody will hear the voice, nor will everybody be able to look upwards through the fog to the summit of the mount. Those who are able to do it must be especially elected to be the bearers of the revelation.

This psychological double-procedure of "revelation" and "choosing" presents a most peculiar and characterizing trait: the first—the Revelation—is, as mentioned above, not a slow, dragging, evolutionary act, but one full of force and vehemence, pushing the chosen bearers with volcanic violence upwards to the summit of the mount. Remember only how unexpectedly and how suddenly the vision of the burning bush changed Moses' entire life; how Isaiah received his revelation by a sudden act of sanctification; how Jeremiah was ordered by an urging vision; how Amos, without preparation, was dragged away from amidst his sheep; how Ezekiel was thrown into the whirl of prophecy by the mystical heavenly apparition—how they and others like them, out of their peaceful life, were aroused by a sudden experience, and, by the force of the unexpected vision, were led up toward the stage of being "chosen." Equal phenomena have happened at all times to all nations. Think only of the sudden transformation of the shepherdess Jeanne d'Arc into the fabulous deliverer of her country; or take as an example in our modern history the sudden appearance of Theodor Herzl among the stars of our firmament, caused by his experience of the Dreyfus Affair. This is the one side of the process.

As for the second—the chosen—the characteristic trait consists in the fact that the elected bearers of revelation have always struggled with all their strength against taking over their task: God tried to persuade Moses to go to Pharaoh and to become the first prophet in Israel, but Moses, according to the Bible, refused by all kinds of reasons, one of which was that he was "slow of speech and of a slow tongue" and not fit to be a spokesman. In the hour of his election, Isaiah cried that he was "a man of unclean lips," and only after undergoing an act of sanctification in the Temple did he yield in accepting his mission. Amos tried to defend himself with the words: "I was no prophet, neither was I a prophet's son, but I was a herd man," and the Lord had to force him and to take him away from following the flock, in order to have him take on his new burden. Jeremiah protested against the election by the famous words: "O Lord God, behold, I cannot speak; for I am a child," and Ezekiel received an admonition not to be obstinate and to take over the task of the prophecy: "Hear what I say unto thee: be not thou rebellious; open thy mouth and eat that which I give thee."

All these remarks show that at first the prophets did not want such a mission and that they even refused it. Why? Because they knew that they might try not to take the task, but that, once having taken it, it would be impossible ever to shake it off, not even in hours of darkest distress nor in years of heaviest reverses. Once having taken up the holy burden they would have to carry it on with all its great happiness and deadly agony, with its glorious joy and its sublime grief. As these men, each of them, knew and felt this, they struggled against it in the beginning, only to accept the mission later on under the compulsion of the Voice. From then on they usually lived as in the solitude of a mountain top, constantly fighting against their own people and against the world. No power in the world could ever help them carry their burden. This double psychological procedure of "revelation" and "choice" brought into the world the stupendous and unique phenomenon of prophecy. Through the gate of prophecy, the World-Spirit—the spirit of the Mount Sinai—entered into history.

By what means and on what account does the World-Spirit live on in history? To answer this question we have to consider another psychological process, equally double and combined in character, the one of "tradition" and "calling." The "chosen" ones themselves have perceived the voice of the World-Spirit during the act of its revelation; they were created to hear this voice from its first source. This is a unique or at least rare favor. Then they teach the ideas of the Voice, communicate them, hand them down from generation to generation and from century to century. This process is called "tradition." It does not work with the dynamic spontaneity of a revelation, nor does it tear men like a flash away from their habitual life to lift them up into an entirely different sphere. This process is rather evolutionary, developing slowly, prepared by teaching, education, and surroundings, and those to whom God grants the grace to hear the voices of the prophecy are the "called" ones among the people. They differ from the "chosen" ones in that they usually do not struggle against their mission. Their talent is cultivated by education and schooling; they are led by the prophets; and usually they serve their cause in great faithfulness. If the first group is called "Prophets of the World-Spirit," this second group is the "Priests of the World-Spirit."

Why do they not struggle against their task, like those who are chosen? The answer is easy: the nature of the appointment is not the same. Priests do not take an eternal oath, lasting up to their death. When the burden of their task gets too heavy and the pressure of their mission too painful, then it happens that they get silent, stretch their backs to throw off the load, and there they are—free. That is why they feel less scrupulous in assuming such a task. They know that they still have a way out. Even our great Jewish national poet, Chaim Nachman Bialik, the greatest we have had, stopped writing one day, the burden of his people and their problems growing too heavy, and stayed silent for more than a decade. Isaiah would not have been able to do so. Just this reveals the whole difference.

II

All we have said about ingenious individuals, be they prophets or priests of the revelation, refers equally to entire peoples of the world. With the revelation at Mt. Sinai, the World-Spirit entered into history, revealing itself to a whole people by an act of proclamation, and choosing Israel, the people who were standing at the foot of the mountain. The Voice addressed the people personally, and, lifting Israel up from her habitual world into a sphere of holiness, God called her to be his prophetic bearer on earth. Israel of course, struggled against the mission, and, only after God had "turned Mount Sinai over them like a vat" and had compelled them, did they answer: "We will do and will obey." Why did Israel do so? Because they knew that primarily they might struggle against such a mission, but that, once having taken it over, they would have to

71

carry it through all the roads of the world, through all the pains of suffering, and through all the gates of history.

As a people of the prophecy we have carried the ideas of the World-Spirit throughout the nations and have taught them. From generation to generation, from century to century, we have prayed them, explained them, interpreted them, and handed them down to the peoples of the world. It is true that among the peoples there have been some, "called" to hear the words, to understand the Voice, and to serve God in faithfulness and honesty. Highly gifted men have related these ideas, sung them or turned them into poetry, sculptured them in stone, set them to music, and taught them from the pulpits. We, the modern ones, then speak of "good literature," of "sublime poetry," of "eternal art," of "imperishable music," and of "immortal religions." The "called" ones bear different names: writers, poets, artists, musicians, and founders of religions. But all these different names have but one purpose: to cultivate and to preserve for mankind the tradition of the World-Spirit, revealed in the prophecy. In the progress of history we Jews nursed the feeling that one day—not even too distant—the World-Spirit's purpose would be realized: the life of nations in justice.

But the great leaders of mankind were only "called"; they did not struggle against their mission, knowing that it would not mean an appointment for ever. When one day the maintenance of conditions became too difficult, some of them stretched their backs to throw off the heavy burden of the World-Spirit, and then they were "free," and no longer priests of the World-Spirit. So it happened that the World-Spirit stopped at a certain point, denied itself, and did not live to see the hour of realization. That is where we are today: on the point of the failure of the European world. There we are standing, we, the prophetic bearers of the World-Spirit, without the priests following us. Europe has quitted the agreement, and this is where all the events of these days, unbelievable and cruel as they are, originate: Europe has killed the World-Spirit.

III

This result, following the efforts, the troubles, and the painful progress of centuries, certainly is alarming, to the world as well as to us Jews. But in spite of that I am not ready to resign and to write Europe off the book of the World-Spirit for all eternity. True, the revelation of Mount Sinai, giving us the World-Spirit, was but a prelude to a great drama, in which the peoples would have had to perform, on the wide stage of humanity, the taking over of the tradition, and in that respect they surely have failed. However, I do not believe that the game is lost. The great German philosopher Hegel once stated that the World-Spirit rules the history of mankind, and does so in the following way: it sets for the world a certain order at a certain time. Hegel called this first step "thesis." Then the Spirit negates this first order and sets the opposite picture of history. The philosopher called this second step "antithesis." He pointed out that at all times of history the Spirit itself has created, out of scheme and counter-scheme, out of thesis and antithesis, a third, more sublime order, which Hegel called "synthesis."

It seems to me that we live now in a time of "antithesis." A few centuries ago, Europe received her order from the World-Spirit. This image has been broken by the appearance of another, an opposite image. But I do believe that out of both these orders a third, higher order will develop, in which the World-Spirit will find itself again and will attain, without repeating mistakes of times past, its goal of realization, one day in the epoch of "synthesis." I do not believe in Europe of today, but all the stronger in Europe of tomorrow. The Europe of the antithesis has renounced to the World-Spirit; the Europe of the synthesis is going to find it again and restore it to the throne of history.

As for us Jews, this time of antithesis may be very sad and may burden our life immensely. But one thing is sure: we Jews will live on in this world, as long as the history of mankind will have sense, or until a voice will sound on Sinai to revoke the mandate once given to us. This mandate is burdened with pains and suffering; on the other hand, it guarantees to our people eternal life. If we only understand this, then we know that all our troubles, strong and agonizing as they may be, cannot lead as far as death and senseless destruction. There is no sorrow so great that it cannot be endured by our people, and no pain so vehement that it will make our people sacrifice its life.

It may be true that the time of the World-Spirit's return

73

still is far away from us and that a long time of suffering will spread between us and that coming "synthesis." That is why our prayer today on Shavuot is the one that we said in the beginning: "These are days that bear in their womb a new world. All the peoples of the earth are standing in judgment, and we among them. Will we all be considered as equal children of one Father in Heaven or will we remain servants of many masters on earth? If we shall be there as children, then have pity upon us, O Lord, as a father pitieth his children. If we remain slaves, then our eyes, full of tears, but also full of hope, will wait on Thee, O Lord, until Thou be gracious unto us and maketh our right radiate as the light." Amen.

MALCHUT SHADAI—THE KINGDOM OF GOD

Kol Nidre, 1946

In the rhythm of the Jewish year, each one of our holidays stands for a definite, well-defined principle. It is as if the religious genius of our people would have formulated a set of ideals and allowed each one of them to find its full expression through the channel of a single holiday. The days of the New Year, the Week of Repentance, and the Day of Atonement are called "The Solemn Days" and are even more permeated with religious feeling than the other festivals of the year. They are emotionally even more soul-stirring, and their theme is, of necessity, thoroughly religious in nature.

What then is the theme of the Solemn Days? It consists of two Hebrew words—*malchut shadai*—and is reiterated in our liturgy like the motif in a musical composition. Its literal English translation is: the Kingdom of God.

What is this Kingdom of God that you and I are asked to affirm and reaffirm year after year? What does it mean to the modern man of the twentieth century? In Jewish conception, the existing order of things is an as yet inadequate expression of God's sovereignty, and the Kingdom of God will be manifest when all nations will believe in Him, when superstition will be eradicated, righteousness established and salvation universal. The law of life which the "solemn days" interpret, imposes upon all of us the perpetual duty to participate actively in the establishment of this Kingdom. The task of mankind is summed up in the famous words of Hebrew tradition: "To perfect the world under the Kingdom of God." But what is a perfect world in Jewish conception? One of the first Jewish philosophers of our history, who lived more than a thousand years ago—Saadia Gaon—gave us the definition: a perfect world is one in which the interests of the individual are harmonized with those of society. This, according to Jewish conception, is the manifestation of the Kingdom of God on earth. In other words, God is here being defined as the power that makes for social advancement, and his Kingdom as the symbol that stands for a better world.

However, God, or the power that makes for social progress, is not outside the world, giving orders which we have to obey. God is imminent in the hearts of man and his presence is evident in the qualities of those in mankind who work relentlessly for social betterment. Affirming the Kingdom of God means thus to ascribe primacy to those qualities within mankind. It means that—in spite of the confusion and darkness of the hour—there are forces that work selflessly for the establishment of God's Kingdom. These forces within mankind work through the individual singularly as through society collectively. There are religious teachings that say that the individual is only a fleeting shadow, a grass that withers; others who conceive him as being a little lower than the angels and the image of God.

Judaism has never experienced the difficulty of these opposing definitions. It has compared human life, with its polarity of individuals and society, to the composition of a book. The average book is composed of letters, words, lines, sentences, paragraphs, pages and chapters. The single letter taken by itself amounts to nothing. It does not even convey a fraction of the meaning of the book. But, by misspelling a word here or there, changing or omitting a letter, one can easily distort the meaning of a whole sentence, of a whole paragraph, of a whole page, and—if one does it too often—of a whole book.

The same is true of the composition of life. The individual taken by himself—without society—amounts to little or nothing. By himself he cannot convey even a fraction of the purpose, the challenge and the tasks of life. On the other hand, society as a whole lives in and through individuals, and they are the vital cells of our social organism. Fathom for a moment a multitude of isolated individuals, letters torn from the context of the alphabet, and you will see that society would not function and the Kingdom of God could not exist. It is in the harmonization of the individual and society that the Kingdom of God finds its true expression. This is why Jews all over the world pray to God in these solemn days to inscribe them in the Book of Life, meaning a world in which the tensions between the individual and the group are solved on a level of a higher, all-encompassing harmony.

As a result of this line of Jewish thought, that proclaims the interrelatedness between individuals and social groups, society owes its members certain debts. A society that manifests the Kingdom of God on Earth will provide the individual with those necessities that make for his betterment: healthful living conditions, balance between work and rest, protection from disease, and economic security. The individual, on the other hand, owes it to society to participate in all its activities that make for social advancement. It is the individual's duty to give himself to causes beyond the interests of his daily life. It makes little difference which of the many causes he chooses, as long as the cause that he has selected can stand the scrutinizing test of the Kingdom of God. Any participation in a cause that works for the advancement of a group as part of mankind, or for mankind as a whole, in its struggle for social progress, means participation in the establishment of God's sovereignty on earth. This is the meaning of *malchut shadai,* the Kingdom of God that all of us are expected to affirm in these solemn days. When the shofar, the ram's horn that is blown on these days, is sounded and Jews listen to it in awe and reverence, it is a "Salute to the King" that we are giving, thus reiterating our faith in the humanly and divinely creative forces in mankind that work for social progress.

You, who gather in the synagogues and temples in these solemn days, might think that this is a rather naive approach to the intricate problems of our time. Our post-war generation is gradually becoming disillusioned, and it is increasingly difficult to blame them or you for it. You look around and discover a world in which a war was won and a peace not yet attained, in which nations, only a while ago united in their hatred of the enemy, are today disunited in their so-called love for mankind; a world in which the leaders of the nations are fighting for strategic positions to frame the world according to their pattern instead of shaping it according to God's design. I know how difficult it is to believe in a progressing Kingdom of God on earth against the background of powers that can sell the blood of Jews down the river of oil of Empires. I know how disappointed and bitter one can get in these days. Still this is not the religious way and particularly not the Jewish way.

Judaism has always refused to believe in the original sin of society. In spite of all the catastrophes that have befallen our people, Judaism has, from time immemorial, clung to its conviction that society is redeemable. We know, of course, that this order of things is not even a beginning manifestation of God's Kingdom. Were it so, God's sovereignty on earth would be manifest today. But there are, in our conception, forces in mankind, and increasingly more so, who give of their energies and devotion to right the social wrongs of our time. All of us, Jews and Christians alike who believe in the redemptive power of religion, have to join forces with them, in order to channelize this, our abiding faith in mankind, into a mighty stream. Judaism teaches us never to judge life by its actualities but by its possibilities. This is why Jewish tradition speaks of the "old heaven and old earth" that God created and the "new heaven and new earth" that he will create at the end of days. This "new heaven and new earth" of human potentiality has to be shaped in our generation and the possibilities of advancement in society are unlimited—if we could only feel that it is in us and upon us to establish God's Kingdom in our days.

It is this message of hope and certainty of ultimate redemption that Judaism brings to a troubled world in these days. Seldom was mankind in so dire a need of such a message. The Day of Atonement is an original Jewish institution, but in its language and in its message it is of universal nature. What mankind needs today, is precisely such a Day of Atonement: to gather in the churches and synagogues of the world and to have the leaders of the nations reaffirm their faith in mankind and their allegiance to the principles for which God's sovereignty stands. May this Kingdom on earth, we pray, be established in our days for the happiness of our generation and the security of your children and mine. At the beginning of the Jewish year, let all of us learn and teach our children the title of a song that has given so much courage to our young generation in the Holy Land: *v'af al pi kein geula,* "nonetheless, redemption."

May this motto remain with us for all the years to come. Amen.

THE TEST OF JEWISH SURVIVAL

From *The Jewish Voice,* September 29, 1950
(An Excerpt from a Holiday Sermon)

"On this day of Remembrance, sentence is pronounced upon countries—which of them is destined for the sword and which for peace: and every creature is brought to account and recorded for life or for death."

It is with a heavy heart, trembling with foreboding, that we approach the new Jewish year. Threatening clouds of war are again on the horizon and our people is unprepared for the emergency. In the four corners of the globe, we Jews are again caught at the crossroads of history.

Let us unfold the picture by beginning at the far end. A wave of terror has recently been unleashed against Jewry in the Moslem country of Afghanistan where the five thousand Jews have been driven into the walls of the Kabul ghetto. The North African city of Tripoli has now become the refuge of thousands of distressed and disease-ridden Jews from all parts of Libya. These Jews who saw their families murdered in the pogrom of 1945 are desperately anxious not to be trapped in Libya when that country, according to a decision of the United Nations, will revert to Arab rule in about a year. Twenty thousand Libyan Jews are anxiously awaiting passage to Israel. Forty thousand Jews are literally rotting in the Casablanca ghetto and on the whole, half a million Jews are faced with moral and physical disintegration in several other North

African ghettos. Many of you will say these places are very far off. But, to quote the song from *Lost in the Stars,* "How many miles to the heart of a child?"

Let us cast a glance on a continent closer to our home and analyze the convulsions that have been overtaking European Jewry. Germany, our newest ally in the cold war, is a place where anti-Semitism is growing and Nazism expanding. Five years after the war, there is not a German who remembers that our people has lost six million souls. The most characteristic story that has come out of Germany and which sums up the entire atmosphere is the one which tells of a German kindergarten in Coblenz in the French zone. It stands on hilly ground and there are stairs leading to it. The stairs are paved with tombstones from the Jewish cemetery of the city and the children are running up and down the Hebrew letterings. To such low estate have we already come that we are permitting a people who killed six millions of our brothers, to trample over their graves.

In the last several months, under the impact of the Korean War, thousands of Jews in Western Europe have registered for Israel. Frantic appeals for passage are reaching us from all over Eastern Europe. The immigration from Romania and Poland is very slow, very limited and even so the permission is only valid until the end of 1950. A conservative estimate of the Government of Israel declares that a minimum of six hundred thousand Jews have to emigrate from Europe, North Africa and Arab countries, especially Iraq, if we want to save their lives before it is too late.

You may ask: why do they not go to Israel? The young Jewish State, though under political and economic siege, is ready to accept them. Said Israel's Ambassador Eban the other day, "If immigration has to bring the State of Israel down—it will go down, but it will seek no salvation for its existing population at the expense of those for whom the State was created." It is obvious that Israel is not the reason why the six hundred thousand Jews are not led to redemption. The only element that stands in their way is the thousands of American Jews who have chosen this year, of all years, not to participate in the Welfare Fund campaign.

The question then arises what will happen tomorrow

when the storm starts again and thousands of our brothers will be caught in the whirlpool? Our present generation has been the witness to the slaughter of six million of our brothers and there was very little one could do to save them. But what excuse will you have tomorrow if you, and you alone, will achieve stoppage of immigration? How will you feel if you will succeed where Hitler, Bevin, and the Arabs failed? How will you be able to live with yourself and to look at yourself in the mirror? What will you say to the fifteen thousand Jewish children in Hungary, where their immigration is still considered illegal and who are roaming the roads of Europe, finding their way into transit camps, anxiously awaiting to go home?

In our Jewish tradition we have a fundamental law called "the ransoming of captives." Our tradition has always considered it the most important Commandment. Said Maimonides: "Whoever postpones the redemption of captives for a single moment where it is possible to facilitate it, is guilty of shedding blood." May the Jews in this area who are shirking their Jewish responsibility remember these words when they come to the synagogue this year and pray for life and happiness of their own families. What makes them so sure that one can have the audacity of asking God for those gifts if one has not procured the same blessings for others? Each one of us prays for compassion to be bestowed upon us by the God of Life, but Judaism has always insisted that no personal prayers are answered unless one prays for others first. Thus repeating the ancient words "inscribe us for blessing in the Book of Life," may be done this year by all of us in the spirit of inscribing the tortured remnant of our people in the Book of Redemption.

THE SEARCH FOR A SUSTAINING FAITH

Date Unknown, c. 1950

The spiritual horizon of our present day generation, which is now entering upon the second half of the twentieth century, is the sum total of all the challenging ideas that were born more than a hundred years ago and climaxed in the revolutionary year of 1848. It was at that time that the ideologies which have shaped and troubled our world to this very day came into existence: nationalism, with its desire for independence of peoples; liberalism with its emphasis on freedom of the individual; capitalism, with its belief in progress through science and technology; socialism with its demand for improvement of the lot of the working man; and romanticism in literature and art, with its protest against deification of reason and its search for a sustaining faith. These were the motivating forces behind the great age of revolution. They are still the background against which our dilemmas, conflicts and tragedies are being played on the international stage and we, the newest shoots of human evolution, are the trustees of their heritage.

Most of these social forces—nationalism and liberalism, capitalism and socialism—have grown tremendously, for better or for worse, during the last hundred years. The only idea that did not survive was the philosophy of romanticism. Had it succeeded in its search for, and the finding of, a sustaining faith, it would have created a synthesis of what is best in the other four ideologies and might have spared mankind its perilous position of today.

What is a sustaining faith? Apparently the question is as old as civilized mankind. It must have been on people's minds in antiquity and obviously in answer to such a question, Isaiah, the great Jewish prophet of the seventh century B.C.E., replied with the words: "The Lord of Hosts is exalted through justice and God, the Holy One, sanctified through righteousness (Isaiah 5:16)." I have always considered this prophetic verse the most important statement in the whole of the Bible. It gives an entire philosophy of life in four lines and places God and man in proper relation to each other. It wants to convey that God is an object of worship only because he is the symbol of all ultimate values and the power that makes for justice and righteousness.

Having thus defined God, the prophet reaches out for a definition of man. Mankind is the highest creature on this globe only because it is the instrumentality through which the divine powers of justice and righteousness can make for a better world and for a more progressive society. God and man are thus conceived as co-workers toward one and the same goal.

81

With deep insight, the great Jewish prophet handed down to us the essence of religion.

Faith in such a God and in such a society can be sustaining, indeed. But it demands as prerequisite the indivisible unity of religion and life, of idea and action, of thought and deed. To separate the two from each other means to divorce God from man. The test of religion is not so much what we believe, but what we do. To love one's neighbor at a service on Sunday morning and to hate him on Monday afternoon because he belongs to another religion, is not "exalting God through justice," but offending him through indecency. To pray to a God of all mankind over the weekend and not to rent an apartment to a human being on week days because he is of another color, is not "sanctifying the Holy One through righteousness" but desecrating the Holy One's name through hypocrisy. Self-styled "religious people" that seem to be able to combine a so-called worship of God with a maltreatment of man, are tearing apart the unity of life and religion, of belief and action, which is the basic principle of classical religions. It is entirely preposterous to call them religious. They are not furthering God's plans, they are hindering them. They may be worshipping a god, per se, but they do not take seriously the God of ultimate values. What our generation needs for its survival is this concept: a God of ultimate values and a mankind which is instrumental in putting them into effect.

This is the sustaining faith for which generations have been waiting, for which romanticism has been searching and which alone might bring redemption to a storm-tossed generation. To shape one's daily life and the actions of the nations on the international scene in such a way as to "exalt God through justice and sanctify him through righteousness," is the great message of Judaism for the second half of the twentieth century.

CHOSENESS AND FORGIVENESS

September 18, 1953

The High Holiday season with its atmosphere of earnestness

and sobriety starts with Rosh Hashanah, is intensified during the Ten Days of Penitence, and reaches its climax on Yom Kippur. As such, the whole season of the Days of Awe actually discusses one and the same subject: the relationship of man to man, and of man to God. Yet, each one of the two holidays has a leitmotif and, consequently, even a vocabulary of its own. The leitmotif of Rosh Hashanah is the Kingdom of God, and its vocabulary is the perfection of the world and the challenging salute of the shofar. The leitmotif of Yom Kippur is not so much the remaking of society as the judging of human nature, and its vocabulary is "sin and penitence, repentance and forgiveness." In the same way, as one cannot understand the essence of Rosh Hashanah without that ancient play of the covenant—one cannot comprehend the very depth of Yom Kippur without a corollary idea which flows directly from the first one, namely, the idea of the so-called choseness of Israel.

You have all at one time or another heard the expression of the Jews as a "chosen people." You have heard it discussed in seriousness or in mockery, or in hostility. The idea was bitterly attacked by the school of higher critics of the Bible and also by a man of the genius of George Bernard Shaw. When, in 1936, the year of the Nürnberg Laws, he was asked to raise his voice against this racist legislation, he replied that the Jews should be the last ones to object to it, because it was actually their own invention. Within the Jewish fold, many secular organizations demanded the removal of this idea, and as great and productive a man as Professor Mordechai Kaplan actually removed any mention of it from the Reconstructionist prayerbook. This "choseness" is then a most controversial subject replete with misunderstandings and considerable ramifications.

This is therefore a good occasion to clarify in our own minds what the subject is all about. We are a Reform Congregation, and in our liberal movement we have discarded many an idea which has lost its meaning in the course of modern history. But before doing so, one has to make a thorough study of the sources, know exactly what was meant by it, and then decide on the merit of the issue proper, whether to retain it or not.

I

In asking the question of what the so-called "choseness,"

or as it is sometimes called, the "election" of Israel means, one has to keep in mind that it is an idea that has had a lasting effect upon Judaism and for that matter upon Christianity, and gave special significance to the relationship between God and Israel. If, in classical Christian tradition the central theme is crucifixion and resurrection, in classical Jewish tradition the central theme is covenant and selection, (or choseness or election), and each is interrelated.

In proclaiming the idea of the covenant, the Bible says "that thou hast acknowledged the Lord this day to be thy God...and the Lord has acknowledged thee, this day, to be His own treasure (Deuteronomy 26:18-19)." In using the term *am s'gula,* meaning that Israel is God's own peculiar treasure, the Bible has already made its first step toward the idea of selection. If a people enters into a rare relationship with God, then it becomes a people peculiar, unique and singled out. From here, there is only one logical step to the idea of selection proper. Thus, the Bible states the case of selection in the following words: "The Lord had a delight in thy fathers to love them, and He chose their seed after them, above all peoples (Deuteronomy 10:15)." This, then, is the source of the conception of Israel's choseness. Either in the words of *am s'gula* or in the term of *b'chira* [choice], the idea is reiterated throughout the centuries of Jewish tradition.

Having said this, one has to keep four things in mind, and give them our utmost attention in order to understand this ancient Jewish concept. First, the purpose: to the student of Judaism it is clear that the idea of selection has nothing to do with racial superiority, favoritism, master racism, or privilege. The prophet Isaiah formulated it most clearly when he said, "Ye are My servants and My witness whom I have chosen, so that ye may know and believe Me and understand that I am He (Isaiah 43:10)." This needs no further interpretation. It means what it says: Israel is God's chosen servant for the purpose of knowing God and believing in him. Yes, there is even more to this purpose of service. It means not only to acknowledge and believe in God, and bring his message to the Jews alone—but there is in it the element of bringing a message of service to all the nations. In the words of Isaiah, "Behold my servant whom I uphold, Mine elect in whom My soul delighteth; I have put My

84

spirit upon him, I shall make the light to go forth to the nations (Isaiah 42:1)." This, then, is the purpose of the election.

Secondly, conditionality: both the covenant and the election, though for the purpose of service, were not given carte blanche, but are conditional in character. Says God to Israel: "If ye hearken unto My voice and keep My covenant, then shall ye be Mine own treasure from among all peoples...and ye shall be unto Me a kingdom of priests and a holy people (Exodus 19:5-6)." Or, "The Lord will establish thee for a holy people...if thou shalt keep the commandments of the Lord your God and walk in His ways (Deuteronomy 28:9)." Should Israel prove to be disobedient and faithless, they would lose the special status and to the universal God they would be no different than the Ethiopians, the Philistines, and the Assyrians.

Thirdly, the reward is punishment: not only is the purpose for service conditional, but the only reward for the election is punishment. Says Isaiah, "I have chosen you to be tried in the furnace of affliction (Isaiah 48:10)." This means that Israel will have to walk on roads of suffering and pain, of martyrdom and exile. The history of our people has proved this to be entirely correct.

Fourth, noblesse oblige: if all this is not enough—the purpose of service, the conditional character and the punishment reward—there was added to the idea of election, the concept that its nobility obliges. Even if Israel does obey the laws of God, stricter obedience to religious ideals is demanded than of anybody else. No special privileges were bestowed upon Israel—on the contrary, special obligations were imposed. In the words of Amos: "Only you have I known from all the generations of the earth—*therefore* will I visit upon you all your iniquities (Amos 3:2)." This means that Israel must not sin in the hope of finding mercy in "the merit of the Fathers." The opposite is true. Because they are chosen, more is expected of them and their activities are judged by higher standards. The Rabbis rightly say that this is the most famous "therefore" in the history of man: Israel is chosen, therefore God demands higher, not lower standards of goodness and will punish lapses more severely. The higher the price, the greater the responsibility.

These four points have to be kept in mind in order to understand the idea of the selection thoroughly. The doctrine of which I speak found its most definite formulation in Deutero-Isaiah, and it could be summed up along the following lines: the Lord alone is God of heaven and earth. He created the universe, controls it by his Law, and in accordance with his purpose he proposes the destiny of mankind, and guides the events of history toward his eternal plan—a united mankind acknowledging him as the One God, and living according to his statutes of justice and peace. In order to attain this goal he has chosen Israel as his servant, his messenger, his witness unto the peoples, his light unto the nations—chosen from the beginning, not for glory, but for service and a blessing unto the nations. Israel has to exemplify this, each generation in its own life, and to teach God's law to all mankind. This service will be attained by suffering; through it Israel will bring salvation to the human race. Israel, the "suffering servant," thus becomes the saviour of mankind. In the words of Deutero-Isaiah, "It is too light a thing that thou shouldst be My servant to raise up the tribes of Jacob, and to restore the offspring of Israel. I will also give thee for a light unto the nations so that My salvation may be unto the end of the earth (Isaiah 49:6)." This is the classical definition of the doctrine of a chosen people. This idea has had its impact not only upon Judaism, but upon Christianity too, for, in his conversion efforts, Paul makes the point that the new converts will become "co-heirs and co-partners in the promise" saying that they, from now on, will be the true Israel, and that they will constitute the chosen ones.

II

I am asking myself what is wrong with this idea if properly understood. I believe it is one of the most fascinating ideas in the history of man. Each nation on earth is attempting to elicit from its own genius the most creative ideas, and to reach high points in which the nation is at its best. When it achieves this goal, it makes a distinct contribution to the totality of mankind.

Let me illustrate this in an example which is close at hand. Western Civilization has its sources in Rome, Greece, and Judea. (Or you can say Rome, Athens, and Jerusalem.) From Rome we derived the notion of government and political administration. The sense of beauty and the spirit came to us from Greece. Our religious ideas and ethical precepts we owe to Israel.

One could easily ask, "Why is it this way?" There is no answer to this question. The fact is that there are three forces that cover the life of man, namely, the material, the intellectual and the spiritual. Of these forces, Rome represents the material, and though mankind owes it its notion of government as a result of Rome's marvelous gifts for political and administrative power—the Roman civilization was not directed toward higher aims but was essentially materialistic. Legend has it that Rome's founders, Remus and Romulus, were suckled by a she-wolf, which reflects the Roman civilization rather adequately. There is a similar story by the Rabbis: two of them were walking down one of the main thoroughfares of Rome, and one of them was admiring Rome's civilization, to which the other one replied that the bridges are for the military forces of conquest and that in the towers innocent people are pining away in the agony of death. Rome had outside splendor but no divine spirit.

The domain of the intellect was that of Greece. The Greeks were imbued with higher ideals than acquisition of power, they strove for something more noble and elevating than the raising of mighty armies, military aspirations and conquests. They cultivated the mind and surrounded life with charm and beauty, harmony and rhythm. They observed and studied nature; their eyes feasted on the marvelous panorama of the universe: the glories of the sunset, the pageantry of the clouds, the grandeur of the heavens, the majesty of winter, the vivacity of youth, and the compassion of old age. These were the themes that this civilization embodied in sculpture and painting, in poetry and song. It was intellectually higher than that of Rome but again the spirit of God was not there. Greek civilization did not evolve the conception of a higher divine being, and the final decay and destruction of Hellas came because of this lack of divine spirit.

The only people in history which came under the domain of the spirit was Israel. From the first, we were determined to build a civilization, distinguished not by its perfection of military institutions, not even by any particular outward beauty and external splendor, but by an essentially spiritual and moral character, endeavoring to found a just social order under the kingdom of God. Following the history of our people through the variegated pattern of its long existence there comes over you a deep sense of its anchorage in the eternal ideals of the spirit and in the forces that make for righteousness. It is this religious character of our people and its attachment to things of the spirit that made us the dynamic force which made for mankind so much that is noble in civilization.

Human civilization rests on three elements: the material, spiritual, and intellectual. As individual Jews we have made contributions to all three, but collectively, our chief contribution was in the field of the spirit. There we have been at our best. As the Bible is a religious book, it speaks of us in the oriental imagery as "chosen" for this particular field of religion— just as was Rome and Greece were chosen for their contributions to the field of government and art. For us it also meant that we were elected for service to others, judged by higher standards, and rewarded with suffering, as is the portion of all who have fought for great ideals. This is the philosophy which a Jew relives when he enters the synagogue on Yom Kippur. It is to this that he pledges himself anew, looking scrutinizingly into his own life in order to find out whether he has lived up to the expectations of our tradition, and to repent if he has not, and to mend his ways.

III

Our Rabbis were fully aware of the fact that High Holidays are what we would call today a "big order." How can a human being actually fulfill all the demands of these awesome days? The Psalmist was frightened and exclaimed: "If Thou, O Lord, shouldst mark iniquities, who could stand (Psalm 130:2)" and his answer was that it is only possible because "with Thee there is forgiveness." The Rabbis in commenting on this psalm say that "at the beginning God had in mind to create the world in the quality of justice, but he saw that the universe wouldn't survive, so he attached to it the quality of mercy," knowing full well "that there is no human being on earth who does constantly good without sinning (cf. Ecclesiastes 7:20)."

It is because of this that in Jewish life we have Rosh

Hashanah and Yom Kippur. Rosh Hashanah is *yom ha-din,* "the Day of Judgement," of law and of justice, and Yom Kippur, on the other hand, is the quality of mercy, the day of forgiveness, of expiation and atonement. On Rosh Hashanah, a heavenly court is judging, based on the principles of justice. On Yom Kippur God answers it and judges man on the basis of compassion. It is the essence of the covenant between God and Israel to be as Holy as he, as compassionate as he, and as forgiving. The demands of the High Holidays are high indeed, and no other people could live up to it, but, says our tradition, the Jews being the elected, are the chosen ones of the covenant for the potentiality of complying with the great request. We, as Jews, can expiate, repent, forgive and be as compassionate as is the Father above.

IV

With the covenant and selection for a motive, the Jews in all generations and in all forms of endeavor taught the ideal of humaneness and compassion beyond the call of duty. In the spirit of the Yom Kippur Day, the following story should serve as an example. It is a rare footnote to World War II and pertains particularly to the idea we have been discussing. It refers to an incident which occurred in North Africa in 1942, reported by the press in a tiny item telling about a certain officer, Ernest Tessier, of the French Foreign Legion, who captured twenty-four men of Rommel's Afrika Corps without firing a shot but by shouting forth orders in German. When the newspapers became curious and wanted to know more about the man they discovered one of the most fantastic stories in the life of our generation.

Before telling you the story, I have to preface it with a few historical facts. You will recall that the minister of foreign affairs of the Weimar Republic in Germany was a Jew by the name of Walter Rathenau. You will also remember that he, one of Europe's greatest statesmen, was murdered on his way to his office in June, 1922. He was the first and the last Jew to hold such a high office in Germany after World War I and he was the first of six million Jews to be murdered by the Nazis. The whole German nation was shocked by this horrible assassination. Over a million people lined the streets and mourned for him on his last journey Unter den Linden. Looking back at it, it is clear that the shot that killed Rathenau gave birth to National Socialism. The police found out the names of the three assassins (two committed suicide before they could be captured, and the third was sentenced to fifteen years in prison.) This is the historical background to the story that follows:

Mr. Tessier was a man of about thirty-nine, who spoke German and French fluently, who did not mix very much with his fellow legionnaires, and remained pensively aloof. There were a number of Jews in Tessier's unit—Europeans who had fled the Nazis and enlisted in the French Foreign Legion. Tessier was strangely drawn to them. When, one evening, he ordered four of them to report to his quarters, they were terrified at first, until they found him amazingly congenial. Tessier told them that the Jews were the only civilized people he had met and that he wanted to be friendly with them. He confessed that he loved the Jews and thought that they were among the finest and most gifted people on earth. On that evening and on subsequent meetings he revealed an amazing knowledge of Jewish history and religion. One evening, when that group and Tessier met again for a discussion they were interrupted by the appearance of a new recruit reporting for duty. The door opened, a young man appeared and said, "Legionnaire Rathenau reporting for duty." Tessier leapt from his chair and said, "Did you say Rathenau? Are you by any chance related to the late foreign minister by that name?" to which the stranger replied, "Yes sir, I am his nephew." Tessier waxed pale and after a few seemingly endless moments said "Rathenau, I am one of the three men who murdered your uncle on June 24, 1922. My name is Ernst Werner Teshow." Then he drew from his inside pocket a faded scrap of paper and carefully unfolded it. It was a letter in German, addressed to Teshow's mother a few days after the murder and written by Mathilde Rathenau, the mother of the foreign minister:

> In grief unspeakable, I give you my hand, you, of all women the most to be pitied. Say to your son that in the name and spirit of him he has murdered, I forgive, even as God may forgive, if before an earthly judge he make a full confession of his guilt, and before the Heavenly Judge repent. Had he known

90

my son, one of the noblest men earth had ever borne, he had rather have turned the weapon on himself. May these words give peace to your soul.

Mathilde Rathenau.

Weeping like a child, he told the young Rathenau his life story. He served five years in prison, was released in 1927 for good behavior, then enlisted in the Foreign Legion. He told him that this letter of Mathilde Rathenau was his most prized possession. It opened a new world for him. In prison he read the writings of his uncle, every word of every book he had ever written. He studied Jewish history, and he studied Hebrew. He soon found out that the Nazis were lying about the Jews, and consequently he has devoted the last fifteen years in order to suppress the evil in his own soul. In the same way as the mother of Rathenau conquered herself when she wrote the letter to his mother, he has tried to master himself. Throughout these years, he has sought out every opportunity to lend a helping hand to the Jewish people. It was actually verified by Jewish organizations that in 1941, dressed as a dock worker in Marseilles, he smuggled four hundred Jews out of Marseilles on Casablanca visas.

This is the meaning of Yom Kippur painted on the scene of contemporary history. Out of hundreds of volumes written on World War II, this is probably the greatest Yom Kippur sermon ever written by life itself on the subject of forgiveness and repentance, for it says that God forgives if man repents, and that man repents if fellow man forgives.

Let us then learn from this Yom Kippur holiday its deep and stirring meaning. Looking into our own souls, searching our own character, asking God for forgiveness and learning to forgive our fellow man. This is the meaning of Israel's election, our purpose and the very meaning of our Jewish life. It is in this spirit that we pray tonight in the hope that God's voice will say "I have forgiven according to your word."

THE TRAGEDY AND THE TRIUMPH

Rosh Hashanah, 1961

The year 5721 just coming to a close was, in Jewish terms, the most dramatic period in the post war era. It manifested the ebb and flow of our destiny in their most extreme forms, of the lowest degradation and of the highest achievement. For it was the year of Eichmann as well as the bar mitzvah of Israel.

The proper name for this year ought to be *The Tragedy and the Triumph.* It is fitting on Rosh Hashanah to reflect upon the two features of the year just entering the annals of history.

The Tragedy. I remember so well and so vividly the two days I spent, this year, at the beginning of May, at the Eichmann trial. There was revealed before one's eyes the picture of terror and mass murder that overtook European Jewry. It was the day in which the attorney general of Israel accused the man who sat in the glass cage and who was the master of the slaughter houses, of conspiracy in the most massive genocide plot human history has ever recorded. A conspiracy, he said, in three phases: first, expulsion of the Jews from Germany; second, the concentration of European Jews in the ghettos, mostly in Poland, in preparation for their extermination; and third, the mass deportation from the ghettos to the concentration camps, with the ensuing results of the burning and the gassing and the cremating, specifically in Auschwitz, the place the attorney general called the "Ashen Planet" which the Nazi put into orbit in the skies of Europe, the soil of which showed a fountain of Jewish blood welling up indefinitely.

When he finished, there came the documents backing up the indictment, giving names, naming places. Then the row of witnesses, representatives of that pitiful remnant of survivors from all parts of the globe, telling their story: the story of the rabbis in prayershawl, the tallis thrust into the fire amidst the mockery of their tormentors; of the hanging of teenage boys to the tune of merry march music played by the camp orchestra; of children snatched from their mothers' arms and dashed against the wall, which the Nazi called the *kinderspiel;* of babies thrust alive into the fire and the bins of the camps filled with little shoes; of whole families falling out of the shower when the door opened, still together, because they died clasping the hands of one another. So it went, endlessly, one after the other, testifying to a plan, the most monstrous ever conceived by men, of wiping out an entire people, deliberately, in premeditation, of six million defenseless men, women, and children.

The attorney general caught the atmosphere of the day, when at the conclusion of the afternoon he said: "I believe that if any man could try to imagine a nightmare, he would not succeed in inventing a tiny fraction of the appalling things that have been presented this afternoon and described here by the witnesses." I admit to you frankly that on the second day I left before the session was over. I admit to you that I could not take it, on the second day, in the afternoon. I could not stand it any longer.

I remember I walked back to the hotel, a long walk, trying to find some measure of self composure, some semblance of balance, eliciting from my own memory the experiences of my own time under Hitler, the stories I just heard. I asked myself, "Has there ever been a lower degradation of a people? In spite of the courageous and heroic acts in some of the ghettos and in the camps; has there ever been a more appalling disgrace, a more humiliating defeat of a great and ancient and cultured people?" I remember that what flashed through my mind was a passage in the Bible, which indicated to me, that it was predicted long, long ago. It is that awesome and dreadful chapter called the *tochacha,* "the Admonition," in which Moses addresses his generation with a vision of the future. He describes a situation which might have been written in 1937. This is the text:

> The Lord will scatter you...from one end of the earth to the other.... Yet even among those nations you will find no repose.... There will be no rest for the sole of your foot. The Lord will give you there a trembling heart and the failing of the eyes and the languishing of the soul. And your life will be hanging in doubt before you; you will be afraid day and night; you will not be leading your own life. In the morning you shall say, "If only it were evening!" and in the evening you shall say, "If only it were morning!"—because of what your heart shall dread and your eyes shall see.   (Deuteronomy 28:64-67)

Moses lived around 1250 B.C.E. His vision was fulfilled in all its dreadfulness and tragic ramifications. You begin to understand the outcry of the medieval author of the penitential prayers still read before Rosh Hashanah, when he reacted to his time and said: "Lord who abidest forever and are holy, look at the disgrace of the distressed."

This is the tragedy symbolized in one aspect of the year. The enormity of the crime committed by a so-called civilized people, in this century, with the rest of the world looking on, believingly or unbelievingly, but doing nothing or very little about it. This is one side of the coin.

There is the other. *The Triumph.* The triumph is reflected in Israel's bar mitzvah. The two are, of course, not unconnected. In historic sequence, it is the tragedy that came first, and the triumph is the result of it. I do not know God's ways more than you do, but apparently in his incomprehensible ways, it needed the slaughter of six million Jews to move the conscience of mankind to grant a homeless people a place in the sun.

Now Israel has done well for itself in these thirteen years. It has developed economically; it has kept its promise to us to keep its doors open to any Jew, any place, anytime; it has extended a helping hand, considerably so, to the newly awakening African continent; it has become a moral voice to be reckoned with in the halls of the United Nations. One can enumerate a hundred other achievements and qualities of these thirteen years, but I believe that no achievement of the thirteen years can measure up to the accomplishment of Israel during the Eichmann trial.

The triumph has two phases. The first phase of the triumph is that you cannot escape the historic impact of what is happening to you: for the first time in two thousand years we have brought to justice a tormentor of our people. After centuries of standing trial as a people before hostile judges and unfriendly witnesses, a revolution has occurred in Jewish life. We have reversed the order. No tormentor ever caught will go free without standing trial in a Jewish court. There have been for us many trials by jury, but this one is for our enemies the first trial by Jewry. This has not happened to us since the days our forefathers left the shores of Palestine in the year of 70 C.E. I do not know what the future holds in store for our people, but one thing I know—Jews will not be slaughtered like sheep anymore.

The historic occasion was felt apparently by the attorney general when, in his summation on August 10, he said, "I am proud that the day has come when a man of Israel can rise and speak the language of the law to the tormentor and evil doer. In this country nobody needs to plead for mercy or pity from an arch murderer. There is no need to flee here and seek protection in any other place. Here there is law." Quoting as he did from the prophet Joel, he prophesied that the day would come in which the Lord will gather the tormenting nations in order to enter into judgment with them in the Valley of Jehoshaphat in the name of the Jewish people and his inheritance, as God says in this chapter, "Enter into judgment with them because they scattered the people so their children remove them from the borders and cast lots of destruction upon them (cf. Joel 4:2-3)." At the end of the chapter, God promises retribution upon the tormentors, to turn it on their heads. Quoting this, he said, "From now on, whoever is apprehended will be judged within the context of the prophesy of Joel." That is one phase of the great triumph of the year, in its historical reversal of the order in our relationship to the majority of nations.

The second, and the last—and maybe even more spectacular than the first—is the fact that the most unforgettable impact of the trial is surely not the man. Aside from the deadly testimony unfolded by the witnesses, the most unforgettable impact is the process of law and of justice in the court. To sit there and watch the scene, giving this sub-human monster days and weeks and months in court, listening patiently to the most grotesque, legalistic arguments of the man who deals with them as if he were discussing a traffic regulation, maintaining sternly the atmosphere of dignity in the court, though it taxes the patience of all concerned to the breaking point. By conducting themselves in this fashion, the judges of Israel have taught mankind, in non-erasable terms, a lesson in the functioning of justice in human society. For the years to come, men will point to these proceedings as a classic example of superhuman decency. The greatest judges and the smallest magistrates will be forever reminded that in a Jewish court, in the city of Jerusalem, a new young nation affirmed the right of the lowliest and most wicked and most wretched of species to the full judicial process of the law. We have been teaching mankind the elements of justice for two thousand years, and anti-Semites have been saying to us, "You are only preaching it because it is such a good protection for minorities." For the first time in two thousand years, there is one place where we are a majority, and we are dealing with justice the way the Bible taught us: *zedek, zedek tirdof,* "justice, justice shall you pursue." Justice cannot be tampered with, not compromised, an element which is taboo, wholly irrespective of who is a witness, the victim, the accused or the accusers. This is the majestic triumph of Israel this year.

Again, this too is the fulfillment of a prophesy. In the same way as the tragedy is a fulfillment of the vision of Moses in the Book of Deuteronomy, so the triumph is a fulfillment of another prophesy. It makes you shudder when you read it. It might have been written after this trial instead of eight hundred years B.C.E. Says Isaiah, addressing himself to Jerusalem in the future—listen to the words:

> I will restore thy judges, as of old,
> and thy counsellors as at the beginning,
> then will thou be called the city of justice,
> the faithful city,
> Zion will be restored through justice,
> and those who return to her through righteousness.
> (Isaiah 1:26-27)

You and I have the great privilege of living in the year of the fulfillment of this prophesy: the judges of Israel restored, the counsellors of the city returned, and the city to be called the city of justice, the faithful city.

This is the tragedy and the triumph, the two features of the year. The tragedy giving birth to the triumph, and the triumph making the tragedy bearable. Now such an extraordinary year imposes upon us great obligations. The history of man is a dialogue between God and man, and at every great important event God is asking a question and what we do is a reaction to it. Such an extraordinary year imposes upon us the obligation to identify ourselves with the tragedy, and to commit ourselves

96

to the triumph. The six million Jews died in unnamed graves, and the only way to bring them back to life is in the unsleeping memory of our generation—in the remembrance. This is a day of remembrance, Rosh Hashanah. They lost their lives only because they were Jews, members of a Jewish people and adherents of the Jewish faith. The only moral, decent answer to this holocaust is the identification—stronger, deeper—with our people and to pay more attention to our faith, to Judaism, to education, to study, to the things that pulsate in Jewish life.

Identification, which is an old Hebrew command, means that those who did not suffer feel the pain of those who did, and that those who are alive hold aloft the spiritual torch of those who are no more.

The other side is commitment. All that we have achieved, speaking in broad historic terms, in our generation, that is positive, all that we were able to create out of the ruins of the ghettos and the ashes of the camps was the old-new Jewish State. Israel will, for the years to come, need much of our time, our energy, our devotion, our substance. Yes, our very assets. It is the only child we have. It has to be cared for, tenderly, longingly, with all the affection of which we are capable, as parents do for an only child. Surely in these days in which thousands of Jews knock again at the gates of the State, with new waves of immigration upon us just now, symbolic identification will not do. Sympathy will not do. Friendship will fail. Commitment to the future of a people—this alone is the commandment of the hour. It is both identification with the past and commitment to the future.

This too is not a brand new idea. This, too, is a prophetic conception with which I am going to conclude what I had to say. The unknown prophet in Babylon, who is the author of the last part of Isaiah, addressed himself to a generation similar to ours—a generation that suffered the tragedy of the exile of Babylon, and which was about to participate or maybe was already participating, in the beginning of the return from Babylon. So the prophet comes to them. Not in so many words, he does not use the words identification and commitment, which is a new vocabulary, but the idea is so clear. Says he to his generation, "For the sake of Zion, I will not be still, and for the sake of Jerusalem not be silent, until her triumph goes forth as brightness (Isaiah 62:1)." He himself is going to see to it that he keeps on giving the message. To make sure his generation remembers the destruction of the state, the suffering in Babylon, before they come to the liberation, he says "I will put watchmen upon thy cities, O Jerusalem. They, too, will not be silent, neither day nor night (Isaiah 62:6)," making sure that the people's memory remains fresh. He then addresses himself to those who already remember and says, "You who now have the memory, you who know the events and feel a part of it, do not allow yourselves any rest, until God has established, and until he has made Jerusalem the glory of the earth (cf. Isaiah 62:6-7)."

So I say to you, the same idea in modern terms—what is upon us in this coming year—is not to be silent for the sake of Zion, not to be still for the sake of Jerusalem, until the triumph of our people goes forth as brightness. First one starts with memory. Memory must lead to identification with a people and a heritage, to take more seriously the synagogue and Jewish education and participation in Jewish community—all the things that make Jewish life worthwhile. Then, I say to you: now that you remember, do not allow yourselves any rest, and do not allow it to your neighbors and friends, until the prophesy is done, until the vision is fulfilled, until we have assured a creative Jewish life here at home and a secure stabilized Jewish State abroad and until we live to see the day that Jerusalem, the City of Justice, emerges as the glorious symbol of a new profile of mankind, a new age of a genuine brotherhood between men and nations. This is our prayer tonight. May it be fulfilled speedily in our days. Amen.

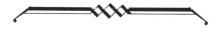

REVERENCE FOR LIFE

September 19, 1961

On Yom Kippur afternoon, just prior to the Memorial Service, when the mood is mellow and the heart is soft, tradition enjoins upon us to read from scripture the strangest book of the Bible, the Book of Jonah. I say strange, because unlike all other prophetic books of the Bible, it contains no vision; it contains no prophesy. It is rather concerned with a story of the prophet, one episode in his life. The book achieved considerable fame, largely due to the story of the whale.

* * *

It does not happen by chance that the greatest of non-Jewish scholars called the Book of Jonah the noblest book of the Bible, because of its wide humanity and deep compassion, because it teaches that God is the God of all peoples, no matter how wicked, that his love embraces all nations no matter how depraved, that the gates of repentance are always open to Jew and non-Jew alike in every generation, and that God is ready to forgive at all times.

This is why this book was put into the liturgy of Yom Kippur and into the synagogue, because the atmosphere of the day of Yom Kippur is exactly the same. It contains a moral horizon which is wide and distant and limitlessly universal. It fits so well into the very liturgy of the prayerbook of the day, a prayerbook which features lines which you and I are repeating during the holidays six, seven, eight, ten times: "Thou, O Lord, extendest Thy hand to the sinners, extendest Thy right hand to those who return. Thou, O Lord, dost not desire the death of the wicked, but that they return and live." Again and again, a hundred times: God hates evil in men, but not men of evil.

If I would sum up the Book of Jonah, and the whole atmosphere of Yom Kippur, I would say: it is the great respect for existence which God himself manifests in Judaism, the love and the compassion and the utter respect for everything that is alive. The clarion call that comes out of Yom Kippur is: to imitate God in human life and to develop what Albert Schweitzer called in our generation, based upon the prophetic heritage, "the reverence for life." If I would have to choose three words that sum up the Book of Jonah and the whole idea of Yom Kippur, it would be "reverence for life."

I am saying all this to you because we are assembling in our synagogues tonight in deep spiritual anguish. The specter of war is hovering over the world again in the center of a divided city, Berlin, replete with concrete block walls and barbed wire fences. The two rival camps are training guns against each other to the tune of a deadly arms race and to the thunder of nuclear explosives. This steadily mounting hostility between the two camps is sending a chill through our hearts tonight, for it indicates an ominous drift to nuclear annihilation, which, in turn, is a testimony to man's failure to control that tremendous force which was born in the ruins of Hiroshima. All this only sixteen years after the end of the Second World War, only sixteen years after the birth of the United Nations created for a very specific purpose; namely, to save future generations from the scourge of war. Tonight the organization created for this purpose is in the throes of hostilities and divisions, with the tragedy only compounded through the great loss and the death of the leader of the United Nations and its secretary general.

Now the problem is doubly serious because we, meaning the West, are faced with a cynical and ruthless enemy and confronted with a strategy of terror and of blackmail. Yet I say to you on this holiest night of the Jewish year, the great danger at the moment still lies within the hearts of men, yours and mine. I look with great anxiety upon a new trend developing within our nation leaning heavily in the direction of an extreme rightist philosophy, which, in turn, spreads fear and hysteria and poisons the minds of millions of our citizens with glib talk and shallow phrases about the inevitability of atomic war.

It has already influenced our press. The free press of a free democracy deals with this subject as if it would be a game in a mathematical experiment. When this inevitable atomic war comes, will it take fifty million dead, sixty million, seventy million? The press is featuring interviews with great scientific minds. Professor Teller, the father of the "A-Bomb," assures us comfortingly that if we will prepare and have all our shelters ready, there is no necessity for eighty or ninety million Americans to die. It may be that only a third of the nation will be in trouble, and the whole outcome of it will be—if we are well prepared—that only ten percent of the nation will be dead. Ten percent of one hundred eighty million people is still eighteen million people. Detached, cool, just amounts.

The press, in columns and editorials, followed up this trend with catchy phrases and cheap slogans: "There is some virtue in a quick atomic war. One should not flinch from the

100

prospect. The sooner we get it over with, the better." There appeared that incredible headline the other day: "What will sudden peace do to the American economy?" You do not believe that intelligent adult people do not know the clouds that are gathering and what is involved.

* * *

I submit to you tonight that Berlin is not good enough a reason, and that the reunification of Germany is not worth the suicide of mankind. To appeal to our generation, sixteen years after the Second World War, to go into either a normal war which may last for several weeks or months or to a nuclear war in order to protect Germany—is sheer madness, a nightmare. To this, visualize that Norwegians, Danes, Belgians, Frenchmen, Dutchmen, who have not forgotten yet the Nazi occupation—the wounds are still open—will now send a new generation which has hardly survived the Nazi occupation, to protect Germany, the country that started the first war, the second, and may be the reason for the third. Is it conceivable for the widows and mothers, who have lost their sons in the Royal Air Force in England under the Nazi blitz and the devastation, to send the Royal Air Force now to protect Berlin? Can one imagine American families that have lost a father, an older brother, in the Second World War where we fought against Germany, to send the younger son and the younger daughter? If this is not a cynicism and cruelty of history, then I do not know of any other example.

To imagine that Jewish young people might again be involved in a third World War, because the reason—the immediate reason for it—is the protection of Berlin or the reunification of Germany, is literally a nightmare. To me as a Jew, as an American who loves this country very well, and who would in time of need give his life for it, I say as a Jew and as an American, and simply as a human being: Germany could not possibly be divided into too many parts as far as the destiny of our people is concerned, as far as the peace of the world is concerned. If I have the choice between our commitments to protect Berlin and the suicide of mankind, I would select the survival of mankind with the best of conscience.

This being the case, coming into a synagogue on so holy an

101

evening, it is good to revert to the ancient wisdom of our people and begin to drink again from the wells of our eternal sources. Admitted that many capitals of the world are the Ninevehs of our day, that their governments are evil, that their leaders are wicked. Should there be no compassion at all for the innocent men, women, for hundreds and thousands of infants who have done no wrong? Even if it would be sure that we could come out as victor, is there no compassion in this whole philosophy now being served to this nation of ours, for the open sky, and open cities, and villages and towns, with millions of innocent people? Ought one not recall the great wisdom of Judaism of hating evil, but not evil men, of imitating God and destroying evil, but not wanting the destruction even of his enemy? All the more that we are dealing with a new threat by which the word victor and victory and vanquished would almost be meaningless. We ought to regain the courage of an ancient religion in order to help our government steer the destiny of the world in the direction which it is taking just now. Building up our strength, and yet cautious step by step, solving every crisis at the time in which it occurs, because every crisis solved means to buy another year, another two years, another three years for the next discussion on disarmament, to prepare another atmosphere for international cooperation, for a hundred things that can happen. It is like borrowing time from the human race to survive. Ought one not regain in the synagogue the sanity of an ancient religion which knew of good and evil, which knew of commandments and of wickedness, but which has said in an eternal answer "Should I not have pity upon Nineveh, that great city, with more than one hundred twenty thousand people that cannot discern between their right hand and the left hand (Jonah 4:11)?"

Should one not learn from the very prayerbook we are using? These days are called in Hebrew *yamim noraim,* "the Days of Awe." These words have never been as meaningful as this year. There are lines which we will be reciting tomorrow which might have been written for this year and this occasion. The lines are:

> All thy creatures, O Lord, pass before Thee,
> And sentences passed on this day;
> Who shall live and who shall die,

Who to the full measure of his life and who before it,
Who shall perish by the sword and who by the fire.

And upon whole nations sentence is being pronounced today: whether to be destined for the sword or to be destined for peace.

Do you need another description this evening of the mood in which we live, the atmosphere which we share, with the whole threat of unleashing the ultimate horror? Yet, does the prayerbook end on this note, in this most moving of prayers when our forefathers used to cry aloud on Yom Kippur afternoon in reading the words? Does it end on this note? It does not. The last line is "Prayer, penitence, and charity avert the final decree." One should learn from these words instead of falling victim to the new fear and hysteria, of allowing oneself to be conditioned by cheap slogans, in an irresponsible attitude which can only be called utter contempt of life.

In contrast, we ought to regain the other side, the deeply felt reverence for life. We ought to see to it that prayer in the weeks and months to come be used as a tremendous weapon. We ought to begin to pray to the Lord of the Universe, as sincerely as our forefathers in centuries gone by, to avert war and to bring peace—because there is no other place to go—and to organize the community of mankind via *our* mass media. Let us suggest to the world, to the churches, to the religious institutions of other faiths, that there ought to be a daily five minute prayer only for this one purpose: to save mankind. If one church will imitate the other, one denomination copy the other, the neutral nations will follow, and finally the churches inside the Iron Curtain will do the same. Then the governments will be ashamed to stand there, seeing the avalanche of mankind and hearing the cry of the potential victims of the holocaust. No power on earth, no dictatorial government could withstand such developments. This is what ought to come out of the Holidays.

We Jews, who bear the scars of so many wars and the wounds of so many battles, have never given up hope that the human mind will not abdicate, that there is another tomorrow, and that the time will eventually come in which charity will reign between nations. We believed in it and believe it to this very day, which means that you respect the difference that divides you, and you seek the common good that unites you. If we hold out steadfastly without losing nerves, without being conditioned by fear and hysteria, but with the inner faith that God could not have possibly meant the creation of this universe only to be blown up by the inventions of the human minds, then this year on the international scene may still be transformed from an utter tragedy to a great triumph. Then we may still live to see the day, distant as it may seem tonight, as the prayerbook promises us. We read: "That the day will come in which all the nations will form one great community so as to do Thy will with a perfect heart."

Let us pray for it. Let us work for it. May God listen to our petition which comes from the very depth of the heart of humanity, and bestow upon us and our generation the blessing of peace and survival. Amen.

OUT OF TRAGEDY—FAITH

From *C.B.S. Church of The Air Program,* August 26, 1962

National festivals, religious holidays, and historic days of mourning commemorated by a people reflect its moral substance, its spiritual outlook and its philosophy of life. More than that, such days are the very key to the soul of a people, reflecting its dreams and aspirations, its visions and its goals.

During the summer season—it fell this year on the ninth of August—the Jewish calendar bids us observe a fast day called *tisha b'av,* the ninth day of the Hebrew month of Av, which marks two great national catastrophes in the history of the Jewish people: the destruction of the first Temple in Jerusalem and of the Kingdom in Palestine by the Babylonians in the year 586 B.C.E.; and then the destruction of the second Temple in Jerusalem and of the Second Commonwealth in Palestine by the Roman Legions in the year 70 C.E.

This is not even all that happened on that day. According to Talmudic tradition, the last fortress of Palestine, Betar, heroically defended by Bar Kochba, also fell on *tisha b'av* in the year 135 C.E. It did not escape the attention of medieval mystics that the expulsion of the Jews from Spain in 1492 also occurred on the ninth day of the Hebrew month of Av. Jews of Eastern European descent cannot possibly forget the coincidence—if coincidence it be—that the first World War in 1914 also started on this historic day of mourning—an event which marked the beginning of the great tragedy of Eastern European Jewry.

It is not surprising that in the Jewish mind this fast day mirrors itself as a particular day of misfortune, bound up with sorrowful events and national calamities. As a result, traditionally minded Jews have for centuries fasted on that day and have recited with heartbreaking chant and mournful tones the biblical Book of Lamentations, bewailing the destruction of the first and second Temple in Jerusalem as well as of the First and Second Commonwealth in Palestine. *Tisha b'av* has, therefore, remained the classic day of mourning through the ages, and to this very day, next to Yom Kippur, the Day of Atonement, the most important *historic* fast day of the Jewish year.

II

But even this remarkable career of the day is only half the story. Judaism is a religion of balance. It never allows for extreme positions of the human soul. It is fully aware that a people cannot live continually on memories of past catastrophes, but must be given faith in brighter days to come and hope for happier years in the future. The mourning over the destruction of Zion and Jerusalem was, therefore, counterbalanced by a philosophy of hope for deliverance. This is why Jewish tradition has arranged the calendar in such a way that the black letter day of mourning is followed almost immediately—this year on the eleventh of August—by a special Sabbath called *shabbat nachamu,* "the Sabbath of Comfort and Consolation." This is a joyous and festive day, named after one of the most inspiring and uplifting visions in prophetic literature, Chapter 40 of Isaiah, which is recited in the synagogue on this day. It begins with the words: *nachamu, nachamu ami,* "Comfort ye, comfort ye My people"; in it the great anonymous prophet proclaims divine forgiveness, the restoration of Zion, and the return of the people of Israel to the Land of Israel.

Moreover, Chapter 40 of Isaiah is the first of seven prophetic readings in the synagogue which are recited during the seven Sabbaths following the fast day of *tisha b'av*—all taken from the second half of the Book of Isaiah and known in Jewish life as the *"Rhapsody of Zion Redeemed."* Together these chapters constitute the message of faith and hope which played so great a role in the history of Jewish survival.

Here are a few examples culled from the *"Rhapsody"* in Isaiah's chapters which are read in the synagogues in these days of the summer months:

Comfort ye, comfort ye My people,
Saith the Lord.
Bid Jerusalem take heart,
And proclaim unto her,
That her time of service is accomplished,
That her guilt is paid off
That she hath received of the Lord's hand
Double for her sins.

(Isaiah 40:1-2)

Break forth into joy, sing together,
Ye waste places of Jerusalem;
For the Lord hath comforted His people,
He hath redeemed Jerusalem.

(Isaiah 52:9)

For the mountains may depart,
And the hills be removed;
But My kindness shall not depart from thee,
Neither shall My covenant of peace be removed,
Saith the Lord that hath compassion on thee.

(Isaiah 54:10)

For as the earth bringeth forth her growth,
And as the garden causeth the things that are sown
    in it to spring forth;
So the Lord God will cause victory and glory
To spring forth before all the nations.

(Isaiah 61:11)

These then are the deeply moving words by the author of the second half of the Book of Isaiah, known in Jewish tradition as the "Great Comforter." Under the influence of these challenging visions, the second Temple was later erected and the city of Jerusalem rebuilt. To this very day, these prophetic lines are recited in our synagogues, again and again, in the weeks following the Day of Lamentations.

III

Even this is not the whole story. But it is a story that allows us to look at Judaism under the aspects of one of its religious customs, in connection with the observance of a historic fast day. It explains many facets in the character of our people which are sometimes puzzling to the outsider: there is first the *stubbornness of memory* with which Jewish tradition has inculcated our soul to a point by which *we often forgive, but never forget,* and with the result that the word *zachor,* "to remember" is the most popular word in the Hebrew language. There is secondly the *proverbially optimistic outlook on life*—balancing tragedy with hope and catastrophe with faith, the bleak yesterday with the joyful tomorrow; never yielding to pessimism, always hoping, striving, aspiring and believing that the future will be better than the past.

Only a people blessed with such religious equipment could survive, in our own days, the Hitler catastrophe with the loss of six million of our brethren in the ovens and concentration camps, and—after this bloodletting—still have the inner strength to fulfill the vision of Isaiah by returning to Zion, building the Jewish State and reuniting an ancient people with its ancient land. We succeeded in this accomplishment because the Zionist dream—the dream that made this miracle possible—was in itself born of memories, nurtured in faith, and carried on the wings of hope. Jewish folklore sensed this uniqueness of our philosophy of life long ago when it stated that *tisha b'av,* the day of national calamities of the past, will, in the future, be the very birthday not only of the salvation of Israel but of the universal redemption of mankind as a whole.

In these days of utter human crisis when the survival of the human race is in question and uppermost in our minds, let us relearn the ancient message of an ancient people. In combining memories of the past with visions of the future, one can still save man from extinction and rebuild our society on solid foundations. May God help us in this undertaking. Amen.

PURIM—THE ANATOMY OF HATE

March 1, 1964

We have just celebrated the Festival of Purim, the story of which is to be found in the biblical Book of Esther. It tells of the narrow escape of the Jewish Community in Persia from annihilation, as plotted by their arch-enemy Haman in the fifth century B.C.E.

The historicity of the event is, to say the least, doubtful. In fact most scholars today agree that it is historic fiction. The book of Esther itself was admitted to the biblical Canon only after much debate among the Rabbis, and tradition considers Purim a Minor Holiday (yMegillah 5:1; bMegillah 7a). It is, therefore, astonishing to find the provocative statement of the Rabbis—reiterated again and again in the poetry of the Middle Ages—that "all seasonal holidays may one day disappear, but the days of Purim will remain forever (Midrash Mishlei 9)."

In order to explain this apparent discrepancy in rabbinic viewpoint, one has to understand that Judaism is an idea-centered religion and that, in consequence, each one of our holidays projects a particular idea, and that together the cycle of our festivals form the galaxy of the classic values of Judaism. Thus, Passover projects the idea of freedom, Shavuot underscores the function of law in society, Succot interprets the idea of human cooperation, and so it goes. Seen against this background, Purim calls our attention to the destructive power *of unfounded hatred* and challenges us to concentrate all our efforts on its elimination, if we ever hope to establish a wholesome society.

There is a paragraph in the Book of Esther which is remarkable for its psychological insight. The whole Purim affair started with a personal incident between two individuals, namely Mordecai and Haman. We read, when Haman saw that "Mordecai bowed not down, nor prostrated himself before him, then was Haman full of wrath (Esther 3:5)." It was, then, nothing else but the hurt vanity of the prime minister that filled him with inordinate rage against one of the citizens. But such is the character of hatred that if that citizen happens to belong to a minority group, it is the group collectively that has to be punished. So the Book of Esther sadly continues: "But it

108

seemed contemptible in his eyes to lay hands on Mordecai alone—wherefore Haman sought to destroy all the Jews who were throughout the whole kingdom of Ahasuerus, even the people of Mordecai (Esther 3:6)." Here the Bible, almost sarcastically, analyzes the personality of the hater and the psychology of anti-Semitism.

History has often confirmed the unfortunate fact that a personal grudge against a single individual leads, on many an occasion, to the wholesale attack against an entire people. We, in our generation, have to remember, for instance, that Hitler's anti-Semitic career started with a personal incident: he believed himself to be a great painter and submitted one of his paintings to the Vienna Academy of Arts. It was refused admission to that illustrious institution because it was third rate art. Quite by chance the man who had to inform him of the decision of the Board of Governors was a Jew. Hitler never forgot it—and the result of this personal grievance was the death of six million Jews in ovens, in concentration camps and in nameless graves.

But this is not all. When personal hatred leads to the plotting of mass extermination, there comes a time when the perpetrator brings forth the rationale, so as to justify the claim in the eyes of others. Here too, Haman was Hitler's most instructive teacher. In presenting to the King of Persia the plan to annihilate a whole people, Haman, devilishly and cleverly, uses "reasoning" and so-called objective facts. This is how he puts it: "There is a certain people scattered abroad and dispersed among the peoples in all the provinces of thy kingdom; and their religious laws are diverse from those of every people; neither keep they the king's laws; therefore it profiteth not the king to suffer them (Esther 3:8)."

Here is the whole abyss of the criminal mind: first comes personal hatred, then intent to genocide, and finally the emergence of some political theory, in order to explain oneself to the world in acceptable terms. That is how it has often been. Hatred is there at the very beginning, then comes the propaganda machine to create the image of the minority as an inferior group, attributing to them the worst qualities of mind and heart and soul in such a way as to make them seem a menace to the welfare of the state. Stalin did it under the heading of

"Jewish cosmopolitans" or "Jewish intellectuals"; Hitler under the slogan of the "inferior Semitic race" which endangers the existence of the "superior Aryan race." Max Nordau—the great Zionist leader—said, more than half a century ago, that *not* the Jewish people is bad and therefore hated by the anti-Semite, but the anti-Semite first hates, and then the Jewish people is made to look bad in the eyes of the world.

It is this curse of "unfounded hatred" undermining a free society that the Holiday of Purim pinpoints and underscores. Too many lives have been lost in the course of history as a result of these maniacal tendencies. In a free society, reason, not emotion, should be the motivating force of all human actions. However, we have not reached this ideal stage yet, even in our own democratic society of the West. Too often voices are still heard, even in our own land, filling the air with hatred against this or that racial or religious minority, because they are in one way or another "different" from the group to which the hate monger happens to belong. Do not be fooled by it. It is not that he reasonably dislikes the other group and then proceeds to the point of hating. It is the other way around.

Let our American people, therefore, not be taken in by venomous propaganda. The matter-of-fact acceptance of differences between groups is the very test of a vibrant democracy. If minority groups should have to pay for their freedom with the abolition of their heritage, democracy would hardly be worth defending. It would mean a cultural and religious coercion, a spiritual totalitarianism which is the exact opposite of a free society in a democratic system. Why should any individual or any group bow down, physically or symbolically, to other individuals or other groups of human beings? We Jews come from a people that has always preferred martyrdom and death to humiliation and spiritual slavery. We have, through the centuries, been a people that has bowed down before God, never before man. Is this religious attitude of an ancient people reason for hatred? No, the "unfounded hatred" of frustrated individuals stands at the beginning. The so-called justification, because of differences, is an after-thought. Such hatred is fundamentally destructive: it kills political enemies, it murders six million Jews, and, in a devious way, assassinates even a president.

110

Seen in this light, the Rabbis were quite right in their provocative statement about Purim. All other holidays may one day not be necessary—because freedom, law, and cooperation may eventually be achieved. But they will be of no avail if, on the deepest layer of the recesses of the human soul, unfounded hatred, per se, is not eliminated and reason put in its place. The Rabbis were aware that this would take a long time, but that the ultimate victory of humanity depended upon it. Redemption for mankind will only come when hatred toward man is entirely gone. May we, then, work zealously for the day in which the Purim Holiday, too, might not be necessary as a constant reminder of humanity's guilt, but that we would celebrate it as a testimony to the final triumph of loyalty and courage over the forces of irrational hatred and evil design. May we see this goal fulfilled in our time—and in our land. Amen.

Arrival in Muskogee, Oklahoma, September 19, 1940

America

WHAT THIS COUNTRY MEANS TO ME!

Installation Sermon, Beth Ahaba Temple,
Muskogee, Oklahoma, September 27, 1940

This Friday-evening service is the second I have celebrated in the United States, but it is the first in my new congregation. Not only this: it is my first service to be celebrated in the English language. Therefore I must apologize for my not yet having mastered this beautiful but difficult language.

I began studying English about one year ago, without any opportunity of practicing it. My Jewish work in Germany did not allow me to devote myself to private studies. I think you will believe me when I tell you that the last seven years that I spent in Germany, as Rabbi of the Great Jewish Congregation of Berlin, were full of difficulties and troubles, of pains and tears, of anxiety and responsibility for my people. To remain there in my place and to fulfill my task up to the last possible minute, although the authorities were eager to make life and work insupportable—this already took all my strength.

You will therefore understand that the atmosphere of that country was not fit for private preoccupation and for studying foreign languages. That is why I ask you to be indulgent. Let me have the time to complete the knowledge of your language, which is now my language, too.

Do not expect me to preach a sermon tonight—I mean a sermon about a special religious or cultural problem. There are too many thoughts and sentiments moving my soul tonight, sentiments of joy and utter thankfulness which will not allow me to deliver a merely intellectual speech.

Remember that after all these trying years, during which I almost forgot that there still exists a pure, human feeling in the world beyond races and peoples, I came to this country and to this town and regained my faith in humanity. We have been met here with helpfulness and assistance, goodness and cordiality, friendship and love.

* * *

The little word, "happy," means so much to us. Perhaps this is a difference between the English and the German languages, for the word, *gluecklich* is very seldom used, and you

114

may guess that we did not use it frequently during these last years. All the more you may be convinced that whenever this word is used, we really mean it.

On one of my last days in Germany, someone whom I happened to meet in the street asked me: "Doctor, will you be happy there, so far away?" I answered: "Far—from where?" He did not know what to reply.

Some people in New York happened to ask me the same question: "Will you be happy, down there, so far off?" I answered again: "Far off—from where?"

The questions, though seeming alike, had a different meaning. The first referred to my former home in Europe; the second apparently alluded to my going far away from the big city. As for the first, we must take into consideration that the tragedy of the Jews in Europe consists in their being deprived of their homes. They became strangers in the very place where they and their parents were born and where God had wanted them to live.

On the other hand, hundreds and thousands of Jews have gone to foreign countries, for instance to America, and they have found themselves—at home! So we wonder what "far away" means in this case. When it means "far from where you feel at home," then we had rather tell this European that he is far away, not we.

As for the second question, concerning big cities, I have found that happiness does not depend on the size of a city or on the largeness of one's sphere of activity. Besides, there is often more loneliness in big cities than in small ones.

* * *

Nevertheless, I cannot deny that it was hard to leave family and friends behind. This is human and everybody will understand it. But there are two more factors which make this painful "far away" less cruel to us. The first factor is the fact of *galut,* the Hebrew word which means "to be spread all over the earth, living among all nations." It was always with deep sorrow that our ancestors mentioned it, because Palestine as a national and spiritual center has always been the dream of our people.

But coming to this country and to this town of Muskogee,

115

we have found for the first time that galut—this negative phenomenon in our history—has its advantages. For we did not come to meet strangers; we have met friends, people whose hearts speak the same language as ours, people to whom we feel as deeply related as though we belonged to the same family. We do belong to the same family: galut had kept us separated up to now, and galut has brought us together. That is one factor which helps us to endure the painful separation from our folks.

The second factor is that the Jewish people, having become homeless in nearly all European countries, have one home which cannot be taken from them, and that is religion. This home, being in our souls, cannot be lost and will always stay with us wherever we are, even when we are "homeless."

* * *

Now one more word about happiness. I have just told you that happiness is not a matter of big cities and great congregations, but rather the result of good feeling and personal contentment. The notion of peace of mind alone does not define the whole contents of the word "happiness." There are some ideas beyond the private and personal sphere belonging to it. These ideas are freedom and peace, the greatest and most precious gifts we have in this country.

There is no doubt that all of you deeply appreciate these gifts of destiny. But do you realize what these words—freedom and peace—mean to me? Freedom for us is freedom of speech—without secret police, freedom of press—without the control of a nationalist party, freedom of opinion—without concentration camp, and freedom of religion—without supervision of the government. This is freedom for us, and there is no happiness in the world without it.

Peace: to walk in the streets, meeting people you are sure are not your enemies and who do not hate you; to see the shop windows of the town without the inscription, "No entrance for Jews;" to take leave of your friends in the evening, knowing that you will see them again the next morning, undisturbed by the idea that some of them or you yourself might be transported to some other place during the night and carried away forever; to stay in one's house with one's family or friends and

116

not to be frightened when the telephone rings or when some-body knocks at your door—this is peace to us, and there is no happiness in the world without it.

Do you see now why we are so unutterably happy to be here? Because we live in freedom and peace, without hatred and hostility, without fear and trembling, but with neighborli-ness and heartiness, tolerance and broadmindedness, with homeliness and religion.

Let me finish by telling you an oriental fairy tale. In the early days of human life, Fortune went around the world look-ing for a partner. At first it found a rich man, who wanted to buy Fortune. But Fortune told him "I don't want you. There are things in the world that cannot be bought even with all your possessions." Fortune went on and found a very strong man who tried to conquer Fortune by the strength of his body. But Fortune said, "I don't want you. There are things in the world that cannot be conquered merely by strength of body." It went on and met a handsome youth. Fortune asked him: "What can you give me to become my partner?" The youth answered: "I own large acres of land, and I am young and strong, but besides this, I want to give you my heart, which is full of love and sympathy for mankind." It was with him that Fortune con-cluded the eternal pact.

America is young. She is rich and powerful, but she has allied herself with Fortune on account of her inner qualities, on account of her golden heart. That is why I want to bring you the regards and the love of all those abroad who suffer the tyranny of nations which likewise were rich and strong but which did not understand how to make partnership with Fortune. All those are looking over to your country, America, and admiring it, and they are calling in their hearts what I am going to call now: it is the old traditional Jewish way of congratulating and celebrating a beloved person; you lift the cup of wine, saying, *l'chaiyim, America!*—"Thou shalt live, America."

America, may your pact with Fortune be eternal! May God bless you with everlasting happiness! You are the only nation in the world to be rich and strong and young and at the same time democratic, tolerant and liberal. You are the hope of mil-lions of men believing that some day the whole world will follow your example, and therefore they all call, as I am calling out of the very depth of my heart: *l'chaiyim, America!*

SINAI—THE CAREER OF AN IDEA

From The Southwest Jewish Chronicle, XV:7 (July 1941)

Excerpts from Sermon on the Occasion of the Twenty-Fifth Anniversary of Beth Ahaba Temple, Muskogee, Oklahoma.

When the Temple in Jerusalem burst into flames, sparks spread all over the world in twos, seeking refuge for a long time. Then, one spark in such a couplet entered a synagogue. As these two sparks belong together, every time Jews enter a synagogue praying from the depth of their hearts, the Temple is built up anew, and the spirit of the old Temple in Jerusalem celebrates its revival.

And so it was that a spark of the Temple entered the hearts of the founders of this temple, and they built it up. The second spark has found its refuge here.

If, today, after three thousand years, we search into the past and look from the United States to Europe, and know Stalin, Hitler and Mussolini and what they stand for, can we say that Sinai—by which we mean Jewish ethics, Jewish morals—was a success, or are we compelled to say it has been a failure?

The question is important in our day because Europe until 1933 was the result of a Judeo-Christian tradition. If you take away the word Sinai from Europe up to the year 1933, you cannot define Europe; for the Bible shaped the cultural form of Europe up to 1933.

What about Sinai? Can we say it is still a success or has it been a failure? Sinai has not lost anything of its great values and ideals, even in 1941. Hitler has conquered a large part of Europe, but nobody in the world, not even himself, can say that he shaped a new spiritual form of the countries he has conquered. Their democratic and religious spirit has never been as strong as in these days.

Hitler's was a physical occupation by military force, and if his program was (and it was!) to destroy the spirit of the first

118

two religions in the world, which came from Sinai, he did not succeed.

* * *

Another example of the success of Sinai is seen in the fact that the few remaining democracies of the world—England, Switzerland and the United States—have never been so aware of the close connection between the political form of democracy and the religious institution of the Church and the Synagogue as at present. The spirit has become stronger and stronger, and millions upon millions of people are now aware of the power of religion and the Church.

We must say with pardonable pride that the seven years of struggle under Hitler show the tremendous success and magnificent influence which the word Sinai has exerted on all the people of the world. That means that even Hitler did not succeed in breaking the chain of tradition, meaning the channel by which the ideas of Sinai penetrated the world.

* * *

What is the mystic power which prompts people in a free country, far from Jewish centers, far from the struggle of the ghetto, to erect a temple? What is this mystic power which takes people and compels them to do things like this? Nobody compelled these people in Muskogee, a quarter of a century ago, to be Jews; it was not even a moral compulsion.

Here again is the same answer. It is a small example of a great idea, namely the unbroken chain of Jewish tradition inherited in blood—a feeling and attitude of Jews all over the world.

How proud we of the Muskogee congregation should be, and how grateful to the founders of the temple! Twenty-five years in a small congregation like this are a chapter of history, and our generation is greatly indebted to those founders. It is our duty to live up to their hopes, hoping that future generations will continue the work of the fathers, because this is the deepest idea of Sinai—that sons should carry on the work and ideals of their fathers.

This solemn anniversary celebration of Beth Ahaba Temple gives us the assurance that, in spite of the past seven years of an embattled religion and an embattled democracy, there will always be an Israel, because there will always be a Sinai. As the Constitution of the United States is to so great an extent founded on the sources of the Bible, we are sure about this also—that there will always be an America!

THE ONENESS OF THE JEWISH WORLD

August 21, 1945

Now that the fight for winning the war is over and the struggle for establishing the peace is commencing, it is good, on the occasion of the New Year, to take stock of the lessons that history has taught and draw the conclusions for the rebuilding of our lives in the years to come.

I

Looking upon the American scene today—a scene filled with the atmosphere of international cooperation and world participation, of Bretton Woods and the San Francisco Charter—one cannot help but remember the same American scene only a quarter of a century ago, a scene filled with the snobbishness of isolation and philosophies of exclusiveness. What a pity that the late Wendell Wilkie could not live to see the title of his book become the cornerstone of the United Nations. For in these twenty-five years, America has turned a complete circle from the point of isolation to the totality of *One World.* These twenty-five years were an epoch of transition that had its vicissitudes, but now that we are concluding this chapter, a child of average intelligence understands that the existence of the United States was defended at Stalingrad, our freedom secured in the battle of Leyte, the American Constitution preserved in the villages of Belgium, and the Bill of Rights perpetuated on the beaches of Normandy. Today, with the atomic bomb in our possession, even staunch isolationists are ashamed to speak openly of their attachment to a philosophy that has become ludicrous on the day of reckoning in Hiroshima.

This is the stern and undeviating message of history for our generation: there will either be "One World" or there will not even be a multitude; there will either be oneness of life or none at all.

II

If one would take a Gallup Poll among five million American Jews, one would easily discover, beyond the shadow of doubt, the adherence of our people to the doctrine of collective responsibility, to America's participation in world affairs, to Bretton Woods and to the San Francisco Charter—in short, to the philosophy of *One World*. Only when we approach the Jewish problem do we discover strongly entrenched minorities within our midst who are still praying to the God of isolationism. The same people who are fully convinced of the oneness of the world on the non-Jewish scene, are particularly impressed with the idea of a separate French, Danish, Norwegian, Dutch, and Belgian problem of Jews. Startling as it may seem, you discover outmoded isolationism in the minds of Jews. It is indeed the most tragic paradox in Jewish life today. We, of all people, have far less attuned our ears to the voice of history than the rest of America. It is time to analyze and correct this tragic comedy of errors in our thinking.

What is paramount in the mind of the average American Jew in these days? Justifiably he thinks of his own security and the future of his children. He is startled and perplexed, he has contributed money to many civic protective agencies, he expected to see results. He was sure that whatever anti-Semitism there was in the United States in pre-war days, it would fade away into nothingness on the day of Pearl Harbor. Now he awakens to the reality that not only has anti-Semitism in the United States not subsided, but it has grown alarmingly and out of proportion in the post-Pearl Harbor days. He asks the question—and rightly so—of how it has been possible. It is high time to give him an answer. It is the first lesson in history that he so badly needs in these days.

What happened to the United States in the last decade, from a Jewish viewpoint, is the result of an anti-Semitic movement that started years ago in Germany and came to power in 1933 in the city of Berlin and a street called Wilhelmstrasse. Beginning with the ascent of Hitler to power, the most powerful short-wave stations have poured anti-Semitic poison into every country on earth, including, of course, the United States,

121

twenty-four hours a day. In addition, millions of dollars have been spent to educate the American people to anti-Semitism. Leaders of the Bund were trained in Germany and sent back to the United States as disciples of the Fuehrer. If a Jew in Los Angeles reads in his newspaper that Gerald L. K. Smith is spreading his gospel of hate in this community, he has to understand that most of it is not of American origin but was born on February 1, 1933, in the Chancellery of a man called Adolf Hitler. The world of hatred, too, was organized as "One World."

If this is true, as I believe it is, the lesson that history teaches follows logically: the destiny of American Jewry is inextricably linked to the fate of the Jewish People all over the globe. Should we, for instance, not solve the European Jewish problem once and for all, there is not the slightest chance for a peaceful survival of American Israel. If the alarming situation of European Jews of today—many months after V.E. day—continues in the years to come, the remnant of that unhappy Jewry that escaped Hitler's gas chambers, will finally succumb in the occupation areas of the United Nations. It will endanger the security of American Jewry. As long as there is starvation and poverty, insecurity and homelessness for Jews in Europe and the American press knows it and the headlines spread it, and the radio tells it, the gentile neighbor becomes gradually, but strongly, Jew-conscious. All this creates an atmosphere which does not spell normalcy and peaceful development. Whether one likes it or not, the lesson of history is simple and clear: there will either be one Jewish world or in the long run, not even multitudes. There will either be oneness of Jewish life or none at all.

III

One may, of course, ask why we do not see to it that the Jewish problem in Europe is finally solved. It is true that our agencies are doing with our contributions whatever is humanly possible to bring about a solution. But the difficulty is that there is no solution for European Jews in Europe. It is so embarrassing to come to one's own people in a time of tragedy and say "I told you so." But many of us who came from Europe warned American Jewry again and again, to awaken to the reality that even with security of the United Nations, the

122

chances for Jewish survival in Europe are slim. We were laughed at and mocked and I wish we had not been right. But the information we have received in the last few weeks about the situation of European Jewry over-shadows by far even our gloomiest fears. The Germans, it is true, have left the formerly occupied countries, but the hatred that they have sown against us is flourishing in countries that knew of no Jewish problem throughout their history. European Jewry, economically impoverished and spiritually broken, has been sending to us, repeatedly, one and the same cry: "Take us to Palestine.... We want to go home.... After the long night of horror, of concentration camps and ghettos, of gas chambers and torture houses, have we not deserved a place of our own in the midst of our people in a Jewish Palestine?"

Here is a solution to the age-old homelessness of our people. Here is the only healing to its bleeding wounds and the voice of history, challenging and strong, speaks to every American Jew to understand the lesson it teaches. Not only is Palestine the only solution for the survival of the European Jewish remnant, but more than that, it is alone in a position to solve the Jewish problem once and for all. By doing this, Palestine is making one of its greatest contributions to the security, normalcy and peaceful development of American Jewry. As the destiny of American Israel depends upon the solution of the European Jewish problem and the latter can be solved in Palestine only, *eretz yisrael* becomes, under a new aspect, a cornerstone of American Jewish security. If the Jewish Commonwealth in Palestine will be re-constituted in our days, as it surely will, a situation will arise that is entirely new in the history of our people. The Jewish people will live in three great centers, none of them a cause of hatred to the other two, but each of them a source of inspiration to each other. One third of our people will then live in Russia, where they are not going to be a problem to us, surely not physically but in all probability not even spiritually; the second part of our people will live in the United States and Western hemisphere, but this time without the European source that feeds hatred for American transmission; and the third group will live in Palestine by its own right, on its own soil, with its own culture and be a blessing to every Jew on the globe.

Yes, I have this vision of one Jewish world in the near future. I believe, with all my heart, that out of this chaos will come the indivisible oneness of Jewish life, the richness of which will be based upon the interchange of experience and spiritual productivity of the three centers of America, Palestine and Russia. It behooves us to dedicate ourselves in this spirit of the High Holy Days to the realization of history's dream: the oneness of the Jewish world.

"IF THERE BE AMONG YOU A NEEDY MAN"

August 18, 1950

If there be among you a needy man, one of thy brethren, within any of thy gates...thou shalt not harden thy heart, nor shut thy hand from thy needy brother; but thou shalt surely open thy hand unto him. Beware that thine eye be not evil against thy needy brother and thou givest him nought; and he cry unto the Lord against thee and it be sin in thee. Thou shalt surely give him, and the heart shall not be grieved when thou givest unto him, because for this the Lord thy God will bless thee in all thy work, and all that thou puttest thy hand unto.

(Deuteronomy 15:7-10)

This passage, from Deuteronomy, was read on Saturday last from every Jewish pulpit in the world. It well brings into focus an alarming situation that has arisen in our community in recent months.

Under the *Displaced Persons Act* of 1948, a total of over one hundred sixty-three thousand immigrants were admitted to the United States and of these close to thirty-seven thousand were Jews. This is, of course, a pitifully small immigration. Arthur Greenleigh, the spokesman for the Council of the United States Displaced Persons Commission, explained the other day, that the flow of immigration was held up by red tape and lack of adequate personnel, but mostly "by the lack of assurance of American citizens willing to accept responsibility for settling Displaced Persons in the United States."

In spite of this situation, it became clear, early in May, that at least twenty thousand individuals could be brought to the United States in spite of the difficulties inherent in the situation. The United Service for New Americans issued an appeal to the Jewish communities on May 8, urging us to issue community assurances for those who are still in the DP camps. As a part of this national campaign, an appeal was issued to the rabbis asking for the mobilization of the entire community behind this drive. The rabbis were asked to set aside a "DP Sabbath" in order to inspire congregations to a supreme effort, in helping our long-suffering brothers and sisters to be delivered from slavery to freedom.

Our Los Angeles Jewish Community accepted the challenge and issued assurances for three hundred fifty-one more DP families which will arrive early in 1951. But then we discovered that there are still hundreds of displaced persons who have been with us for quite sometime, without jobs and for whom our local Jewish community has to assume responsibility. Together with the three hundred fifty-one families of next year, these people will become objects of charity and an unbearably heavy burden upon the community. This is why our community is engaged in a city-wide emergency job-finding campaign. Our American Jewish community is now summoned to demonstrate its ability to fulfill its obligation to those whose lives depend upon our generosity. We have always prided ourselves that in the course of our entire history we have always taken care of our own people. This is actually what we promised the American Government and guaranteed the immigration authorities.

It is unthinkable that we should turn our faces away from the uplifted arms of our suffering people who look toward us for a haven. It is not charity that is asked of us but constructive help—to give the newcomer a job so that he can help himself. In our factories and in our offices, wherever we employ people, room should be made for one of the new immigrants. It is very little that is demanded of us compared to the superhuman efforts of the State of Israel in caring for four hundred thirty thousand newcomers within two years, almost three times the number of immigrants admitted to the United States during the same time.

We, the people of the Book, are expected in these days to translate the Bible into the reality of our daily life. Ladies and gentlemen, there are among us needy men; they are our own brothers and they are within the gates of our city. Do not harden your hearts and do not shut your hands from our needy brothers, but let us open our hands unto them. Be aware that our eyes be not evil against our needy brothers, so that we give them not what they need; they will cry unto God against us and the sin will be ours. Our hearts shall not be grieved when we give them the tools for rehabilitation, because it is for such humane attitudes that the Lord will bless us in our own undertakings and in all that we put our hands unto. May our hearts be attuned to this biblical voice and may we live up both to the heritage of our people and the expectations of our times.

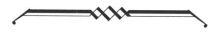

SENTIMENTS

February 18, 1951

In a letter dated January 16, 1813, Goethe, the famous German classic author, wrote the following lines to his friend Jacoby on the theme of human brotherhood:

> Sentiments are what unites people; opinion what separates them. Sentiments are a simple bond that gathers us together; opinions represent the principle of variety that scatters. (The friendships of youth are founded on the former; the cliches of old age are to be blamed on the latter.) If we could only realize this early and arrive at a liberal view as regards others in motivating our own attitude of mind, we would be more conciliatory and try to collect, by the bond of sentiment, what opinion has dispersed.

In these lines, the sage of European Civilization states the oft-forgotten truth, that opinions may sometimes separate us but sentiments will always unite us. The classical tradition of Judaism—and its daughter religions of Christianity and

Islam—have indeed, from the outset, been aware of the gulf that divides groups, races and creeds from one another because of ideological differences. Yet an abyss, even when broad and deep, is only a cleft in the earth's surface and its walls can be joined by a common ground below and by a bridge from above. However deep the differences of the mind, the unity of the heart runs deeper; no matter how fierce the conflict of ideas, the kinship of humanity is stronger.

This was exemplified in a most dramatic event that took place eight years ago this month. On the third of February, 1943, the American troop-ship, Dorchester, was torpedoed off Greenland with only three hundred survivors. Among the six hundred men lost were four chaplains: two Protestant ministers (George L. Fox and Clark V. Poling); one Catholic priest (John P. Washington); and one rabbi (Alexander P. Goode). They stood on the deck of the doomed ship and discovered that there were not enough life-jackets to go around. Without a minute's hesitation, the four chaplains in uniform gave their life preservers to the fighting men, locked their arms together and intoned the prayers of their respective denominations until the icy waters closed over them.

This is a magnificent symbol of what Goethe meant by the "unity of sentiment" in spite of "diversity of opinions" and what classical religion meant by the "unity of the heart that runs deeper than the differences of the mind." Each one of these four chaplains represented a different church and stood for a definite theological viewpoint. The rabbi intoned his prayers in Hebrew, the Catholic priest in Latin, and the two Protestant ministers in English. But beyond all ideological differences, motivating them from beneath and bringing them together from above, was the kinship of humanity that met the challenge with an act of selfless nobility.

It is this spirit in human relations that we have to evoke during this Brotherhood week and make it last for all the days to come.

CAN CONSERVATIVE AND
REFORM JUDAISM MERGE?

From *The Reconstructionist,* XXII:14, November 16, 1956

I am convinced that the merger of the two denominations is more than feasible let alone desirable—it is inevitable.

I believe that in another ten or twenty years there will be on the American scene only two types of Jewish living: the Orthodox, on the one hand, and the Liberal, on the other.

The minute you accept the principle of "change" which is basic to all non-Orthodox manifestations of religion, you have moved away from the Orthodox platform. This is the fundamental step. Whether you interpret "change" under the aspect of evolution or revolution, moderateness or radicalness is actually a matter of degree, and is of secondary importance.

Therefore, even theologically, the two main streams of non-Orthodox Jewish life are bound to meet, and as a matter of fact are quite advanced in the direction of that goal.

The characteristic signs on the American scene in recent years have been a more positive attitude toward an acceptance of meaningful ceremonies in Reform services and a more courageous attitude toward the elimination of Orthodox vestiges in Conservative synagogues.

Already there are some Reform synagogues in the United States which use as much, if not more, Hebrew in their liturgy than do the Conservative ones. In recent years, there has even been an increase in the number of Reform synagogues which have reintroduced the yarmulke, at least for the rabbi and the cantor on the pulpit.

Study the personal lives of the younger generation of rabbis from the viewpoint of observance and you will have great difficulty in distinguishing between the Reform and the Conservative ones. I know, personally, of quite a few Reform rabbis who still maintain kashrut and of quite a few Conservative ones who do not.

It can easily be seen from all this, that the boundaries are not fixed and the demarcation lines are quite fluid. It all comes down to the point that real Orthodox Jewry is observant, whereas Conservative and Reform are not, or, where they observe, they are doing so by free choice.

This is why I believe that Orthodox Judaism will remain what it is, but, out of the merger of Conservative and Reform Judaism, will sooner or later emerge an American form of liberal Judaism.

However, one should not passively allow history to take its course, but should actively help in shaping the future. There ought to be established points of contact between the two groups and mutual advisory boards on both the regional and national levels, in order to act in unison on such points—and there are many—on which consensus of opinion could easily be achieved.

Rabbinical bodies should, from now on, have at least one session to which they invite the other group, and at which matters of common interest may be discussed and official pronouncements released to the public in the names of both organizations.

Let this happen for a decade or so, let us get to know one another better, and the American Jewish community get accustomed to see us together, and we will achieve what is indeed not only feasible, but desirable—a unified liberal Judaism born out of the fusion of Conservatism and Reform.

It would, in my opinion, turn out to be a blessing for American Jewry.

TO PERFECT THE WORLD

From *Hollywood Jewish News*, XXIII:9 (September 1957)

The theme of Rosh Hashanah is the belief that human society can be remade and constantly improved upon—in the words of our tradition "to perfect the world under the Kingdom of the Almighty." This is why a religious Jew can look upon each successive year against the background of this theme, and measure its quality from the height of this leitmotif.

Using the Rosh Hashanah theme as criterion, I am happy to say that the year 5717, now passing into history, was a year of considerable achievements. It had, as do all other units of time, its negative moments and disappointing hours, tragic days and apprehensive weeks; but weighed in the scale of

129

totality, it was a year in which the forces of good won out on many fronts, in which human conscience asserted itself, and in which free society stood its ground. In short, it was a year in which we progressed. We have not achieved the goal, but we took steps in the right direction. We have not reached the "Kingdom of God," but we came closer to touching its hem.

On the international scene, it was the year of the Suez Campaign. In it Israel wrote a glorious chapter of heroism, forced open the Gulf of Aqabah and brought relative tranquillity to the border areas of the Middle East. It was also a year of unprecedented immigration of Jews to Israel from hitherto closed areas behind the Iron Curtain. The political and military crises, both in Hungary and in Poland, bestowed upon Israel the gift of highly-skilled and well-trained professional immigrants, experts in many fields of human endeavor. The year 5717, finally, ends on a note of good and friendly relations between Washington and Jerusalem, and with the strong bond of steadfast friendship that has so blessedly developed between France and Israel.

The same is true of our own situation as Americans here at home. Today, as I am dictating this column, the Congress has just passed the Civil Rights Bill. Weakened and diluted as the measure may be, it is still a liberalizing step brought about by the progressive forces within our American community. In the Jewish conception of the "Kingdom of God on Earth," there are no separate compartments for races or different color. On this Rosh Hashanah, therefore, when we pray for the perfection of mankind, we will do it with the feeling that the America of today is, morally speaking, slightly better than the America of yesterday.

The Jewish year just approaching its end also saw the maturing process of American Jewry. The annals of history will proudly record the indomitable spirit with which the American Jewish community rose up, with unanimity and dignity, against the evil forces which attempted to impose sanctions against Israel during the time of the Sinai invasion. Future generations will remember that in the year 5717 American Jewry had come of age.

INVOCATION:
DEMOCRATIC NATIONAL CONVENTION

July 13, 1960

Heavenly Father.

We humbly invoke thy blessings upon the representatives assembled here in convention, upon the members of this organization throughout the land, and upon our beloved nation which gave birth to free institutions by which a free society is governed.

We are meeting at a time in which mankind finds itself living in an atmosphere of uneasiness and discontent, even of distress and despair caused by fear of wars of self-destruction and co-extermination—wars which may result in an utterly disgraceful end to man's long experiment on earth.

In this moment critical for the survival of mankind—with a bewildered generation unsure of itself and uncertain of its future—the world is in dire need of an America with a new image: an America motivated by historic purpose and possessed of a sense of destiny; an America that recognizes the moral summons within her and is capable of moral response; an America that is ethically committed, and which reflects the ancient principles of our common religious heritage. It is for such an America that we pray tonight:

Thou, O Lord, who revealest thyself in the workings of the mind, in the stirrings of the heart, and in the aspirations of the soul; thou who directest the destinies of men and nations and who hast bestowed upon this country the manifold bountiful blessings of overflowing abundance—cause us, we pray thee, to be worthy of our noble legacy by kindling a veritable light to illumine a world in darkness, and to set an example to be emulated by others:

May we, in the future, spend as much energy in the attainment of spiritual values as we have, in the past, on the acquisition of material goods;

May we give to our own citizens of all races and all religions the rights and liberties that we so self-righteously demand of our adversaries for the inhabitants of their lands;

May we labor as zealously for the duty to pursue justice as we have so diligently for the right to pursue happiness;

May we select for leadership men of inner integrity, creative vision, and moral responsibility;

Men who will remember tomorrow what they pledged today, and fulfill after elections what they promised at conventions;

Men with passion for social justice, with devotion to universal brotherhood, and with dedication to greater humanity;

Men who will thus fulfill the dreams of the Founding Fathers of this Republic and guide our nation along the highway to genuine, effective, and well-deserved world leadership.

Paraphrasing a commentary of the Sages of Ancient Israel on the meaning of the Priestly Benediction in the biblical Book of Numbers (6:24-26), we prayerfully invoke God's blessings, tonight, in the spirit of our common religious tradition:

May God bless us with material possessions and guard us from having them possess us;

May the Lord make his face of spiritual enlightenment and moral insight to shine upon us, and give us grace in the eyes of other nations;

May the Lord turn his countenance of tender care and loving attention unto this our land, and bestow upon us the blessings of security and tranquillity, of harmony and peace—with all men, here and abroad. Amen.

JEWISH PEOPLEHOOD:
IDENTIFICATION AND COMMITMENT

February, 1966

In modern sociology the word "people" is defined as a group of human beings whose ancestors lived at one and the same time in one and the same place, and whose descendants succeeded in surviving by some mutual bond. The Jews are such a people, because our ancestors lived for many centuries in an area called Palestine, and we, their descendants, have achieved survival via the mutual bond of Judaism. This, in turn, means that Jews wherever they live—East or West, North or South on the globe—are members of one and the same historic family called the Jewish People.

132

This being the case, the question arises as to the relationship of the different parts of our dispersed people to one another and of the relationship of each part to the totality of Israel. In the course of Jewish history, there have been numerous manifestations of such relationships, expressing themselves in acts of sympathy and mercy, of philanthropy and rescue—acts which have been based upon the Sages' dictum: "All Jews are responsible for one another." Actually, however, we have never grasped the basic philosophy of Judaism in this area of relationships, and it is high time that this fundamental position be made crystal clear to our present day generation.

For the relationship of the parts of our people to one another and of each part to the whole, as enunciated in our ancient tradition, calls for far more than sympathy and philanthropy—it calls for *identification*. This is a uniquely Jewish way of life, which demands of each one of us to identify ourselves with the people as a whole in such a manner as to make of the individual Jew and the collectivity of Israel one indivisible entity—as demonstrated in the seder ritual at which a Jew has to recite the verse: "It is incumbent upon every man to look upon himself as if he himself went out of Egypt." Our Rabbis say that if a Jew has not fully understood the meaning of these words, all other Passover commandments he might fulfill are of no avail. They mean that it is not enough to tell and retell the story of the Exodus, but to identify ourselves with the generation that fought for freedom to a point by which we are telling the story in the first person of the "I" and the "We." More than that, the symbols of the Passover table are there for the purpose of undergirding this injunction for identification: the Jew is commanded to eat of the maror as well as partake of the matzah, so as to make sure that he identifies himself with the misfortunes of slavery as well as with the blessings of liberty. Whenever, then, we speak of the concept of "Jewish Peoplehood" we have to understand that it is not only a matter of acknowledging with one's mind the existence of the eternal collectivity of Israel, but also of complete spiritual and emotional identification with the Jewish People as a whole, here and abroad, in Israel and in the Diaspora.

But even this is not enough in terms of Jewish tradition.

For in the same way as the acceptance of the doctrine of "Jewish Peoplehood" leads to spiritual identification with the whole household of Israel—*identification,* in turn, leads to *commitment.* This means that Judaism demands of us not only to accept the idea of "Jewish Peoplehood" and to pledge our loyalty to it, via the process of identification on the spiritual and emotional level, but also to commit ourselves personally to serve our people with all our heart, with all our soul, and with all our might in all areas of its welfare, with deeds and actions on the practical level of day to day work.

This idea of commitment was dramatically espoused by the Book of Esther when Mordecai sends his classic message to the queen, who apparently hesitated to get involved in the destiny of her people. Said Mordecai to her:

> "Think not with thyself that thou shalt escape in the king's house, more than all the Jews. For if thou altogether holdest thy peace at this time, then will relief and deliverance arise to the Jews from another place, but thou and thy father's house will perish; and who knoweth whether thou art not come to royal estate for such a time as this (Esther 4:13-14)?"

This biblical passage is fascinating from the viewpoint of the topic under discussion. Note that the first sentence— "Think not with thyself that thou shalt escape in the king's house, more than all the Jews"—is an affirmation of *identification,* while the rest of the message is an appeal to *commitment.* He threatens the queen that if she would not both identify herself with and commit herself to her people, there will be divine intervention for the liberation of the Jewish people, hand in hand with punishment upon her as an individual for having violated the two basic laws of Jewish survival.

It is, therefore, not astonishing that Jewish tradition esteemed so highly the commandment of "the rescue of prisoners" which obligates a community to use all its resources for the liberation of fellow-Jews in lands of persecution, even if it has to be done at the expense of local religious institutions, including the building of a synagogue. So strong and overriding then is the obligation to our people which flows from our identification with it. It is basic Judaism. Whosoever has not familiarized himself with this fundamental attitude of our Jewish people has never understood the aspirations of its soul, the workings of its mind and the stirrings of its heart.

II

It is this philosophy—the concept of *Jewish Peoplehood* leading to *identification* and *commitment*—hallowed by centuries of Jewish tradition, which we have to recapture in our own days, if we want to live up to the historic challenge of the hour. The task is not easy—but its difficulty is the very test of genuine Jewishness.

This is the year of 1966. Behind us are twenty-one years since the end of the Second World War; twenty-one years after the liberation of the German concentration camps; three decades since the proclamation of the Nürnberg Laws, and thirty-three years after Hitler's assumption of power in 1933. All these events emaciated our strength and reduced our numbers from 18,500,000 in the pre-Hitler period, to 13,500,000, in our own days. The concentration camps, the ghettos, and the ovens caused a blood-letting from which we have not yet recovered and will not for generations to come. Whether we like it or not, all of us are the product of our generation's tragedy.

On the other hand, it is eighteen years since the establishment of Israel—the most dramatic event to come out of the holocaust and of the Second World War. Israel has been an independent State and a going concern, with open doors, to which have flown the streams of over 1,250,000 refugees— only this time refugees finally going home as free citizens of a Jewish State. The dreams, the visions and the aspirations of untold generations have, thus, been fulfilled in our own days. At no other time in our history has one and the same generation gone from such defeat to such victory, from such catastrophe to such redemption, from such ebb to such tide in the flow of Jewish destiny. We are then not only the generation of tragedy, but also the one of triumph. What is needed, now, is the identification with the tragedy and the commitment to the triumph. This is the mitzvah for 1966.

III

Fortunately for our generation, there is an instrumentality

in Jewish life, today, that makes the fulfillment of this mitzvah possible. I am referring to the United Jewish Appeal which to me and, I know to many of our colleagues, has been the noblest expression of the philosophy of Jewish Peoplehood. More than that, it has, throughout its history, been the very symbol of *identification* and *commitment.*

To understand the total picture of the problems facing us, one has to become acquainted with some of Israel's difficulties. The most critical human problem which Israel faces, in the coming year, is to make substantial progress in the absorption of thousands of Israel's newcomers who are socially and economically disadvantaged. Despite Israel's preoccupation with security, it has given haven to 1,300,000 Jews—250,000 in the last five years alone—and has shouldered most of the financial burden of absorbing the newcomers. The enormity of the continuous immigration is straining Israel's back to the breaking point, and with an expected immigration over the next five years, again from 200,000 to 250,000, the absorption problem will be aggravated even more. If we do not make a strong effort to solve the problem *now,* we may soon have on our hands two Israels—an advantaged and a disadvantaged one—and then it will be too late for any solution we might design. This absorption problem is most acute in the twenty-one new development towns, where ninety percent of the Oriental newcomers have been settled during the past decade—a large proportion of whom are illiterate and bereft of any training in industrial or economic opportunities.

This, in short, is the story—the needs, the problems, and the program to solve them. Will American Jews say that it is an impossible task? This depends on one's viewpoint. With small charity or even with mild philanthropy, little will be achieved. But if we will approach the challenge with a concept of Jewish Peoplehood and with its corollaries of *identification* and *commitment,* the solution is at hand.

If we will look upon ourselves as if we, personally, were in Dachau and Bergen Belsen; as if we, personally, were beaten and tortured, and miraculously rescued at the last minute; as if we, ourselves, lost our parents, our brothers, our sisters in the ovens or in nameless graves; as if we, ourselves, went through many liberation camps and were finally redeemed and brought to the Land of Israel; as if we, personally, live in one of the border settlements of the Negev, or in one of the twenty-one new frontier towns, and it is through our windows that the El Fatah is shooting; and if we will feel the pain, the same pain of an Israeli who sees his country surrounded by one hundred million Arabs armed to the teeth by both East and West—then, if we have identified ourselves completely with our people, with the Jewish State, with the places and the events, and one will be able to say "we," instead of "they," and, then, translate, this identification into sacrificial commitment—then we will have achieved the greatest victory for ourselves and be justified in considering ourselves Jews of conscience.

IV

All this was summed up long ago by a prophet who addressed his fellow Jews in Babylon about their reunion with the Land of Israel. It was his vision that Israel will emerge from the graves of the exile, renew its life on its own soil and open a new era of moral and spiritual regeneration. Said Ezekiel,

> "I will take you from among the nations, and gather you out of all the countries, and will bring you into your own land.... A new heart also will I give you, and a new spirit will I put within you; and I will take away the stony heart out of your flesh...and I will put My spirit within you...Ye shall dwell in the land that I gave to your fathers; and ye shall be My people, and I will be your God...And I will multiply the fruit of the tree, and the increase of the field, that ye may receive no more the reproach of famine among the nations.... Thus saith the Lord God: I will cause the cities to be inhabited, and the waste places shall be builded. And the land that was desolate shall be tilled, whereas it was a desolation in the sight of all that passed by. And they shall say: this land that was desolate is become like the garden of Eden; and the waste and desolate and ruined cities are fortified and inhabited. Then the nations that are left round about you shall know that I the Lord have builded the ruined places, and planted that which was desolate; I the Lord have spoken, and I will do it."
>
> (Ezekiel 36:24-36).

Here we have the whole ideology of Jewish Peoplehood, and the philosophy of *identification* and *commitment,* which flows from it. It is as if Ezekiel were addressing himself to the Arab League of our time, when he refers to the nations around Israel who will come to recognize that the Jewish State is the fulfillment of a divine promise. This is, then, the challenge which is upon us in these days: it is upon us to identify ourselves with our people to such a degree, as to take them out of lands of despair and plant them on the soil of Israel and to increase the produce of the fields and the factory, so as to make sure that what was neglected and destroyed will be rebuilt and restored. Let us, then, make the nations of the world look up and see that this was the land that was wasted and neglected and ruined, and that the Jewish People had rebuilt it, opened the gates, admitted the pitiful remnants of our people, and transformed the country into a garden of Eden. The Eternal One of Israel has promised and has fulfilled. It is upon us, as Jews, to imitate God and to fulfill our commitment by rescuing our people, by rebuilding the Jewish State, and by making the name Israel a blessing to mankind.

"THE ECLIPSE OF GOD"

September 22, 1968

Excerpt from a Rosh Hashanah Sermon

There are periods in human history in which the evil that men do assumes such proportions that God, as it were, grows angry and says, "I will hide my face from them...for they are a generation given to perverseness (Deuteronomy 32:20)." Motivated by this biblical image, Martin Buber speaks of periods in which God withdraws his presence from history. This occurs when a generation breaks off the dialogue with God and is left entirely to itself. Buber calls such times "the eclipse of God."

In such an age do we now live, and the year 5728 may serve as its symptom: the war in Vietnam has continued unabatedly with disastrous results in human lives—28,000 Americans dead and 200,000 wounded; in cost—thirty billion dollars a year; and in prestige—loss on the international scene. The Soviet Union would not have dared invade and suppress a small country like Czechoslovakia were it not for the fact that our moral authority in world-affairs is at a low ebb. It is for the same reason that Russia took advantage of this psychological situation and provided the Arab states with tanks and jets, missiles and rockets, so that the Arabs, in turn, may be properly equipped for another round of war in the Middle East. It is clear to any student of contemporary affairs that even Nigeria would not have had the audacity of defying a whole world in its bid to halt the starvation of the Ibo tribes, were it not for the utter erosion of moral values in our present day society. Thus, "the eclipse of God" extended its shadow, last year, over Asia and Europe, the Middle East and Africa.

It was a period of turmoil and turbulence within our own borders. It was a year of assassination and of riots, of protests and demonstrations. Underlying the whole atmosphere of restiveness is the fact that here at home we find ourselves in the middle of a triple revolution of the black against the white, the poor against the rich, and the young against the old. They are all interrelated in their protest against the social immorality of our "establishment," but mostly centered around the problem of the Negro in a white society. Our black brothers are caught in a vicious cycle of despair and hopelessness, and they are determined not to live any more in the slums and ghettos of poverty or to play the role of second class citizens. They want to see our promises fulfilled in the areas of equal education for their children and decent housing for their families and adequate jobs for themselves. Unfortunately, they have learned from experience that riots and protests are the most effective methods to awaken the white community to their desperation.

A recent study made by an independent group of sociologists and churchmen called *Hunger USA* proves that within our most affluent society, there are ten million Americans who suffer from hunger and malnutrition—the majority of them Negroes. Other studies show that of the so-called better placed black citizens, over half live on an income of less than $5,000 a year. Is it then surprising that they are so impatient with our slow response and so desirous of a change of status? Is it so

139

strange that they are groping for identity, searching for self-respect and struggling for a positive philosophy? "Black is beautiful" so they say. And it is. We as Jews, particularly, should be the first ones to appreciate this "Zionism in black."

A majestic Jewish tradition looks down upon us, challenging us during this High Holiday season to translate social ideals into daily reality. When confronted with the fright and pain, the hunger and the misery of a destitute minority of twenty million Americans, let us read Isaiah:

> Hear, ye deaf,
> And look, ye blind, that ye may see...
> Here are people robbed and spoiled,
> They are all snared in hovels and hidden in slums;
> They have become a prey—and none to rescue,
> A spoil—with none to say "Restore";
> Who among you will give ear to this?
> Who will hearken and hear for the time to come?
> (Isaiah 42:18, 22)

Isaiah gives his own answer:

> Learn to do well;
> Seek justice, relieve the oppressed,
> Judge the fatherless, plead for the widow.
> (Isaiah 1:17)

When confronted with the abject poverty of the ghetto, with anger and aloneness and with resentment and rage—conditions that make it impossible for a Negro to enter the mainstream of American life—let us reread Jeremiah,

> If one practices justice and righteousness,
> Then it is well with one;
> If one champions the cause of the poor and the needy,
> Then all is well;
> For this is, indeed, to know Me saith the Lord.
> (Jeremiah 22:15-16)

In a year of "the eclipse of God," this is the only way to make his face shine upon us again in the days that lie ahead.

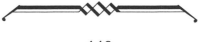

ISRAEL AND AMERICAN JEWISH YOUTH

Excerpt   April 6, 1971

To our children in the seventies we must say that you and I and they are sons and daughters of a historic family called the Jewish People, extending from the dawn of our history to our great-grandchildren of tomorrow and the day after tomorrow; that though the Jewish People lived in different settings—a nation in Israel, a nationality in Eastern Europe, and a religio-cultural community in the West—all its parts, in spite of the differences in their style of living, are components of an indivisible entity called the Jewish People.

This being the case, the time has come to change the whole concept of the *religio-cultural community,* as we call ourselves in the West. I sincerely believe that in this decade where the vocabulary is rootage and identity, we ought to say to our students as well as to the American environment what we historically really are, namely an *ethnic-religious community.* We are part of the Jewish People and we are part of Judaism. Therefore, we are both, and we should say so openly and frankly.

Throughout the centuries we have been living as an ethnic community which has a religion of its own. I believe, therefore, that the time has come to state this position in clear terms, not alone because it is the only language that a young generation understands, but because it is the honest truth. What is wrong in this decade of the seventies with being an ethnic minority in the United States? We are part and parcel of the Jewish People—and this is ethnic. We are part and parcel of Judaism—and this is religious. I repeat: this position is honest; it is straight; and a young person will easily understand it.

Secondly, I suggest that we begin to talk about Zionism and change our vocabulary in defining it. Courses on the history of the Zionist Movement have to be offered in our religious schools and explained as the *movement of liberation of the Jewish People.* This is exactly what Zionism is. Once a young person understands that he is part of a people, a people that has been persecuted for centuries and a people which has undergone the most cruel of experiences in the Diaspora, he will easily come to the conclusion that such a people needed a home and a place to call its own. A people which has suffered so much not only from a barbaric society, but also from the so-called civilized world—read for instance Hans Habe's book, *The Mission*, about the 1938 Conference in Evian where the whole Western World could not come up with a single answer of how to save European Jews—such a people has a right to demand of history a return to the place from which it was forcibly ejected. And, again, this fully coincides with the vocabulary of our decade. It is rootage. It is anchorage. It is identity. This is what the Zionist Movement is all about.

Lastly, I would like to see a shifting of ingredients and of emphasis in our presentation of Judaism as a whole. Not enough attention has been paid by us to the fact that you and I come from the most non-conformist people on this globe. We have had the courage to say "no" throughout the centuries to so many things that other people considered us in a state of utter madness. We even had the courage to say "no" to the God of the Universe himself. Show me a parallel to the biblical chapter in Genesis in which Abraham, the founding father of our people, throws into the face of the Almighty the challenge, "Should the Judge of the whole earth not do justice himself (Genesis 18:25)?" Where is there a parallel to Isaiah's majestic summation of religion: "The Lord of Hosts is exalted through justice, and the Holy One sanctified through righteousness (Isaiah 5:16)?" God is either the ultimate in justice or he is quite super-fluous, and, on the other hand, the only way to serve him is through righteousness. I ask, again, where in the whole of religious literature of antiquity or our own days, East or West, will you find any saying even approximating the level of Isaiah? And, again, where else will you find a parallel to the challenge of Rabbi Levi Yitzhak of Berdichev, who, on Kol Nidre night after a pogrom, could say to God, "Lord of the Universe, I am warning you. With your help men, women and children were killed. This has to stop! Because without us, where will you be tomorrow?" I am wondering in which religious tradition such audaciousness would even be allowed. This on the holiest night of the Jewish year, and by the saintliest of Chassidic rabbis!

Yes, we have said "no" to God and to whole civilizations which offered us the easy way out by getting baptized and living happily. We said "no" to the beauty which was Greece and the glory which was Rome, because we did not accept their moral thrust, though they represented an alluring and sophisticated civilization. Yes, we have used the word "no" more than any other group on earth. We have said "no" to the status quo and to the so-called "establishment" of many generations. Judaism, therefore, has to be presented in the seventies as the revolutionary religion that has challenged man's injustice, and his violence and his shedding of blood; and that we did it stubbornly throughout our history because this was our substance, and in substance we have remained inflexible.

This is, then, what I wanted to present to you tonight: changes in our vocabulary and emphasis upon certain elements of Judaism which are in tune with the seventies. It is within this frame that we should teach Jewish Peoplehood, Zionism, Israel and the social ethics of Judaism.

All this was summed up long ago by the prophet Isaiah, who lived almost eight centuries before our time. In order to answer the question, "Why did God allow the Jewish people to survive?," he gives three reasons and formulates them in the following way: "I covered you with the shade of My right hand: to plant heaven, to lay the foundations of the earth, and to say to Zion: You are My people (Isaiah 51:16)." If I take these words of the prophet, reading them in reverse, but without adding or subtracting a single word, then you have before you the whole program which I tried to outline for your consideration. It is also a guideline of what Jewish education ought to be in the seventies: our generation ought to know, first, the meaning of Zion and the Jewish State, and the meaning of Jewish Peoplehood via its Zionist ideology. Secondly, it must be our task to educate our young generation "To lay the foundations of a new earth," in our American society as well as in our Jewish community, in the spirit of social justice and Jewish responsibility. Thirdly, the great task before us is "To plant heaven"—a most felicitous explanation in the Hebrew language to which there is no parallel—meaning to put the best ideas and the finest sentiments into the hearts of our children and by doing so planting a piece of a new heaven.

As we are all teachers, this, then, is the definite approach for the decade that lies ahead. The identification with Israel and the Jewish People, the elevation of society to a new moral platform here at home, and to plant ideas that are good and decent and humane in the hearts of our children. If we should accomplish this goal, for which I prayerfully hope—you and I could not receive a greater reward than that later generations will say about us that we planted a new heaven for our ancient Jewish heritage.

INVOCATION IN HONOR OF
SENATOR GEORGE McGOVERN

September 26, 1972

Lord of the Universe,
We humbly invoke thy blessings
upon the distinguished citizens of our community,
assembled here at this banquet,
in the determination to change the American reality
by recapturing the American dream.

We invoke thy special grace, O Lord,
upon our guest of honor tonight.

He is a man of faith and of vision,
of integrity and of humaneness.

He believes, as do we,
that America is too *great* to be offensive to the weak,
and too *mighty* to be unjust to the downtrodden,
that America is too *noble* to persecute the poor
and too *compassionate* to oppress the lowly.

He is an inspired and righteous leader
who believes, as do we,
that a just society in our country must mean
that those who do not suffer feel the pain of those who do.

In this crucial hour in our nation's destiny,
we pray thee, O Lord, that we may stand by
this genuine representative of social idealism.

May we, in our daily pursuits
in the weeks that lie ahead,
through generous sympathy and personal sacrifice,
help him in the building of the better world of tomorrow.

Zionism, Israel, and
"Outside the Land"

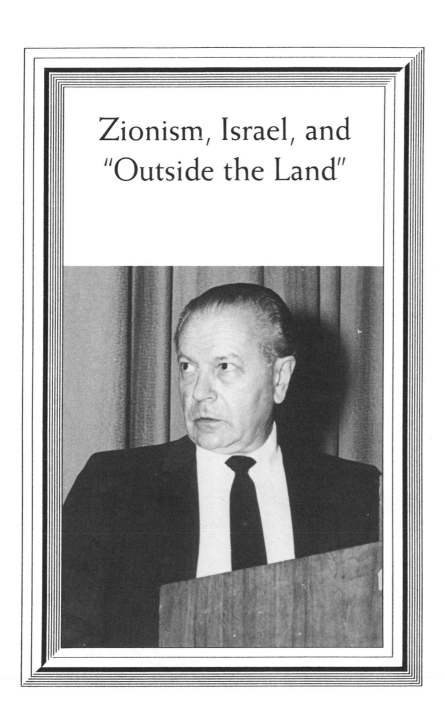

With David Ben-Gurion in Israel, 1962

MODERN ZIONIST RABBIS

Breslau, 1928

Until now, the Zionist world has paid very little attention to the theologians. Very little effort has been expended to attract them or to influence them. This lack of interest by the Zionist world has of course had a bad effect. Rarely have rabbis come out officially for the idea of national peoplehood. Yes, even those rabbis who were Zionists were satisfied to carry their opinion privately deep in their hearts, without ever announcing it to their congregation from the pulpit. This is without a doubt the result of the disinterest of the Zionist world. For if it had demanded it, the rabbis would have given the necessary response. Theologians are by nature religious people. At least most of them. Theologians are also born leaders. At least the best of them. But religious leaders always defend their ideas with all their heart and soul. If they did not do so in our case the reason is obvious.

II

Zionists, you have to pay more attention! Rabbis, you have to change! Change, but how? What should the modern rabbi be like? What type should the modern, Zionist rabbi represent? What should be his task?

To the first questions I offer several answers: the modern rabbi has to be a person whose Weltanschauung is Zionism. Weltanschauung is the sum total of a man's thoughts and his image of the world—its events and his relationship to them. All this is the content of his inner life. Provided he has a Weltanschauung, all his thoughts and ideas are interconnected, forming a closed circle. Within it he can move with complete safety. It represents a spiritual fount from whose core he can survey the world and its problems, can assort and explain them. This is what Zionism must mean to the modern Zionist rabbi. It cannot be just one political credo next to many others, must not have its place somewhere at the periphery of his realm of thoughts, but must be its very center from which all references to life and to the world must radiate. Zionism has to embrace it all. A Zionism, of course, that is not only the aim to establish a national homeland for the Jewish people, but comprises— and answers—an entire complex of questions outside *eretz yis-*

rael, like the question of education, preparation, language, and the relationship to the outside world. Zionism must be the content of his life, his moral and religious support, the guiding star illuminating brightly the path of his struggle to prevail. This then is the modern Zionist rabbi.

III

What kind of rabbi should he be?

Well, he has to abandon the highbrow-aristocratic-pulpit-pose of the previous generation of preachers, who from up on high talked down to the people. The modern rabbi must be a true leader. He has to stand in the middle of the people, share their lives and loves, their pains and suffering. From here he must chart the way to a national religiosity.

If he wants to have influence on his congregation he must not stand aside but be one of them; not stand at the shore watching ships coming or disappearing in the distance, but he himself has to brave the waves and emerge victorious—not just follow the stream of the developing vitality of Jewish Peoplehood, but pay it his personal tribute. Such has to be his character.

IV

And his task! If the modern rabbi is indeed the leader of his people, then his task is two-fold: the education of the old and the education of the young.

As for the old: be he Conservative or Liberal, he will stress the traditions of the *Shulchan Aruch*—or at least part of them, not much differing from previous rabbis. But the modern Zionist rabbi has to look beyond. In addition to the traditional Code of Law he will consider—and even observe—a National Shulchan Aruch. To this day the purely nationalistic circles—projecting a Zionism severed from any tradition—do not understand what, even from a national viewpoint—is allowed and what is forbidden. This has to be determined by a National Code. It ought to include positive and negative directives: *you must not intermarry; you must not have a Christmas tree; you must not assimilate!*

However, you must give your children a Jewish education; they must learn Hebrew. You yourself have to learn Hebrew— so that you can understand your children. You must preserve the cultural heritage of our people. In other words: you must nationalize yourself. No matter what one thinks of laws, and even if one is against all strict dogmas and rejects them for our time, one has to admit in all honesty that these laws have their tremendous merits. Even the most intellectual members of our people cannot maintain their individuality without laws by which to live.

I believe that if we had a National Code, evolved by the Zionist Congress, our Zionists, disciplined as they are, might actually prefer Jewish partners for their marriages. For such and other similar national postulates, just as for his religious ones, the rabbi has to fight with the strength of his personality. Without the framework of a national peoplehood there is no religious content.

Now a word about education of the youth. If the rabbi is a popular leader his activity must not be confined to the synagogue, but must span all areas of Jewish life, even outside the synagogue. The most important of these areas will have to be the education of the young. The hardest part will be to gain contact with them, and there is only one way to do it: the rabbi has to share their everyday life. The modern rabbi must not look down on the young from the exalted perspective of his own life, but has to search and find the way to them from their own vantage point. Not his everyday life but theirs he has to try to experience.

These lines do not presume to develop a program for the future. They are only an attempt to suggest a reformation of the modern rabbi for today and tomorrow.

ARE WE READY FOR A
JEWISH COMMONWEALTH?

1944

The question is rhetorical. Thanks to the character of our people, to the discipline of our young generation and to the glorious achievements of the *yishuv*, the Jewish Palestine of today is in fact a Jewish Commonwealth. As far as we are concerned, the matter is very clear: here is a land promised to us by the

Bible, assured by providence, reinstated by the modern civilized world, formulated in documents, given to us as a challenge—and we responded with the dignity of a people of so ancient a civilization. The elements that in history make for self rule and independence are already there: the soil we have bought, the language we have revived and the economy we have created. All we ask of a so-called Christian world is to allow the developments to take their natural course.

Is the world ready for a Jewish Commonwealth? This is the question. Nothing could have proven more clearly the impact of galut with all the curses that this notion involves than the recent attitude of Britain and its Labor Government to boot. It demonstrates clearly that in all the changing movements of history, our people are being sacrificed for one or the other "ism," but the principle of sacrifice remains consistent. Six million Jews were sacrificed for a Hitler appeasement at Munich. The pitiful remnant of European Jews are being sacrificed today for an arranged Arab appeasement in London. The name has changed, the principle remains the same. If our generation needed one more example of how much trust you can put even in a so-called Progressive Socialist Government, the last few weeks hammered the reason home to us.

Each generation in history is asked a question by providence and expected to give an answer. The inquiry of destiny today reads: are the Jews decided upon the solution of the Jewish problem through a Jewish Commonwealth? If the reply is adequate and wholeheartedly yes, Palestine will be a Jewish Commonwealth when the British Empire will be a mere memory. It is to this task of assuring the future of the Jewish Commonwealth that all of us should dedicate our energies, our devotion, and our very lives.

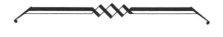

A BIRTHDAY PARTY

April 22, 1950

This is a birthday party, the second one for a child called Israel. We, American Jews, together with all other Jewries of the world, are giving the party and receiving congratulations.

We do not come to the celebration as distant or even close relatives, but in our capacity as parents. This is why the American Zionist Council, which is composed of all Zionist organizations of this community, and of which I have the honor to be the Chairman, is your host tonight, inviting you to share this hour of joy with us.

I have made this introductory remark for obvious reasons. The Hebrew date of the fifth of Iyar, which is the date of the establishment of the State of Israel, has already secured its place on the Jewish calendar. From now on, year after year, Jews all over the world, including, of course, American Jewry, will participate in a global birthday celebration. Within a decade, "Israel Day" will probably be as much a feature of American life as St. Patrick's Day has been now for several decades. In both cases, ethnic groups, while loyal citizens of this great republic and an integral part of American civilization, pay homage to the lands from which their forefathers came and reaffirm their affection for the religious-cultural heritage that originated in their ancestral homes. The only difference is that there has been a land of Ireland in historic continuity, inhabited by the Irish nation, so that the Irish groups in the United States are the sons and daughters of the reborn Eire. In the case of Israel, a diaspora took place, from which a part of our people had to return in order to make the independence of the state possible. This means that Jews all over the world are not the sons and daughters, but rather the parents of the newly born republic of Israel. It is in this capacity that we take great pleasure in sponsoring this celebration tonight.

The point we just made is more than a homiletical image. It is the historical reality of our Jewish life. For all we are and have is the result of one of the most alluring romances between a people and a land that has ever occurred in the history of human civilization. At the dawn of our history, a marriage took place between the people of Israel and the land of Israel. Out of it came judges and kings, priests and prophets, sages and teachers. Out of it came the rich spiritual heritage of Isaiah and Jeremiah, of Amos and Hosea, of the Psalms and the Proverbs, of the Lamentations and the Song of Songs. Out of it came the ideas of monotheism and of social justice, of the brotherhood of man and of international peace. In short, this marriage resulted

151

in our great heritage which became the cornerstone of Western Civilization. But in the year 70 C.E., a historical tragedy necessitated a separation of the people from the land. Since that time, the two parents went their own ways: the land suffering from the curse of desolation and the people enduring the hardship of exile. But not for a moment was there forgetfulness. It was a separation, but no divorce. Constantly and uninterruptedly we have been yearning for each other.

We, the people, remembered Zion, our beloved Zion. We remembered her in every phase of our daily life. We spoke of this love for her on every page of our prayerbook, sang it in our hymns, recited it in our poems, discussed it in our books, and preached it in our sermons. Nowhere else in the history of mankind has such great and undying love been expressed in so many forms of spiritual, religious and cultural activities. Finally, on the fifth of Iyar, 5708—May 14, 1948—the great moment of reunion arrived on the horizon of our modern Jewish reality. Twice separated from each other, a new wedding took place. The people and the land stood again under the chuppah and God himself, as it were, smilingly bestowed His blessings upon the new couple. It was on that day of the wedding that an ancient name was restored to a young child and a new name of "Israel" given unto him. Until three years ago, there was a Jewish people and a Holy Land; there were Jews and there was Palestine. The names Zion, Jerusalem or Israel were mere symbols. Today there is a new reality: out of the newest marriage between the Jewish People and Palestine has come the shoot of Israel.

This is why this occasion fills us with joy and happiness. It is in gratitude to the God of Life, who has seen fit to single out our generation to become the parents of this promised and promising child, that we say a prayer of thanksgiving at this birthday party. Tonight, we American Jews who have given of our energy and devotion and financial resources to make this reunion of people and land possible, pledge anew to stand guard over Israel so that it may develop sound in body and spirit, be a blessing to its parents and to the family of nations.

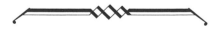

ON MAY 15, 1948

May 6, 1951

On May 15, 1948, Jews gathered in their synagogues and read—as they have done for centuries—the haftarah, the prophetic portion assigned for that day. It was the prophet Amos who spoke to us in the following words:

> In that day will I raise up
> The tabernacle of David that is fallen,
> And close up the breaches thereof,
> And I will raise up its ruins,
> And I will rebuild Zion as in the days of old....
> And I will return the captivity of My people Israel,
> And they shall build the waste cities, and inhabit them,
> And they shall plant vineyards, and drink the wine thereof,
> They shall also make gardens, and eat the fruit of them.
> And I will plant them upon their land,
> And they shall never be removed again
> From the land which I have given them,
> Says the Lord.
>
> (Amos 9:11-15)

There was nothing particularly new about these words that have been a part of the synagogue ritual for that Sabbath morning for many centuries. Only that this time, the passage was imbued with a new meaning, because the night before, Israel had been established and the president of the United States had recognized the new-born State. It was a day which the Lord has made and Jews all over the world rejoiced in it.

Many of us in Reform Judaism have nurtured the hopes and aspirations of which the prophet spoke. True, this attitude has not always motivated the official thinking of our movement. Thus, the Pittsburgh Platform of the Central Conference of American Rabbis in 1885 abolished the hope for the return to Palestine, because our early Reformers believed that "in the modern era of universal culture of heart and intellect, the approaching of the realization of Israel's great Messianic hope

153

for the establishment of the kingdom of truth, justice and peace among all men" was just around the corner. But between 1885 and the time of our own generation, the world has changed so radically that the *Guiding Principles of Reform Judaism,* adopted by the Central Conference of American Rabbis in Columbus in 1937, made an entirely different statement on the very same subject:

> In all lands where our people live, they assume and seek to share loyally the full duties and responsibilities of citizenship and to create seats of Jewish knowledge and religion. In the rehabilitation of Palestine, the land hallowed by memories and hopes, we behold the promise of renewed life for many of our brethren. We affirm the obligation of all Jewry to aid in its upbuilding as a Jewish homeland by endeavoring to make it not only a haven of refuge for the oppressed, but also a center of Jewish culture and spiritual life.

Beginning with this year of 1937, an even larger number of leading Reform rabbis and an even greater majority of our liberal congregations participated actively in the upbuilding of the Holy Land. This is why we join, this week, with all other Jews, and with thousands of Christians all over the world in the celebration of Israel's Independence Day.

Looking back upon the three years of Israel's existence, it fills us with pride to have been found worthy to witness the redemption of our people. The State of Israel has not only miraculously withstood the attacks of seven Arab neighbors; has not only come into existence under the barrage of enemy bombs; but has, which is even more important, successfully absorbed a half million Jews fleeing either the Iron Curtain of the East or the concentration camps of the West. This is an unprecedented story of immigration, unequaled in the annals of Western Civilization. In spite of all the difficulties, in the fields of economy and security, it has made tremendous strides in its cultural institutions and in its religious creativity. Thrilled with pride, we extend our heartiest congratulations to the new State of Israel, the only real friend the United States has in the Middle East. Thrilled by the knowledge that Israel today is a beacon of light and a democratic bastion in the Middle East, we Liberal Jews promise to do our share in helping to fulfill the vision of the prophet. We pledge to do our utmost to raise up the tabernacles of David and to rebuild Zion as in the days of old; to help return the captivity of our people so that they may rebuild the waste cities, plant the vineyards and make the gardens; to the end that they may be planted upon their land, and never be removed again from the land which the Lord has given them.

Next year, when we assemble again for the celebration of Israel's Independence Day, may we be able to say that the dream of the prophet has been realized, our people rescued, Israel secured, and mankind redeemed.

WILL ZIONISM SURVIVE ISRAEL?

June, 1951

I

There is an extraordinary phenomenon in our present day Jewish life which has not attracted the attention it deserves. I am referring to the spectacular career of the idea of Israel's statehood on the one hand, and the gradual deflation of the prestige of the Zionist movement on the other.

There was a time—and not so long ago—in which the Zionist movement grew in proportion with the achievements of the Jewish Agency for Jewish Palestine. The more immigrants we sent and the more colonies we built—the more Jews joined our Zionist ranks and the higher soared the reputation of our movement. This process has now been completely reversed. The State of Israel has become not only the triumph of our Zionist yearnings, but, far and beyond it, the only point around which the public opinion of American Jewry is marshalled today. There has never been anything like it in the history of our Jewish community. Even the American Council for Judaism—that insignificant little group which has fought our movement with tooth and nail—has already accepted Israel, recognized it *de facto,* and speaks of it as our American "ally in

155

the Middle East," and as the fulfillment of "biblical visions." Israel today is the only idea that unites the overwhelming majority of American Jews on one platform. Yet, hand in hand with this triumphant conquest of the minds of our generation by Israel, there is the noticeable downward trend of the Zionist movement in the United States. Fundamentally, of course, it is only the other side of the medallion: as Israel's needs for the present lie in the economic field of either the philanthropic or the investment dollar, the appeal has to be made to the entire Jewish community. If the community responds—and American Jewry has been doing it—the functions that have been exercised by the Zionist movement over a period of more than half a century, are gradually being taken over by the larger community, and in this process of center-shifting, Zionism is being emptied out of the programmatic projects which it has originally initiated.

This state of affairs, sad as it may be for many a veteran Zionist, would not be tragic, were we convinced that neither Israel nor the Jewries of the Diaspora needed the Zionist movement any more. But the facts are that both Israel and *chutz la-aretz* are, and will be for a long time to come, in need of the Zionist movement. Bonds may be bought by a few non-Zionists in the upper echelons of our society—and I hope their number will increase and their financial investments grow— but in order to conclude the drive successfully, the masses of American Jewry will have to participate. Who else will do the job unless the Zionist organizations will mobilize their forces? If, God forbid, it should come to a world conflagration between East and West, and Israel should decide to remain neutral— who will have the courage of conviction to explain Israel's position to the American public? I doubt whether the American Jewish Committee can be relied upon to do the job. Those in Israel who have been displaying the attitude of "The Moor has done his duty, the Moor may go," should take time out to ponder this question very seriously.

The same is true of the role of the Zionist movement in the Diaspora. If the downward trend persists and the Zionist movement continues to lose prestige, it will be a mortal blow to all the aspirations of Jewish survival. Actually, whatever positive Judaism we have in American Jewish life today, has been either originated or motivated, guided or enforced by Zionist ideology. Remove the Zionist movement from American Jewish life and our community councils become welfare agencies slanted toward assimilatory tendencies.

To sum it up, hand in hand with the phenomenal ascent of the State of Israel, there is a saddening decline of the Zionist movement. This, in spite of the fact that both Israel and the Diaspora are, and will for a long time to come be in dire need of the Zionist movement, and despite the fact that within the frame of our own organization, the present administration has been diligent and forthright and led the cause with organizational skill.

II

Is there a solution to this problem? I believe there is, if our forthcoming "Convention of Implementation" will make this problem the central theme of our deliberations and take some drastic steps to lead our movement toward new vistas.

Foremost is the question of our relationship to Israel. Here the issue of *chalutziut* cannot be avoided any longer, first because it is a basic Zionist principle and, secondly, because Israel requires it. The ZOA Convention at Atlantic City must come out with a positive statement on our American attitude toward the principle of *chalutziut*. As we are, more or less, an organization of the middle class, American *chalutziut* must not necessarily copy the *hachsharah* centers of Eastern Europe of previous years. It should be an institution, not mainly of agricultural, but also of industrial and commercial character. Young people who want to go to Israel and to identify themselves with the new Israeli nation, should have the opportunity of preparing themselves for agricultural, commercial, and industrial enterprises. Israel cries out for technicians in many fields, and we have the possibility of replying to this request. In addition, *chalutziut* happens to be an area which the Zionist movement can carve out for itself, unafraid of competition of non-Zionist groups who, I am sure, will be most reluctant to follow us on this road. The Bond campaign of recent weeks has literally revitalized the ZOA in every community. This shows that given a project, the Zionist movement can still be a vital force. An expanded program of an American edition of *chalutziut* in the fields of agriculture, commerce and industry,

157

may again provide a project that might serve as the spark plug of our Zionist movement for many years to come.

The same is true of our relationship to the Diaspora. Already last year, at the convention in Chicago, I pleaded for the abolition of the Zionist party system and advocated an integrated Zionist movement. The more I think of it, the more I am convinced that our party affiliations are gradually, but surely, becoming an anachronism. But as long as the present structure continues to exist, the ZOA could play a tremendous role within American Jewry, by injecting into our Jewish life those elements that make for Jewish survival. There are several areas which, because of our constant preoccupation with political emergencies, we have either neglected or not undertaken at all. The time has come to transfer these plans from the realm of speech into the world of reality. For instance, one cannot continue to speak of a "bridge between Israel and American Jewry" without implementing a program of Hebrew culture at least for the members in our own ranks. Very few of our Zionist officials in many Jewish communities know the meaning of the Hebrew alphabet. Unless we transform the Zionist movement into a Hebrew speaking and Hebrew reading organization, all the programs of "building bridges" will be of no avail. The goal of making Hebrew the second language of every American Jew must be proclaimed at this forthcoming convention, with the definite understanding that every member of the ZOA is expected to serve as an example in his community for his own study of Hebrew, for the Hebrew education of his children, and for the establishment of Hebrew Adult classes as one of the main activities of the local Zionist groups.

Within the frame of this program to revitalize Hebrew in the United States, several additional steps should be undertaken. The convention should go on record that it is the desire of the Zionist movement to establish chairs for the Hebrew language in every American university, and our local groups should be made to understand that the implementation of this program in their own region will be their sole responsibility. A similar project should be developed for all American junior and senior high schools, at least in the larger metropolitan areas of our country. By doing this, we might be in a position to raise an American Jewish generation that will speak

Hebrew and read the literature emanating from Israel. They, themselves, will then become the strong "bridge" of which we have been speaking for so long.

But, beyond that, and equally as important, the ZOA should arrive at a functional coordination of activities with the American Jewish Congress—as I suggested at our last convention in Chicago—thus projecting into the lives of our members the importance of the fight for Civil Rights and equality, for first class citizenship and dignity of the American Jewish community. These are problems that affect each one of us, and without their solution, there will be no healthy Jewish community in the United States. The whole complex of activities in which the American Jewish Congress is engaged is indigenous to our Zionist work and basically a fundamental principle of our Zionist philosophy. Here, too, our movement is in a position to make a magnificent contribution to the Jewish life in the United States and, in addition to it, provide projects for the day by day activities of our entire membership.

III

I pray that our convention in Atlantic City may rise to the occasion imposed upon it by history. The fate of the Zionist movement is in the balance. The destiny of the Zionist movement will be in the hands of the delegates. From the depth of my heart, I believe in the mission of Zionism and stand in awe before the many tasks that lie ahead of us. If our delegates will be motivated by this missionary ideal of Zionism and its historic importance for both Israel and Diaspora, the convention in Atlantic City may go down in history as having been the "Convention of Implementation."

BANKRUPTCY OF WESTERN FOREIGN POLICY

Excerpt   October 26, 1956

It is quite clear by now that what we have witnessed in recent weeks is a complete bankruptcy of Western foreign policy, aided and abetted by our own State Department. Were the situation not so tragic, we could, with justification, come and say "we told you so."

The position of the Zionist Movement on the problems of the Middle East and the solutions we have proposed for years have now been proved correct from beginning to end. Unfortunately, it needed the tragic turn of events at the Suez to hammer this truth home, even to some members of the present administration. Were it not so tragic, it would be a comic spectacle: an administration spends a full four years on wooing the Arabs, cultivating their friendship, providing them with ammunition, sending them military and technical aid, begging them to accept millions of dollars in gifts—all this in order to tie them into the Western orbit and erect a fence between them and the Soviet Union. Now after four years of this policy of "imagination" and "statesmanship," of "wisdom" and "vision," Russia has emerged as the most potent force in the Middle East, the official friend of the Arabs and their spokesman at the United Nations, to a point by which the whole Suez Canal discussion will turn out to be a flop because of a Russian veto. A greater bankruptcy of policy has never been seen in modern history of man.

The situation is doubly tragic because there have been many liberal voices, here and abroad, warning the State Department of the treacherous road it is traveling. Principally among these voices was the one of our own Zionist Movement which, again and again, has been warning and pleading, demonstrating and begging, calling attention with facts and figures—without making a dent.

When we said that Iraq will never be bought by the West, in spite of the millions of dollars in guns and ammunition, nobody believed it. When we analyzed Nasser, at the very beginning, and predicted that he would develop into a Hitler of the Middle East, the politicians laughed. When we petitioned to redress the wrong of the stoppage of Israeli shipping at the Suez Canal, in spite of the Convention of 1880 and two resolutions of the Security Council, the "statesmen" turned a deaf ear.

160

EASING OF EAST-WEST TENSIONS

From *The American Zionist* (October-November, 1959)

To us, as Jews, the dialogue between East and West as exemplified by the Eisenhower-Khrushchev meeting has an additional significance. No other people has suffered more from the split of our society into two hostile camps than have we in the post-war period. The three million Jews behind the Iron Curtain are completely sundered from the main body of Jewry, separated from the State of Israel, and detached from the eight-to-nine million Jews living in the free world. All attempts to establish contact between the three main branches of our people's existence have ended in failure. If this is not enough, what we have learned recently at the International Assembly of the World Jewish Congress in Stockholm proves that the Soviet Union is determined to eradicate the spiritual and religious content of Russian Jewry under a policy of forced assimilation.

Russian Jewry today, the largest reservoir within the pitiful remnants of European Jewry, lacks even the privileges accorded to other religious communities in the Soviet Union. The word "Jew" is stamped into every passport of a Jewish citizen and carries with it negative implications. Jews are officially considered members of a nationality and yet there is nothing in the spiritual, cultural, or religious life of Russian Jewry to correspond to this high-sounding title.

Therefore, I submit that should there be a relaxation of the tensions or at least what the president called a "melting of the ice," there is hope that the Soviet government will, at least, make a gesture in the direction of freedom of religion and Jewish identification to those who want to stay, and freedom of movement to those who want to emigrate. The prayers of all Israel will, therefore, accompany the president of the United States, both in his discussions in Washington, as well as on his forthcoming trip to Moscow.

To us, as Zionists, any improvement in East-West relations would amount to a three-fold benediction. For it is obvious to every student of contemporary history that every single phase of international policy is influenced by the atmosphere prevailing between Washington and Moscow.

This is doubly true for the problem of the Middle East: the hostile attitude of the Soviet government to Israel, the viciousness of the Soviet radio which has intensified its propaganda recently, calling openly upon the Arabs to do away with the State of Israel and naming the latter the "51st state of the United States"—all this wooing of the Arab League in order to attach them more and more to the Eastern camp, all this is in itself the direct result of East and West tensions. It even influences the attitude of our State Department both vis-a-vis Israel as well as vis-a-vis Nasser—the sudden outpouring of love and millions of dollars in order to salvage the Egyptian economy and to widen the Suez Canal, irrespective of Egypt's flagrant violations of international commitments and its recent acts of piracy executed in utter shamelessness. On the other hand, the advice of our State Department to Israel not to raise the issue of the Suez blockade at the Security Council for fear that Russia will veto any motion put on the agenda—thus projecting herself in the role of playing the defender of the Moslem world—is indicative of the impact which the struggle between the two giants is exerting upon our foreign policy.

Again, in an atmosphere at least devoid of bitterness if not of hopeful cooperation, neither East nor West would be in the desperate need of playing up to the Arabs at the expense of Israel. Nasser would be deprived of his favorite game of blackmailing Washington by flirting with Moscow or threatening Moscow by flirting with Washington. In an atmosphere of cooperation between East and West, Israel could devote its abundant energies to building and reconstruction, to the liquidation of the galut, and the ingathering of the exiles. It is an exciting and challenging dream, and I only hope that our generation will live to see its fulfillment.

Lastly, any positive outcome of the discussion between the Western and the Eastern powers would make a real contribution to the many unfinished tasks before us. Relieved of the pressing burden of the cold war, the Zionist Movement, here and abroad, could dedicate its willpower and its resources to peaceful, constructive causes, both in Israel and in *chutz la-aretz.*

One does not have to spell out to Zionists the almost unlimited possibilities or the many things we could undertake

162

for Israel, the very existence of which is the central core of all our aspirations. But I would like to say a word about one aspect of our activities in the Diaspora which we have hardly begun to consider. There is a deeply challenging problem of Jewish identification, not only in the communities living behind the Iron Curtain, but unfortunately also in many Jewish communities of the free Western world of *chutz la-aretz*. It was deeply moving for me, as I am sure for many other members of the American delegation, to listen for hours to the many pleas of the representatives of the smaller Jewish communities in Western and Northern Europe, as well as to the delegates of the Far East and North Africa, and even of the Western Hemisphere, literally begging for positive Jewish leadership, for trained teachers, organizers of schools, reading material, books and pamphlets in their respective languages—expressing the hope that the salvation in form of manpower and material will come from Israel and from the Free World, specifically from the United States.

Each one of them told the same story: that if their communities are left to shift for themselves, the emptiness of content on the one hand and the erosion caused by assimilation on the other will cause them to disappear from the Jewish scene within another decade or two.

Having just lost forty percent of our people in the Nazi holocaust—can one witness a further diminution of our small people numbering only eleven million souls today? It is a gigantic problem requiring large resources of funds, extensive planning, and concerted effort. In this connection, I have not even touched upon our own problem here at home, in filling the emptiness of American Jewish life behind the glittering facade and thus suggest to the young generation of our American Jewish community a way of life which spells positive identification with Israel and the Jewish people as a whole.

Freed from the fetters of the cold war our energies could be used for the fulfillment of our Zionist ideal; namely, the upbuilding of Israel and the unification of the Jewish people in the far-flung corners of the earth. Thus, even the destiny of the Zionist Movement and its very program is inextricably bound to the East and West conflict. This is why as Americans, as Jews, and as Zionists, we will, in these coming weeks, be praying and

163

working for the dawn of East-West understanding, so that our harassed generation may know again tranquility and peace.

THE ZIONIST MOVEMENT
IN SEARCH OF AN IMAGE

Excerpt   From *The American Zionist,* June 29, 1960

The Zionist Movement has recently been under attack from two opposite quarters: the assimilatory forces in the United States on the one hand and members of the Israeli Government—particularly the prime minister and foreign minister—on the other. As far as the American Council for Judaism and their sympathizers are concerned, it is, by now, completely superfluous to rehash old arguments or even to dignify them with a reply.

The uncompromising attack on the Zionist Movement by the prime minister of Israel, however, is an entirely different matter and has to be given serious consideration. At the Mapai Central Committee meeting early in June, Mr. Ben-Gurion said that Jews all over the world agreed that other Jews may find a haven in Israel and that in this respect "There was no difference between Zionists and non-Zionists." He then went on to ask "will the Zionist Movement in America organize aliyah which is Israel's most pressing need, or Hebrew education, which is what Jewry elsewhere needs most?" Apparently concluding that the Zionist Movement will do neither, he climaxed his remarks by saying that the Zionist Movement "creates a gulf between the younger generation of Israel and the Jewish people—for how can we explain to the young generation that there are two sorts of Jews, Zionists and others?" Thus, Mr. Ben-Gurion's latest utterance on the future of Zionism.

There is, it seems to me, a basic fallacy in the prime minister's logic: in spite of appeals and much oratory, of public declarations and even denunciations, there will be no *mass* immigration to Israel from the American Jewish community. American Jews, and that goes for Zionists also, look upon

164

themselves as living in *chutz la-aretz,* (a historic term used in the Talmudic Age to denote free and creative communities outside Palestine) and do not feel that their existence in the United States is characterized by *galut.* The American Jewish community feels solidly at home in these United States and considers its members first class citizens, functioning normally in the fabric of America. The sooner this realistic view is accepted by some Israeli leaders, the better for Israel and the better for us.

To make aliyah the only criterion of a Zionist in the United States is, therefore, not only unrealistic, but simply naive. In spite of this, however, the Zionist Movement in the free world is a historic necessity not only for the lands of the Diaspora, but specifically for Israel itself. For what the prime minister does apparently not understand is the fact that every great cause in history needs a dedicated army in order to translate its vision into reality. It is true that, with minor exceptions, the whole of American Jewry is sympathetic and friendly toward Israel, but there is a vast difference between sympathy and commitment—and American Jewry, with all its friendship, is not committed to Israel; the Zionist Movement, however, is an organization of commitment. There is a great difference between organizations which were founded for an entirely different purpose and which have now added an Israeli project to the many projects they had undertaken before—and a movement which is wholly devotedly and zealously committed to the conception of Jewish Peoplehood and the centrality of the Jewish State. This psychological difference has emerged clearly, again and again, and especially during the critical period of the Sinai Campaign when many of the so-called friends manifested a negative attitude towards Israel's move, whereas Zionists—and Zionists alone—stood firm and proved to be Israel's only reliable allies.

The young Jewish State will, therefore, be in need of a strong and influential Zionist Movement for decades to come, because Israel is a great historic cause and needs not only friends but allies, not only sympathy but commitment. The Zionist Movement is the only organization in the free world that can fulfill this requirement. When the political thinking will reach the state of greater maturity, even some Israeli leaders will come to the conclusion that the Zionist Movement is not a gulf, but a veritable bridge between the Jewish State and the Jewish People.

ZIONISM AND HERZL

From *The Washington Examiner* (July, 1960)

The National Executive Council of the Zionist Organization of America is meeting this time between two historic observances: the seventeenth anniversary of the revolt of the Warsaw Ghetto, which we just commemorated in tribute to the six million martyrs, and the twelfth anniversary of Israel's independence. To round it off, we are remembering these two historic events—one of tragedy at the very depth of degradation, the other of triumph at the very height of redemption—against the background of the centennial of Theodor Herzl, who foresaw the tragedy and predicted the triumph.

The two events are, historically speaking, not unrelated. It is painful to state that six million Jews had to die in order to move the heart of the world to pity and to cause the leaders of nations to recognize the debt that mankind owes a persecuted people, at least to the point of restoring its ancient homeland—but the historic truth is that this is exactly the way it happened. It was the unspeakable catastrophe which stirred the conscience of the world to repay our people for the many blunders and mistakes that were made even by the Western nations, at a time when millions of Jews could have been rescued had there been an open door anywhere on the globe. It is not easy to grasp the enormity of the historic connection between the two events, but somehow in the mysterious providence of the Divine Ruler of men, it has come about that the blood of six million Jews cemented the very foundations of the Jewish State. This being the case, it is incumbent upon us to tell and retell the story of the Jewish tragedy, year after year, "even if all of us were wise, all of us people of understanding, all of us learned in the Torah," as we have been duty-bound throughout the ages to tell the story of Egypt. We of the Zionist Movement have to undertake a solemn oath for ourselves never to

166

forget and not to allow either the Jewish people or the world-at-large ever to forget what happened in Warsaw, Majdanek, and Treblinka. Nowhere was this formulated in a more impressive manner than in the words of a modern poet:

> Let the memory be cold as ice, clear as glass and
>   bright as diamonds!
> For every child killed, for every body flayed,
> For every tear wept, for every moan, every scream,
>   every pain,
> For every naked body in a mass grave,
> For every cut and bruise,
> For every oven where flesh became ash, for every
>   gas chamber,
> For every diabolical device,
> For every gallows where the bodies, swaying, mea-
>   sured the wind,
> For every ignominy, for every wrong,
> Let there be no forgetfulness,
> Let there be no dimming of the memory.

"Let there be no dimming of the memory," and let us see to it that we in the Zionist Organization become the responsible custodians of this collective historic memory.

As in the tradition of our people nothing ever concludes on a minor key, we go from here to the second event—from memory to vision, from galut to redemption. We, the representatives of a revolutionary and state-creating movement, can look with great satisfaction and inner happiness upon the child to whom we gave birth and who now celebrates her twelfth birthday. History has proven us right in our analysis of the Jewish problem and the necessity of an independent state for the very survival of our people. We have not been disappointed either in Israel's accomplishments during these years or in the stature she has achieved in the capitals of the world. We are privileged to live in a generation chosen to witness the emergence of the Jewish State, and we rejoice with the young state in the place of honor she occupies among the nations.

We send our heartiest mazal tov from here to the president, the government, and the people of Israel. May her birthdays multiply throughout the generations and may her days be long upon this earth. As leaders of the Zionist Organization of America, we pledge ourselves to continue our work of rebuilding and the marshaling of public opinion, of strengthening Israel's economic position, as well as her political security for all the years to come.

We are remembering the one event and celebrating the other under the aegis of Theodor Herzl, who analyzed the problem of anti-Semitism so correctly and astounded the world with his historic answer of the *Judenstaat.* Under the impact of the Dreyfus case, he wrote: "Until that time most of us believed the solution of the Jewish question was to be patiently waited for as a part of the general development of mankind. But when a people, which in every other respect is so progressive and so highly civilized, can take such a turn, what are we to expect from other peoples which have not even attained the level which France attained a hundred years ago?" With this keen observation, he gave the by now classic answer: "The Jewish State is a world need...I believe that for me life has ended and world history begun." Thus did the founder of our movement envision the events both of destruction and of rebuilding, of catastrophe and redemption, of tragedy and triumph. It is upon us, the heirs of this precious heritage, to see to it that the fruits of his vision remain in good hands, cultivated and nurtured along by our movement.

On the international political scene our voice ought to be heard in these days, asking the leaders of East and West alike, to discontinue arming the Arabs of the Middle East and, without enforcing any edict upon either Israel or the Arab States, to proclaim to the whole world that in their opinion nothing can be as beneficial to the peace of the world than the beginning of dircct ncgotiations between Israel and her neighbors.

On the Jewish scene, as veritable heirs of Herzl's legacy, we have to begin earnestly the reshaping and reconstructing of our organization, and devote ourselves to the "reselling" of the Zionist philosophy to the American Jewish Community. Whether some members of the Israeli Government believe it or not, we still are and will, for decades to come, continue to be Israel's only reliable ally. It is, therefore, highly in the interest of the Jewish State that the Zionist Movement advances from strength to strength and commences again to play its role of leadership in this largest of Jewish communities. The recent changes, both in the Jewish Agency, as well as in the American Zionist Council, offer us a rare opportunity for the strengthening of our movement and for a new vigorous battle in behalf of those Zionist ideals, without which we cannot conceive of any form of positive Jewish life in the countries of *chutz la-aretz.*

May we then—under the injunction of remembrance, under the impact of redemption, and in the spirit of Theodor Herzl—dedicate our very lives to the achievement of these noble goals.

THE FUTURE OF ZIONISM

February 19, 1961

The recent debate on the future of Zionism—and that includes specifically this week's editorial in *Life Magazine*—is based upon an almost incredible misinterpretation of the very nature of the Zionist Movement, on the one hand, and upon a completely unrealistic approach to the complexities of Jewish life, on the other.

Zionism is a Jewish philosophy of life which believes in the indivisible oneness of the Jewish People. This, in turn, means that Jews, though living dispersed all over the world and rightly counted among the most loyal citizens of their respective homelands, are inseparably held together by historic, religious, and cultural ties, which make of them members of one and the same people. In order to guarantee the survival and the unity of this Jewish People, a Jewish State had to be established as the very instrumentality for the achievement of this goal. Israel of today functions in this capacity and fulfills its historic design by offering a place of refuge to those who flee, a land of fulfillment to those who settle, and a source of inspiration to those who stay.

Zionism is much more than work in or on behalf of Israel. This in itself would be no more than Israelism, but Zionism is Israelism plus the Jewish People in the Diaspora, meaning that we cannot conceive of the future of our people without the spiritual centrality of the Jewish State. To us as Zionists, every new project in Israel and every new undertaking by a Jewish community, in the far flung corners of the earth, are both manifestations of the same Jewish will to live and the self same expression of the creativity of our people's spirit. Precious as the State of Israel is to our generation—and it is the most glorious achievement in our history—even more precious is to us the peoplehood of the Jews, for the survival of which the State was created in the first place. Zionism is the floor that gives Jewish life its basis; the walls that hold it together; and the ceiling that gives it its crowning dignity. This is what Theodor Herzl, the immortal founder of our movement, meant when he said that "Zionism will never die."

This being the case, there is no other organization in Jewish life that can possibly take its place, because there is no other organization to compare with its basic philosophy, its majestic past, its classic achievements, its high visions, and its future goals. Where else in Jewish life can a World Zionist Congress be duplicated, a congress to which delegates from every part of the world and every continent come—with the exception of the Jewish communities behind the Iron Curtain—to participate in a gathering which is the veritable assembly of a whole people? The disappearance of such a movement from the Jewish scene today would amount to a real tragedy, as Prime Minister Sharett so rightly stated the other day, because it would create a vacuum to be filled by no one except by the assimilatory and isolationist philosophies on the periphery of Jewish existence.

We have only recently signed an agreement with the Government of Israel for mutual undertakings in the field of Hebraization in Jewish communities, building of projects in Israel, and fostering aliyah in the Western countries—undertakings which, by their very nature, are destined to cement inextricably the different parts of our people, both in Israel and the rest of the world, into the eternal entity of Jewish peoplehood, with Israel serving the Jewish people as a shelter for its body and a sanctuary for its spirit.

These tasks are great, the goals are high, and the vision universal—let us then invite friends and sympathizers to join with us in the strengthening of the Zionist Movement, so that it may continue to contribute in the future, as it has so nobly

170

done in the past, to the freedom of our people and the redemption of mankind.

STATEHOOD AND PEOPLEHOOD

March 19, 1963

Excerpts from a speech at the Actions Committee of the ZOA

Now, a few words which I feel have to be said here tonight about some fundamental issues which were raised in the speeches of Dr. Goldmann, Mr. Sharett and Mrs. Halprin. Again and again the words *heshbon ha-nefesh* were used, and I believe it is about time to do *just* that, though it has not been done yet. For if not now and here, within the Zionist family, when else and where else?

When Herzl came upon the modern scene of our history, he enriched our vocabulary with two words—which have been, of course, an old possession of our people, but he coined them anew for modern usage. These two words were *statehood* and *peoplehood*—in this order. This meant that it was imperative to create a Jewish State in order to guarantee the unity of the Jewish People. *Ein Volk, ein Volk,* "A People, One People," was Herzl's motto. This in turn has meant that in our Zionist history we did not create a state just for the trappings of ministries and armies and navies and flags—but that we created the State as the best instrumentality for the preservation of the cohesiveness and the unity of the Jewish People. *The State was created for the People, not the People for the State. The Jewish People was organized to create the Jewish State, so that the Jewish State could be organized to preserve the Jewish people.* This is the classic Zionist philosophy. Not the other way around.

What happened when we reached the first plateau of this development? In 1948, the Zionist Movement in the Western World, surely in the United States, was at the very height of its influence, its strength and its membership—the ZOA itself had a quarter of a million members in 1948—and all over the world, Jews flocked into its ranks. It was a time in which we had even considerable financial resources and, what is even more, tremendous prestige. In 1948, it was fashionable to be a Zionist.

171

With Golda Meir, Prime Minister of Israel, c. 1970

Then, suddenly, an unexpected development occurred—something which has been plaguing us now for fifteen years. We expected the Jewish State, the child of the Zionist Movement, to say to the world that it was the majestic movement of Zionism that had the dream and the vision and the aspirations to work for the establishment of the State and to accomplish its task; that, therefore, this Zionist Movement will, for the years to come, remain the very symbol of the unbreakable unity between the State and the People in all parts of the world; and that this movement has, therefore, a special status in Jewish history—and fully deserves the dedicated support of all Jewish communities in all parts of the globe. This is what we expected. Instead, exactly the opposite occurred.

* * *

We have done all this work and will continue to do so, not for any personal glory, but because we deeply believe in the concept of Jewish Peoplehood. We are afraid that this concept is going down the drain because of the existing split between Israel and the Zionist Movement abroad.

I remember that as a student in Germany, I once listened to Jacob Klatzkin delivering a speech in the Beit Am, in Berlin, on his philosophy of *shlilat ha-gola,* "negation of the Diaspora." It made a deep impression upon me. He assured his audience that sooner or later the Jewish State will be born, but predicted that when this happens, there will occur a division within the Jewish people, so that the one who will want to remain a Jew will be going to the Jewish State, and that those remaining outside will assimilate very soon thereafter. There will be no line of communication between the two communities. Moreover he added, in two or three generations, there will be no Jews abroad altogether.

At this time I thought that this was an exaggerated prediction. But the shades of this philosophy are already with us. Israel has a problem now with its young generation which says that they are Israelis and not Jews. We, on the other hand, have a teenage generation of American Jewish youngsters who are obviously not Zionists and do not have the slightest intention of changing their status.

This being the case, I am asking you tonight in all frank-

173

ness: against the background of all the dreams and aspirations and visions which were ours when we set upon the goal to create a shelter for our people's body and a sanctuary for its spirit—is this the result that we wanted to achieve?

ISRAEL AND THE ARABS

Excerpt   September 27, 1963

Here are two nations which have had a long and common history. There is no ideological problem between them. Communism is not the issue between Israel and the Arabs. There is no racial conflict. There is no language conflict. The two nations speak closely related Semitic languages. In the course of history, the Moslem world was often much more hospitable to our people than the Christian. When we lived together with the Arabs, in Spain for example, we created a literature and culture of such quality that we called this period the Golden Age.

If it is possible to bring together two nations as opposite as the United States and the Soviet Union on some issues, should it not be possible—among peoples living in the same neighborhood, who have had a history of amity and good relations on and off throughout the centuries—to take this conflict off the battlefield and bring it to the table of negotiations? Yet even yesterday, the president of Iraq echoed what his delegates said at the United Nations, that his only aim in life is the annihilation of the Jewish State!

In the time of Isaiah the prophet, the empires of Egypt and Assyria—the Iraq of today—were the mortal enemies of Israel and of each other. It was a tense era; the feeling of international hostility was so thick that it could be cut with a knife. In the midst of such conflict, Isaiah—standing in the marketplace of Jerusalem itself, delivered this speech:

> [Thus saith the Lord]: "In that day there shall be a
> highway out of Egypt to Assyria, and the Assyri-
> an shall come into Egypt, and the Egyptian into
> Assyria; and the Egyptians shall worship with
> the Assyrians. In that day Israel will be the third

174

with Egypt and with Assyria, a blessing in the
midst of the earth; for the Lord of hosts hath
blessed him, saying: 'Blessed be Egypt My people and Assyria the work of My hands, and Israel
Mine inheritance.'"   (Isaiah 19:23-25)

If, so long ago, a prophet could rise above hostilities and
enmities to utter such a vision of peace, should not two brother nations, Israel and the Arabs, be able to speak to one another today?

Do not think that only an ancient prophet could utter such
words. Let me share with you one of the most moving poems I
have read in a long time. I came across it by chance when I was
in Israel this summer.

> Not far away from my home in Israel, there passes
>   the border line.
> Beyond it there is an Arab country.
> The same rain falls here and there.
> The same locust invades the corn.
> From the same water pool the flocks drink.
> Each morning when the sun rises, I can see on both
>   sides of the border workers go to work, farmers
>   in their fields, children on their way to school.
> They get up after a night of terror, and they shall go
>   to sleep behind closed gates and barbed wire
>   fences.
> Do not say "It is not in our power to grant them a
>   life of peace and security."
> Do not say "Words will not change things."
> But say "There is no peace without human affection,
>   without people talking together, without a talk
>   face to face."
> Do not say "The time has not come, and not we shall
>   decide the fate of our countries." But do say,
>   "We are the people, this is the place, now is the
>   time to sow the seeds of peace in the fields of
>   hate. Sow the seeds of peace, and in time to
>   come there will grow a peace-tree, bearing fruit,
>   bestowing shade for all."

175

This is not an Isaiah living centuries ago speaking, but a man of our time whose very life is lived on the borderline. His name is Rashid Hussein, and he is an Arab poet living in Israel. He tells all of us to "sow the seed of peace in the field of hate." We desperately need a new dialogue in the Middle East between two nations—descendants of a common ancestor—so that the tree of peace may grow and bring shade to Arabs and Israelis together.

WHAT DOES ZIONISM MEAN TO THE YOUNG AMERICAN JEW?

From *The American Zionist,* LVII: (November 1966)

Every national and state-building revolution is a quest for identity. In this quest, the revolution goes through two distinct psychological phases: one, the building of independence, in order to be on a par with all other nations, to achieve the same status as have the other nations—a status, the symbol of which is statehood. In other words, in the first phase, the revolution emphasizes the desire to be like all others. Once independence is secured, the new nation progresses to the second stage: evaluating itself against the context of its own history, linking itself to older roots, establishing itself as the climax of decades or even centuries that preceded it, gradually defining its characteristics as a race or a nation, and then, projecting to the world its particular image.

In short, national revolutions commence with the idea to have the same rights, the same freedoms, the same privileges as all the others and to be like them. Once this frame is constructed, the new nation will dig deeper in order to come up with the elements which are its very own, the ingredients that make it different, so as to announce to the world what makes it unique.

All African revolutions of our own generation are a good case in point. They all started with the burning desire for independence from colonial rule, be it Britain or France. Once they achieved statehood—meaning the status symbol of nationhood—they began to concentrate almost immediately upon the "African personality," African literature, African history, and

176

African art. Now before our own eyes, the process goes even further. A new vocabulary is being born: the Burmese personality, the Nigerian identity, and so on. The tendency is to rediscover the roots of the past; and the purpose of all these revolutions is to show us not how similar they are to everybody else, but how different they are in character and in outlook from the rest of the world.

It is interesting in this connection that even the Negro revolution in our own country follows this pattern. It started out with a cry for equality and for the same freedoms and privileges that the White population has. But to the student of contemporary Negro literature, it is quite evident that these goals are stressed, not in order to assimilate among the Whites, but on the basis of their Negro-ness, the recognition of their distinct contributions as a particular race. The quest here, too, is not for assimilation but, on the contrary, for racial identity.

The psychological truth stated above has much bearing upon the question of what Zionism means to the young American Jew. Zionism was a national state-building revolution. It was a quest for Jewish identity. When it began, it spoke of Jewish homelessness and demanded the right to have a state of our own like all others, and it concentrated, therefore, on the building of a Jewish commonwealth. So much did we emphasize independence, nationhood, statehood, that our adversaries accused us repeatedly of a desire "to be like all other nations." It was the privilege of my generation to bring this dream to fulfillment and to live to see the establishment of the Jewish State.

Now that the State exists, and its support by the whole Jewish people is assured, there is a "searching of the heart," both in Israel and in the Diaspora, for the meaning of this event, for defining the Jewish profile and developing the *particular* image of the Jewish personality – in short, a quest for Jewish identity that digs deep in our ancient roots.

It is true that the Canaanites in Israel are still with us and what they want is nothing but statehood—*k'chol ha-goyim*, and nothing else. There are still many sabras who agree with them. But there are significant things going on in Israel even in the curricula of government schools, and in discussions, debates and symposia, on the subject of our particular traits as a people—not biologically, but spiritually. There is, unquestionably, a shifting from *k'chol ha-goyim* to *goy echad* (a unique nation) or *am echad* (a unique people).

We have, then, moved to the second phase of our revolution: from the general idea of having a territory like all others to the specific idea of a particular state; from the first phase of being normal to the second phase of being different; from the quest for a Jewish State to the search for Jewish uniqueness. This process, in turn, leads us, by necessity, from the phase of statehood to the phase of peoplehood. It seems to me that herein lies the hope for the preservation of Jewish unity.

It was Jacob Klatzkin who, decades ago, warned us that out of the establishment of a Jewish State would emerge two different nations which would not even understand one another. This danger is, to a certain degree, still with us. But if this process of the second phase of the Zionist revolution is allowed to develop, the Israeli youth will soon discover, as some of them already have done, that they are not only Israelis, but Jews. Our own young generation, here, will soon learn that they are not simply Americans of Jewish persuasion, but members of an indivisible entity called the Jewish People. It is on this basis, and on this basis alone, that the young generation, here and in Israel, can meet as members of one and the same family and therefore as partners, and together, begin the difficult task of building the Jewish People.

The building of a people is much more difficult than the building of a state. Unlike the latter, it has no glamour, no uniforms, neither army, nor navy, nor consular corps, nor embassy status. It is a daily grinding job, and yet the time has come to undertake it if we want to fulfill ourselves within the Zionist revolution.

There are several steps that can be undertaken. As far as the Israelis are concerned, much is being done in this area by the Ministry of Education as well as the Army. But in a recent symposium held in Brussels on the subject of State-Diaspora relationships, I suggested to Israel one additional point. Young Israeli students should not be allowed to come to the United States without any preparations and without any government plan. There are many programs in the United States sponsored by high schools, colleges, universities and, directly, by our

State Department, and American students do study for a year in Germany or in France or in England. Israel could take a leaf out of this program to see how carefully this is planned, how the background of the student as well as the one of his European host is scrutinized, in order to make sure that the young American gets the most out of his European study year. Israel ought to do the same and, most important, guide the student who comes to the United States to stay with a Jewish family which is active in Jewish life and committed to Jewish values. A young Israeli would suddenly discover that the Jewish people is a larger sphere than the State of Israel and that he is part and parcel of a large entity.

Only the other day, Bernard Postal published an article, "What Israeli Youth Leaders Learned About North American Jewry." Speaking of an experiment launched by the National Jewish Welfare Board and the Jewish Agency last year, he says, "The realization for the first time that they are part of the Jewish people at large, not just of the Israeli people, is the major discovery of six Israeli youth workers and teachers who have just completed a full year of living and working in countries where Jews are not the majority." Living for a year or two in the positive atmosphere of a Jewish home would help build the concept of Jewish Peoplehood in the minds of young Israelis.

Second, we here in the United States could undertake several practical steps to begin the building of our people. First, teaching the concept of Jewish Peoplehood which is still unacceptable to the non-Zionist world. The average American Jew identifies himself, if at all, with the Jewish community of his own city, possibly with the American Jewish community as a whole. But the philosophy that he is a member of the Jewish People, as he is a member of his own family, is quite distant from his mind; that Israel plays a central role, within this concept of Jewish Peoplehood, is even farther away. Philanthropy for the Jewish State and investment in it and even an emotional attachment to the Holy Land should not be equated with centrality in the building of the Jewish Peoplehood.

Third, we have to give the classic word aliyah its definition in American terms. We are doing much to expose American teenagers and college students to the great romance of the Jewish State, but it is not enough either in quantity or in quality. Thousands of young Americans ought to be visiting Israel either for the summer or, even more important, for a year's study—and ten times the number that we are sending for these purposes now. Such contact with the land will, by necessity, strengthen identification with our people, the love for the Jewish homeland, and deepen the consciousness for living a Jewish life. All this, in my concept, is aliyah—some of it of short duration, some of it of long duration. Many will, undoubtedly, return and become genuine *olim*, if the experience of the year is challenging and deep.

Lastly, it is, I am convinced, the task of the young generation to find its way to commitment. We have spoken so often of the spread of Hebrew, and this is undoubtedly important. But I speak here of commitment not to a language, but to the things of the spirit of which the language is only the symbol. And, here, one cannot avoid anymore the whole question of the role of religion in the personal life of our young generation. Important as the learning of Hebrew is—and I have always belonged to its fervent advocates—one has to remember that it is the religious and cultural heritage of our people which makes us unique and gives us our particular image. Take Judaism away from us, and there is nothing left that is special, different or unique. This, in turn, means that one cannot build Jewish Peoplehood without commitment to the great spiritual values which our ancient tradition so majestically created.

Sooner or later, each one of the young Jewish generation has to force himself to genuine confrontation: does he want to be a Zionist because we have a State or does he want to be part of the second phase of Zionist fulfillment and lead the type of Jewish life which is meaningful in spiritual terms?

It was Leo Baeck who said once that "every generation is a question which God addresses to humanity; and every people must answer for its own sake and for the sake of humanity." If I should give the answer to the historic question addressed to the rising generation, I would say that the task of their life is identification with our people, the center of which is the Jewish State, and commitment to its spiritual values, for the challenge of history to the new generation is the building of Jewish Peoplehood on the eternal foundations of its majestic heritage.

THE GLORY AND THE CHALLENGE

From *The American Zionist* LVII:10 (June, 1967)

The year 1967 is a Zionist year par excellence. It is the seventieth anniversary of the first Zionist Congress convened in 1897 by Theodor Herzl, in Basle, Switzerland. It is, also, the fiftieth anniversary of the Balfour Declaration issued by the British Government in November 1917. The two events are logically connected with one another as are cause and effect. There is a direct line from Basle to London, and the two events combined brought about the 1947 decision of the United Nations to partition Palestine and the 1948 decision of the Jewish Agency to establish the Jewish State.

This is, then, a year filled with anniversaries and replete with historic turning points. The ancient vision of the prophets "to raise the tabernacle of David that has fallen" and "return the captivity of our people," so as "to plant them deep upon the soil of Israel (Amos 9:11,14,15)"—this ancient prophetic vision became the political dream of Theodor Herzl, and his Zionist dream, in turn, achieved its first historic breakthrough in the Balfour Declaration, by which a great power recognized the association of the Jewish people with the Jewish land in terms of international law.

To this glorious chapter in our movement's history has been added—in the second week of June—the spectacular campaign in which the young Israeli army broke the backbone of Arab might in a blitz of sixty hours. Fighting for their very lives, their homes and their families, they had the God of Israel on their side who manifested himself by giving victory to the few against the many. Here too, Herzl's prophecy that once we return to the ancient soil "a wondrous generation of Jews will spring into existence—the Maccabeans will rise again" was fulfilled, only the other day, before our very eyes. The glory of Zionism reached its high point on the sands of Sinai and in the Straits of Tiran.

There is a second aspect of this Zionist victory: the attitude of the Jewish people throughout the globe and, specifically, of the American Jewish community. Future historians will write a saga about our people, and our grandchildren will believe they are reading fiction stories. The outpouring of sentiment, the manifestation of solidarity, the utter identification with the

181

Jewish State, the sacrificial giving, not only of the rich and well-to-do, but of the poorest among the poor, is an event of staggering proportion.

Nowhere in the history of man is there a parallel to a dispersed people, citizens of other countries, standing up in such multitudes and volunteering large donations, by borrowing from banks or by ridding themselves of their hard-earned savings, as did the Jewish community during the month of June. Not even the year 1948, in which the State was established, can serve as a parallel to this phenomenon. From one end of the country to the other, Jews did not even wait for official appeals. They telephoned their contributions. They sent their checks by mail or brought their donations, personally, to the offices of the UJA and the Bonds, or both.

We, as Zionists, have always proclaimed the centrality of Israel and have always dreamt of the unity of the Jewish people in support of the Jewish State. But even we were overwhelmed by the selfless response to and the complete identification of the American Jew with Israel in its hour of need. The rallying, not only of individuals, but of organizations, yes, of the total Jewish community in America, to the defense of Israel's right to existence, is almost as dramatic a victory as the military sweep of Dayan's army through Egypt, Jordan and Syria. All this would not have been possible were it not for the teachings and instructions, for the enlightenment and the persuasion bestowed by the Zionist Movement upon the American Jewish community in the course of seven decades. This too, then, is a triumph of Zionist ideology of which we may be rightly proud.

This shining glory of Zionist achievement has its counterpart in the burden and the challenge for the years that lie ahead. If Zionist attainment means only attachment to and identification with Israel, the victory is already ours. In listening to Zionist and non-Zionist speakers, at mass rallies in different communities—including the one at Lafayette Park in Washington—the speeches were easily interchangeable. The non-Zionist addresses already use the same vocabulary coined by us and familiar to us. There is no special function for the Zionist Movement in this particular area, unless the one of remaining the conscience of the community and the source of continuous vigilance for the future of the Jewish State.

There are, however, areas vital to Israel's survival which the others have not touched and will not grapple with in the foreseeable future. There are two such areas: one is aliyah to Israel, and the other is Hebrew and I mean Hebrew—not only Jewish—education here in the United States.

The greatness of our movement has always consisted in the fact that we had the vision to look beyond today to tomorrow—to be pioneers in ideas not popular at the time, but crucial to the future. So it is with the two areas mentioned above. In both cases, we have paid only lip service to these ideas, and it is time to be honest and admit it frankly.

The Zionist Movement is the only one that could motivate aliyah from the United States—and the older the Jewish State gets the more will it be in dire need of Western aliyah. Thousands of young people across the nation visited Israel consulates and volunteered for service in the Jewish State. We ought to take advantage of this deep-rooted sentiment and spend most of our budget on motivating aliyah of the old and the young, but especially of the younger generation. We have never succeeded in telling the exciting story of Israel to our young American-born generation. In human terms, it is a story vastly more exciting than any to the found in the Peace Corps movement.

The glory of Zionist achievement in the year 1967 should challenge us to heroic efforts in concentrating all our powers and all our means on giving the Jewish State what it needs most—aliyah of young people from the United States. This aliyah has to be undertaken in a flexible method—for a year, or two, or three, or permanently. The people are available. The idea is exciting indeed, and it would be the greatest contribution to Israel of which the Zionist Movement is capable in our generation.

The same is true of the deepening of Hebrew knowledge on the teen-age level in schools and on the more mature level of adult education. Most American Jews are interested in a general religious education, but Hebrew as a language—which alone guarantees the continuous line of communication between the dispersed Jewries and Israel—is still a stepchild, even with Jews who belong to synagogues and are active in Jewish life.

Here, too, is an area for which non-Zionist organizations

will show very little enthusiasm. But to us, it is another element of unity in Jewish peoplehood and an indispensable brick in the wall of Jewish survival. If we could convince the members of our own movement of the historic challenge to make the knowledge of Hebrew language and literature a Zionist mitzvah to be fulfilled in our days, we would erect the second pillar upon which to build solidly a Zionist future for decades to come.

This program of aliyah and Hebrew has great potentialities and could be very successful, but only on one condition: the unification of our Zionist forces into some form of an *American Zionist Movement.* Our parties as they exist today are anachronistically outmoded, and the ideological differences between them—on the American scene—are without any importance or validity. If we could rise above narrow confinements, unify our scattered forces, avoid the waste of time and energy and substance in duplication of work, agree on an overall Zionist program on the American scene and do it together in the name of an integral American Zionist Movement, we could attract many new members, appeal to the young ones, especially to the college student, raise the prestige of Zionism, and capture the imagination of Jewish communities with constructive projects.

The mentality of the American Jew is such that he will readily join a Zionist Movement with a challenging program. He is not inclined to join one of many Zionist parties. We of the ZOA, who have always prided ourselves on belonging to the General Zionist Movement, ought to be the first ones to applaud the atmosphere which is now prevailing in America. We have always wanted one single Zionist Movement and we have always envisioned it as a unitary entity. Now that the Commission for Reorganization is making a similar suggestion, we ought to be in the forefront in leading the other organizations and persuading them to accept the unification of our forces—something which has been our ideal from the very beginning. Let us hope that we will find the wisdom to recognize that this is the only way to secure the future of our movement, and to act accordingly.

The year 1967 is a year of Zionist glory. May it also be, I pray, a year of Zionist fulfillment.

184

STATE AND RELIGION IN ISRAEL

August 30, 1968

Israel is at the moment beset by many external and internal problems: the surrounding Arab States and the El Fatah terrorists, Russia and the United Nations, and a host of others. But aside from these vexing problems of its security and survival, no problem on the inner front, is more complicated than the relationship between religion and state. And this for three reasons:

There is first the historic fact that the Jews are a people, but that the essence of its "peoplehood" is the spiritual heritage of Judaism. Peoplehood and religion are so interwoven in the four thousand year old history of the Jewish People that a complete separation of the two is beyond the realm of possibility. Secondly, the Turks who ruled Palestine for four hundred years bestowed upon the Church, the Mosque, and the Synagogue the exclusive rights in matters of marriage, divorce, and personal status, especially inheritance—and any religious establishment that has such powers is bound to dominate the life of the nation. As the rabbinate in the Middle East has always been Orthodox—no other form of religious expression has ever been introduced to that area—it has always been the halachah, Orthodox Jewish law, by which the rabbinate has been guided. To this has been added the fact that similar to the pattern in many European countries, the rabbinate is not only a religious establishment but the exponent of a political party. As all governments in the history of the young Jewish State had to be a coalition of parties—because no single party is strong enough to form a government by itself and the Orthodox group had to be included in every government—a price had to be paid for their participation. The price consisted in the procedure that more and more of the laws of halachah were gradually, by an act of the Knesset, made into the law of the land.

As a result of these three reasons, religion and state are not only not separate from one another, but Orthodoxy is, in a large measure, dominant in the life of the State, in spite of the fact that the Orthodox group constitutes only fifteen percent of the population. This situation has provoked a counter-move by militant secularists on the other side of the spectrum. Between

185

the two extremes, there is a majority which belongs to neither but is deeply disenchanted with the status quo which allows the official religious establishment to impose its particular form of religious expression upon an unwilling population and upon a young generation in revolt.

Israel desperately needs on the spiritual level what the late and beloved Martin Buber called "a third religious front," meaning new forms of religious expressions, be they Conservative, Reform, or any other home grown liberal approach to the problem of religion in the twentieth century. It is here that the World Union for Progressive Judaism, (the International Movement for Reform Judaism) with the help of the American Reform Movement, has pioneered in recent years in establishing progressive congregations, of which there are now seven in existence, in addition to some others established by the American Conservative Movement.

If the American Jewish Community, which was raised on the ideal of the separation of church and state, will go out of its way in assisting these struggling congregations financially, we may bring "a new light to shine upon Zion." Time is all the more on our side, as formidable voices inside the Orthodox camp are now heard, in favor of separating religion from politics. (Professor Isaiah Leibowitz, Rabbi Efrayim E. Urbach, Dr. Ernst Simon and many others.) There is here the beginning of a new chapter in the discussion of this topic. The future looks promising in the years that lie ahead. Israel, which has solved so many insoluble problems in recent years, will eventually find the right answer to this complex question.

Separate religion from politics, allow it to battle its own way in the marketplace of ideas, and you will see what a beneficent role religion could play in the Jewish State. Give it a liberal, non-orthodox form of expression, and it will attract Jews in the hundreds of thousands. American Jewry will go out of its way to help such a struggling and courageous movement which may bring a new light to shine upon Zion and which would guarantee the survival of the State as a Jewish State and its people as a Jewish people.

Germany, War, and Post War

WE ARE AT WAR

May 24, 1942

We are at war. We, the United Nations. And we Jews all over the world, are part of this fight for Democracy.

Within the United Nations, the British Empire has been at war against the ruthless aggressor for now almost three years; Russia for a year; the United States for about six months; but we Jews—for now nine consecutive years.

This is why there will be a special Jewish problem in the post-war world. I admit that an economic crisis will prevail in the United States and the British Empire once this war is over; that much hardship will have to be endured by the smaller nations; but all this stands in no comparison to the tragedy which will befall millions of Jews in Europe.

The continent of Europe will be exhausted. Germany will have lost its second war within one generation. The German youth, educated to believe that the Jews were the cause for Germany's defeat in the first war and have been the reason for this Second World War, will react accordingly. There will be disappointment and bitterness in innumerable homes. Europe will have to put itself together, socially and economically. Who else will be considered guilty of that predicament than we Jews, the classical scapegoat.

All the other nations, even the smaller ones, now Hitler-occupied, will go home. Where will the European Jews go? To what kind of a home, after having been deprived of everything they possessed? Will they try and find out the names of millions of Nazis who have stolen their property and killed their children or parents in concentration camps and in ghettos, and sue them in court?

I do not think this is a solution. Having been at war with Hitler longer than the other nations, our casualties count higher than the others. Europe today has ten million Jews, and with exception of those in England and Russia and the inconsiderable groups of Switzerland and Sweden, these millions of European Jews live in ghettos, concentration camps and dungeons of the Gestapo. We, a nation of seventeen million people in the whole, have lost already nearly two million lives—the highest casualty list of any nation so far. Those who will sur-

188

vive in Europe—if there will be any—will not surpass the number of three millions, and even those will be economically broken and psychologically disabled. Where will they go?

It is in this connection that Palestine lends itself to become the only possible solution. We in America—the country which has always given its assistance to persecuted nations and suppressed minorities—must not cease to proclaim and demand Palestine as a Jewish commonwealth, whose immigration policy be controlled by the Jewish Agency only. In order to achieve this goal and to make Palestine a part of our new tomorrow, we Jews want to share officially in the burden and the responsibility of this war. Thousands of Jews are fighting today in the four continents, on the seven seas, and in the air all over the world. But we do this as Americans, as Englishmen, as Russians, as Dutchmen, Belgians, and so on. Palestine, however, is the Jewish National Home of today and the Jewish commonwealth of tomorrow. This is why we as a nation want to have the opportunity to fight for it under our own flag. Palestinian and stateless Jews have been waiting for months and years for the building of a Jewish army. It is the American public opinion that can help us in achieving this aim.

In a threefold way we are at war with the axis: as Jews against whom Hitler declared a war of extermination nine years ago; as lovers of Palestine, against which the axis wage a war of annihilation, and finally as Americans and citizens of the United States whose democratic way of life Hitler seeks to destroy. It is in this threefold attitude as Americans, as lovers of Zion, and as Jews in general, that we appeal to the public opinion of the American people. There will be no justice in the world of tomorrow unless the Jewish problem is solved once and for all. Let us see to it that the most homeless nation of the world may acquire their most cherished home on earth: Palestine. Let us together build a new world order, in which there will be no oppressor and no oppressed, no persecutor and no persecuted, but a world of free men and free nations.

WHY WE FIGHT

Undated (c. 1943)

I came to this country in August, 1940. For eight consecutive years I watched the growth of National Socialism in Germany. I was a rabbi in Berlin during all those years and studied carefully the literature and ideology of Hitler's movement. As a result of this and my experience, here is what I have to say.

National Socialism is not a political movement but a religion. In its ideological system of education and so-called philosophy it is definitely of pseudo-religious character. Being totalitarian in substance, it covers the lives of human beings from the cradle to the grave, beginning from kindergarten, through grammar and high schools, throughout universities, labor fronts and army service. Like every genuine religion it accompanies the life of man from the beginning to the end with "religious" symbols of its own: baptism formulas, kindergarten instruction, "religious" education in grammar and high schools, "religious" radio services and lectures in universities. All of them are based on National Socialistic principles and are presented in a "religious" framework.

This is the reason why Hitler's *Mein Kampf,* the swastika, and the naked sword could be offered as substitute for the Bible, the Christian Cross and church symbols. This is why the National Socialistic movement could establish a church of its own called German Christians, with the Minister Mueller, who is an old member of the party, as its head, and with Hitler's *Mein Kampf* as the basis of each of his sermons. This is why the hatred of National Socialism for church and synagogue is so deeply rooted in the minds of its leaders and their followers. After centuries of history in which three great religions, Judaism, Christianity and Islam, have dominated the scene, a fourth religion came into being which cannot go on and live as long as the other three exist. It is not a question of persecution in Germany, it is rather a question of extermination.

We are speaking to you under the sponsorship of the National Conference of Christians and Jews, and let me make a statement which may surprise you. If we, in Europe, had had a National Conference of Christians and Jews, the history of our generation might have been changed and you would not be in

190

uniforms today. But we did not have the atmosphere for the creation of such a movement. Each religious group lived its own life, confined to its own followers within the walls that separated each group from the others. Hitler knew and took advantage of this fact. He proceeded to exterminate his religious enemies along the lines of his policy of conquest outside the German borders. He started out by crushing us, the smallest minority of five hundred thousand Jews within a German population of eighty millions. This was easy and not much heroism was needed.

Meanwhile, the Catholic Church was assured that nothing would happen to it because National Socialism did not have anything against Christianity. So the Catholic Church stood aloof and watched our destruction. Not that Catholics agreed with the government, but being afraid of their own fate, they kept silent. Six months later the German press started a campaign of the wildest accusations against priests and nuns and their allegedly immoral lives. This was the psychological preparation of the German people for the attack to come. It came with clock-like precision: Catholic churches were closed, their treasuries confiscated, and Catholic youth groups disbanded.

During this time the Protestant Church also stood aloof and looked at the destruction of the Catholic Church. Not that Protestants agreed with Hitler, but they were assured that they, being German in substance, would not be touched if they did not interfere with state affairs. The peace for the Protestant Church lasted only a year. The Nazis found means and devices to crush them in another way. They established the Church of German Christians and required the rest of the Protestant Church to join that movement. The Protestant Church in its turn discussed the issue—some Protestants accepted the solution imposed upon them, but most of them did not. During that year the headlines of the German press were full of those discussions. Allegedly, the government was heartbroken that there was no unity in the Protestant Church. The discussions pro and con were given prominent space in the magazines. Finally, the government issued a statement that it was not in a position to see such tragic disunity within the majority denomination of the German people in times of emergency.

The attack came in the same ruthless way as it happened before to the Jews and to the Catholics. Churches were closed and taken over by the army. Protestant youth groups were disbanded. Protestant services had to be changed and held at a later hour on Sunday in order to allow the Hitler youth to attend Nazi meetings. The victory was complete. The three major religious groups which from a religious aspect were, and still are, the greatest danger to the "Brown Religion" of National Socialism, were officially brought to their knees.

If the three major faiths in Germany had stood together from the very outset, much of the tragedy that has befallen all three of us could have been avoided. Why am I telling you this? Because this war, in its deepest meaning, is a religious battle. The decision that has to be reached is whether the new church of the "Brown Religion" should dominate the world or whether the three older, genuine religions should remain in power. A religious answer is the only reply to a religious challenge. When this war is over, you, the American youth of our three faiths, will undoubtedly meet the German youth, thoroughly trained for the last ten years in "Brown Religion." Their background and knowledge of that religion of hatred is tremendous. We have to see to it that you who are going to meet them are imbued with the same thorough knowledge of the religious roots of our democratic American system. Only so will we be in a position to counteract their training of the last decade.

The National Conference of Christians and Jews is a great religious voice and, simultaneously, deeply American. From our aspect, we fight for this very principle—that the three major faiths of the world may live, each according to its own laws, in harmony and togetherness. Our enemy stands for one nation, one party, one fuehrer and one church. Here is the major issue of our struggle. Hitler is right: both ways of life cannot live in one and the same world. Only one can survive. It must be ours!

THE ROLE OF ORGANIZED RELIGION IN THE POST-WAR WORLD

Excerpt   January 1, 1943

The peace that comes at the end of this war must be a religious peace, led by organized religion. We therefore demand:

192

1. UNIVERSAL DEMOCRACY. The Bill of Rights of the American Constitution must be applied to all men. This will end all colonial empires and assert the equality of all individuals, all classes and all races.

2. INTERNATIONAL WORLD ORDER. We believe in the necessity of creating a Parliament of Nations or some other international organization which will adjust differences between nations, and to which countries should yield some of their national sovereignty.

3. GLOBAL DISARMAMENT. If such a Parliament of Nations will be built, disarmament could gradually be achieved by the supervision of an international police force. We know that for a certain number of years the United Nations will have to remain equipped with all the tools of war. This, however, should be a temporary measure only, covering the interlude between armistice and peace. The ultimate goal should be complete disarmament of the peoples of the world.

4. ECONOMIC AND SOCIAL JUSTICE. The natural resources of the world must be put at the disposal of all nations. The problem of unemployment, of economic insecurity, of child labor and other social evils will have to be solved through the agencies of that international organization of the governments of the world. This demand for social justice must lead to economic equality.

5. A WORLD COURT. We urge the institution of a World Court where nations, minority groups or individuals could plead their causes and receive justice.

6. ETHNIC AND CULTURAL PLURALISM. We believe that the rebuilding of a war-torn world can be based on freedom of minorities and smaller nations only. The right to live after their own conceptions, traditions and cultural development comes from God, and this right is therefore the inalienable possession of each nation or group, race or color, large or small, in Europe or in the United States. We demand, in definite terms, justice for the Negro and the solution of his problem in the United States.

7. A SOLUTION OF THE JEWISH PROBLEM. Last, but not least, we urge the United Nations to solve, with our cooperation, the most complicated problem of our age. This religious war was declared first against the Jewish people. We, a people

193

of seventeen million, have lost more than two million members in this war, although we are not fighting this war officially as a state. This is the highest percentage of casualties of any group of the United Nations in this war. We do not know yet how many will survive Hitler's hell in the jails, ghettos and concentration camps. We know, however, that at least four million Jews will be homeless after this war, in the deepest meaning of the word "homelessness." We ask organized religion all over the world to help us in the solution of this problem. This is not a Jewish problem—it is a world problem. If public opinion in the United States, especially within organized religion, will be strong in favor of rebuilding Palestine, we will save millions of lives, which otherwise may, by Divine miracle, survive Hitler's war, but will not, without human intervention, survive the victory of the United Nations.

BERLIN—CITY OF DECISION FOR WAR OR PEACE

Excerpt   1959

Berlin symbolizes the East-West conflict. You go down to the street which leads to the Brandenburger Tor, and you see the sign, "You are now leaving the British Sector," and you understand exactly what is happening. All the discussions in Geneva and those between Khrushchev and Eisenhower come into focus. This divided city with the hostile frontier is a symbol of the deep-seated conflict in our generation between East and West.

Berlin is the city of decision, and the decision is along three lines, the way I see it. Firstly, you have read in recent weeks and months many statements in the American press that everyone wants the reunification of the two parts of Germany. *There is no truth to it.* The Russians surely do not want reunification of the whole country, because they do not want to lose the Eastern part which is a Communist State. They know that by reunification, the Communist Party will get lost in the shuffle. Even more fascinating is the fact that Bonn does not want it either. Actually, the only ones who really want unification are the Americans and the French, but particularly our State Department. Bonn is using the slogan of unification, but the people in the political life of Germany today who know the score say that no one is going to sacrifice himself for reunification. No one actually wants it too badly. The simple reason is that the coming in of East Germany to the Western Republic would, in the case of unified elections, mean the upset of the apple-cart of the balance of power between the Reichspartei of Adenauer and the Social Democratic Party. No one knows how the East Germans are going to vote.

What each one of the two sides does want is Berlin. That is ten times more important than unification. To the West, to the Republic, which has Bonn as a temporary capital, the going back to Berlin of the German Parliament would be a symbol that the West is here, and that West Germany means Germany as a whole, once again.

To the East, to the Communist Regime, which has a continuous territory from Russia to Poland, to Breslau, to East Germany, and to Berlin—Berlin would be a symbol that they are there to stay. Whoever possesses Berlin possesses Germany in the eyes of millions of Germans, and in the eyes of the whole world. Therefore, the whole unification debate is a smoke screen.

RECONCILIATION BETWEEN MAN AND MAN

October 11, 1959
Excerpt of a broadcast on Voice of America for the Day of Atonement

Was deshalb die Versoehnung zwischen dem Deutschen Volk und Gott anbetrifft, muss das Deutsche Volk heute selber wissen, wie am besten dieses Ziel zu erreichen ist. Aber bezueglich der Versoehnung zwischen Mensch und Mensch— was in diesem Falle bedeuten muss die Versoehnung zwischen dem Deutschen und dem Juedischen Volk—muss man offen und ohne Vorbehalt sprechen. An diesem heiligsten Abend unseres Jahres sage ich, dass es nie zu einer Versoehnung zwischen Deutschen und Juden kommen wird, es sei denn, in

195

den Worten unserer Weisen, dass das Deutsche Volk Abbitte leistet und uns durch Taten der Versoehnung von seinem guten Willen ueberzeugt.

Das Deutschland der Nachkriegszeit hat bereits einige Schritte in dieser Richtung unternommen. Ich habe es besonders auf meinem letzten Besuch im Sommer in der Stadt Berlin empfunden. Aber was man von Berlin sagen kann, gilt noch nicht fuer die Deutsche Republik, wo es noch starke reaktionaere Kraefte gibt, die noch immer von der Pracht des nationalsozialistischen Deutschlands traeumen. Wir hoffen sehr, dass die guten, anstaendigen und progressiven Kraefte, die es heute wieder in West Deutschland gibt, in diesem gewaltigen Ringen um die deutsche Seele die Oberhand gewinnen werden. Nur dann wird es zu einer wahren Versoehnung kommen koennen.

* * *

Therefore regarding the reconciliation between the German People and God, the Germans themselves have to know how to reach this goal. But regarding the reconciliation between Man and Man—which in this case is synonymous with a reconciliation between the German and the Jewish peoples—one has to speak openly and without reservations. On this the holiest night of our year, I say: it will never come to a reconciliation between Germans and Jews until the German people ask forgiveness and convince us by *deeds* of repentance of their inner sincerity.

Postwar Germany has already taken certain steps in this direction. I felt this strongly during my last visit to Berlin this summer. But what is true of Berlin is not necessarily true of the German Republic, where strong reactionary forces are still virulent and are still dreaming of the splendor of National-Socialist Germany. We fervently hope that the good, decent, and progressive forces existing today again in West Germany will prevail in this momentous contest for the German soul. Then and then alone, a true reconciliation could be forthcoming.

196

THE STATUTE OF LIMITATIONS FOR
NAZI WAR CRIMES

Excerpt   March 11, 1965

For the last twenty years the West German Government has tried desperately to change Germany's image in the eyes of the world. The reparations agreements, which it faithfully carried out, and the economic and military aid, which it generously extended to Israel, were part and parcel of a carefully planned endeavor to establish the "new" Germany as an entity separate and distinct from the "old" Germany of the Nazi period.

Yet, throughout these two decades, there has been evidence of a continuous line of appeasement either to public opinion within or to political pressures without: Germany refused to establish diplomatic relations with Israel—an act which would have been the very symbol of its regeneration—because of Arab pressure; it did not act, in spite of many promises, on the recalling of German scientists from Cairo for fear of offending Nasser; to this day, it could not see its way clear to extend the Statute of Limitations, because of the organized hostility of right-wing and former Nazi groups who are determined to lower the curtain of history upon the greatest crime of genocide ever committed in human history; and now, to round out the picture, Bonn has decided to break its word and discontinue its aid to Israel because of Nasser's threat to recognize East Germany. Thus the line of appeasement was woven into the tapestry of the "new" Germany, amounting again and again to a policy of surrender to blackmail—and this to such a point that even the support it did render to Israel was kept top secret from the Germans at home and the world abroad.

The Jewish Community of the United States—and for that matter the Jewish Communities all over the free world—has no intention of taking this dangerous development lying down. We voice our sense of shock that Germany, a country which under Hitler slaughtered one-third of our people, should now, so callously by its action, pave the way for the immunity of Nazi criminals, on the one hand, and for the destruction of the surviving remnants, at the hand of Arab aggressors, on the other. The halting of aid to Israel, coupled with the continued employment of West German scientists in the production of missiles for Cairo, places West Germany in a role of actually encouraging Nasser in his plans to destroy Israel, and thus finish the job which Hitler began. We stand aghast at the spectacle of Nasser succeeding in coercing West Germany in discontinuing aid to Israel for defense against aggression by Egypt— a country which is being deluged by a steady stream of Soviet armaments. All these actions of the Bonn Government are a blot on the conscience of the "new" Germany, and its government and people should bow their heads in shame at these acts of moral and legal bankruptcy.

We will not rest and will not pause until Germany undertakes in repentance the following acts of atonement: the establishment of diplomatic relations with Israel; the recalling of the German scientists from Cairo; the extension of the Statute of Limitations; and the resumption of aid to Israel. We will mobilize all forces, Jewish and non-Jewish in this country, and all men of good will wherever they are, to bring about the victory of morality over expediency, of commitment against surrender, and of moral responsibility against political blackmail. Let us hope that Bonn will see the light before it is too late.

BONN, ARABS, AND THE STATE DEPARTMENT

From *The American Zionist,* Vol. LV, No. 6   (March-April 1965)

The State of Israel is now facing the most critical period since the days of the Suez Campaign in 1956. Three major factors are involved in the present crisis which pose the gravest threat to Israel's security. These are: the position of the Bonn Government, the renewed outbreaks of Arab intransigence, and the stand of our own State Department.

It is the State of Israel more than any other nation—ironic as it may sound—that has helped Germany revise her image in the eyes of the civilized world. The reparations payments agreed to by Israel, the voluntary acceptance by Israeli kibbutzim of hundreds of young Germans who left their country to help in the pioneering labors of Israel, the visits by German professors and political figures for lectures at Israel's highest institutions of learning, the existence of the Israeli Purchasing Mission in Cologne enjoying quasi-diplomatic status—these and numerous other actions on the part of Israel contributed in a decisive manner to helping Germany rehabilitate herself in the eyes of humanity.

Viewed against this background, Germany's change of heart will be judged by the American Jewish community and humanity as a whole by Germany's action in the following four vital spheres: the extension of the Statute of Limitations against Nazi war criminals; the establishment of diplomatic relations with Israel; the recall of German scientists employed in the production of missiles and rockets in Egypt; the continuation of military aid to Israel to help the surviving remnants of the six millions of our people, massacred by a German Government a quarter of a century ago, to live in security and freedom within the boundaries of an independent State.

The recent steps undertaken by Bonn for the extension of the Statute of Limitations and its offer to Israel for the establishment of diplomatic relations are cause for satisfaction. While long overdue, they may open a new chapter in Germany's relationship with Israel, as well as with the Jewish People. We look to the German government now to go all the way toward solving the remaining two problems which cry out for redress, namely, the resumption of military aid to the Jewish State and the recall of the German scientists from Cairo.

These problems have assumed a transcendent urgency in the perilous situation which Israel now faces because of the dire threats of the Arabs and the growing influx of Soviet arms.

Nasser's blueprint for Israel's destruction, which he has publicly unfolded in recent weeks, provides for the siphoning of the headwaters of the Jordan in Lebanon and in Syria, to deprive Israel of its rightful share of vitally needed water. This plan is designed to maneuver Israel into making the first military move, in defense of its very life. In the eyes of the world Israel would then be branded as the aggressor and Nasser would assume the posture of the defender. Nasser also fully counts upon Soviet Russia's backing for his devious scheme.

This demoniac plan is fraught with the danger of war in

199

the Middle East, aggravated by the uncertainty of action by our own Government to avert such a catastrophe. Information from reliable sources indicates that U. S. Ambassador Averell Harriman's mission to Israel was primarily aimed at pressuring Israel to refrain from making any move against the diversion of the water sources by the Arabs. This is a policy of dubious morality.

We therefore appeal to our State Department to desist from this immoral policy. At the same time we address a serious plea to the president of the United States to take a personal hand in solving this problem by using the good offices of the American Government to persuade the Arabs not to go through with the water diversion plan, an undertaking of sheer spite and hostility which would not yield the slightest benefit to their own countries and their own populations.

We have the utmost faith in the great abilities and good will of President Johnson to exert all his powers to prevent a conflagration in the Middle East which in turn may ignite the spark of a third world war.

We rely upon the sense of fairness of President Johnson to counterbalance the massive arms shipments of the Soviet Union to Egypt and Iraq through the sale or grant to Israel of military equipment, to prevent a dangerous imbalance in the Middle East. The supply of weapons, particularly heavy armaments, which Nasser is receiving from the Soviet Union is making inadequate the defensive United States Hawk missiles and the tanks which Israel received hitherto from Germany. Thus, in terms of armaments which are essential to defend a new and small country from annihilation, Israel is rapidly losing out. The new developments relating to Germany and the Middle East are a challenge to the United States to change its policy by fully equipping Israel with the military means required for its defense.

In this connection, a serious warning must be sounded against a new tactic of anti-Israel propaganda launched by Arab agents in this country. Taking the cue from a statement by President Nasser made last week, the newest line of Arab propaganda opposes the maintenance of a military balance in the Middle East on the ground that Israel with a population numbering only two and a half million is not entitled to equal arms, because it is no match for its Arab neighbors with a combined population of one hundred million. Israel would thus have to rely on the mercy of Nasser and other Arab rulers, who day in and day out publicly avow their intention of destroying the little state. It is significant that the newest Arab propaganda line was launched in the same week when Nasser, in a public address before a cheering crowd in Cairo on March 8, warned: "We shall not enter Palestine on a path of sand and flowers; we shall enter Palestine on a path of blood."

The Israel Government has not only time and again extended the hand of peace to Arab neighbors, but also has warmly endorsed proposals for the disarmament of the entire Middle East. It seeks an arms balance in the Middle East only to deter aggression against its sovereignty and its territorial integrity.

WHITHER GERMANY?

From *World Jewry, II*, 10 (March/April 1967)

My visit to Germany in January differed in character from my previous trips. Two years ago, I went on the invitation of the German Government, and a year ago on that of the City of Berlin. This time, it was at the request of the *Keren Hayesod* (United Israel Appeal) which conducts a yearly campaign among Jews still living in Germany. The thirty thousand Jews in the German Federal Republic have been raising an average of half-a-million dollars a year for Israel, and this year they will in all probability contribute six-to-seven million dollars to the Jewish State. Compared with British or American Jewish Communities, they are doing, per capita, better than most of us in affluent societies.

Needless to say, I took advantage of my mission to make contacts with representatives of the government, the church and the press, in order to learn of their reaction (a) to the Chancellorship of Dr. Kurt Kiesinger, and, (b) to the neo-Nazi NPD.

As far as Dr. Kiesinger is concerned, the problem is more a matter of psychology than of actual background. I spoke to people who have known him well for many decades, including the saintly Reverend Heinrich Grueber, who rescued hundreds of Jews at the risk of his life, was thrown into a concentration camp, and almost beaten to death, and they all testified that during those bitter days of Nazi persecution, there was a handful of nominal Nazis who were extremely helpful in rescue work and that Dr. Kiesinger was one of them. The problem, therefore, is not his actual background and the things he did. The damage is psychological, because it suggests Jewish approval of his membership in the Nazi party. People, even in Germany, know little of his connection with rescue work, but they do know that he was a member of the Nazi party. This cannot be wished away, either by his anti-Nazi attitude after the war or even by his positive involvement in the establishment of diplomatic relations with Israel. It remains true what Guenter Grass, probably Germany's most prominent novelist, said in a letter to Kiesinger, before the latter's appointment to the highest office in the land:

> What arguments will the young people have against the National Democratic Party (NPD)...if you, with your past record, accept the post of Federal Chancellor? How can we properly honour the memories of the tortured and murdered resistance fighters, and those killed at Auschwitz and Treblinka, when you, the Nazi-fellow traveler of yesterday, lay down the political line of today? You will have the responsibility; we shall have to bear the results and the shame.

In this letter, Guenter Grass gave expression to the psychological damage created by Kiesinger's appointment—and the damage is serious.

But, even so, analyzed from a Jewish viewpoint, Dr. Kiesinger is not a problem. Because of the stigma attached to him, he has leaned backwards in manifestations of friendship to the Jewish community in general and to Israel in particular. What does constitute a problem, and will occupy us for quite some time, is the emergence of the neo-Nazi party called the NPD. The danger consists, first, in the fact that a large part of its membership comes from actual Nazi ranks and from two previously dissolved neo-Nazi parties and, secondly, from the vaguely, but cleverly drawn-up program, with many heterogeneous points calculated to impress large segments of the nation with one or another part of the manifesto. When the NPD, for instance, speaks of the honor of the German women that has to be re-established in German society—millions of conservative people who are deeply unhappy about the low level of their popular sex magazines can only applaud; when the NPD makes the point that twenty years of colonialism and subjugation to the United States are enough—millions of Germans who are by now quite anti-American will secretly say "Bravo"; when it proclaims that there must be an end to the war crimes' trials because they undermine the essence of German nationhood—all Nazi and pro-Nazi elements will accept it with utter joy; and when the NPD shouts from the rooftops that the Jews and Israel are bleeding Germany to death through the payments of billions of dollars in restitution—the sentiment is popular in Germany.

Fortunately for us, the situation is different today from what it was before Hitler came to power. In discussing this matter with representatives of the government, the church and the press, I came away convinced that they are deeply concerned with the new development, watch it diligently, and are determined to eradicate this evil before it takes root in larger segments of the nation. The democratic forces during the advent of Hitler were weak and disorganized, whereas today they are in much better shape. The trade unions and the churches have already undertaken a counter-offensive and so has the majority of the press. Therefore, it is incumbent upon the leaders of Germany today not to be satisfied with defending the status quo against the neo-Nazi movement, but to go over to the offensive and deal with them from strength.

The danger at the moment is not only the NPD, but the nationalistic voices which are allegedly in opposition to the NPD. The report I heard in Germany, over and over again, is that the conservatives are attempting to defeat the NPD "by passing them on the right," meaning that they are using the same nationalistic slogans and repeating the same demands without associating themselves with the NPD. In an offensive *for* democracy this facet too must be taken into consideration. There is a difference between giving the younger generation a national consciousness—which is normal all over the world—

and fostering nationalism as a philosophy of life which, in German history, has always had the overtones of militarism, narrowness, and hatred for everything that is not purely German. But, again, if the democratic forces really mean what they say, this danger, too, could be overcome. The idea of a United States of Europe and of the exciting values of the democratic way of life could easily fill the vacuum.

For the first time during all my visits to Germany in the post-war period, I came away with a feeling that there exists today in the West German Republic the greatest potential danger; yet I also left with a feeling of more hopefulness that the danger can be overcome.

DID THE GERMAN NATION KNEEL IN PENANCE?

Excerpt of a sermon delivered in Berlin   January 15, 1971

This evening, with its historic ramifications and stirring emotion, can only be understood if one evaluates it under the aspect of three Hebrew words, each one of them expressing an ingredient of our people's time-honored tradition.

The first word is *kaddish.* We remember tonight all those who lost their lives during the Holocaust—from the six million in Europe to the sixty thousand in Berlin; those who were removed to the concentration camps and returned in the form of small urns containing their ashes over which we, the last rabbis of the city, had to recite the Kaddish; and those who did not return at all and who are buried in unmarked graves of the trenches of Dachau and Auschwitz. We remember tonight all those in the top leadership of German Jewry who, selflessly and dedicatedly, fought the battle of rescue, until they themselves became the victims of the evil forces of Nazism. May their souls find eternal rest in the shelter of God's love.

The second word is *todah,* meaning "thanks," or even better, *Mizmor Todah,* a "Hymn of Thanksgiving," which is the phrase used in the Book of Psalms. We are obliged tonight to express our deepest gratitude to Dr. Hans Erich Fabian, the first president of the post-war Jewish Community, and to Mr. Heinz Galinski, the current president, and to their associates

204

for the incredible achievement of the last quarter century. When the Second World War was over, there was literally nothing left of the once great and noble Berlin Jewish Community. They had to start from scratch and to create out of nothing. What they have accomplished in these short twenty-five years is utterly astonishing: the four functioning synagogues, the Old Folks' Homes, the apartment houses for Senior Citizens, the Religious School, the Jewish Kindergarten—the best in the city and the envy of other religious denominations—the rich cultural activities in art, music, literature, exhibitions and lectures on a remarkably high intellectual level; the radio and television programs covering the Jewish holidays and Jewish affairs generally; the fully functioning departments of the *Gemeinde* Administration, providing—among other things—a full Jewish program for the young generation on different age levels, and completing the whole circle even with a new cemetery owned and operated by the *Gemeinde*—all this is a spectacular accomplishment within one generation, and is one of the stirring sagas in the battle for Jewish survival.

The last word is *shehecheyanu*. This is not the time to enter into the debate whether Jews should or should not live in Germany. For many of us living outside, it may often be difficult to comprehend the psychology of a Jew living in Germany today. But one has to start from facts. Jews do live in Germany in 1970, and a small Jewish Community will, undoubtedly, be here for years and possibly decades to come. This being the case, one has to give them a Jewish frame of reference, attach them to the mainstream of Jewish life, and connect them as deeply as possible with the romance of the Jewish State.

Our generation has gone through the greatest catastrophe in Jewish life, but it has also emerged as the most remarkable generation in Jewish history. For the very same generation of Dachau and Auschwitz somehow succeeded in raising itself out of the ashes, gather its pitiful remnants, re-establish communities all over Europe, battle for Jewish independence, create the State of Israel and bring the Jewish People into the membership of the United Nations—all this within twenty-five years following the Second World War. It is, in other words, a generation that went from deepest humiliation to the highest ecstasy, from utter degradation to the loftiest heights, from tragedy to triumph, and from Auschwitz to Jerusalem within two–and–a–half decades. The emergence of this small Jewish Community in Germany has to be seen in this light in order to be fully understood. If the kneeling of the chancellor before a Jewish Memorial Monument in the Warsaw Ghetto is symbolic of the kneeling of the German nation in its quest for forgiveness, then I would not like to see Hitler's will accomplished beyond his grave—by making Germany *Judenrein.* If Germany is interested in becoming a permanent member of the Western World, it has to create an atmosphere and conditions that make Jewish life possible for those who want to stay and live here.

It is in this spirit—in the light of rebuilding Jewish communities all over Europe, under the aspect of the great miracles of Jewish survival and the building of the Jewish State, on this historic occasion, in this City of Berlin—we utter the ancient benediction praising God "who has kept us alive, sustained us, and permitted us to celebrate this joyous event."

Essays, 1940-1952

HOW JEWS LIVE IN GERMANY TODAY

From *ORT Economic Bulletin,* I:4-5 (July - October, 1940)

The continued survival of thousands of Jews in Germany cannot be denoted by the term "life." For this word implies certain intellectual and spiritual factors, called imponderables, which are wholly lacking within German Jewry today. A life led by a community without the least trace of freedom on the one hand, and without a chance to be moulded by music, plastic art, the theatre, the movie, and so on, hardly deserves to be called life. One cannot even speak of the "being" of these people, for this, considered in its human aspects, requires at least a framework of civilization—I am speaking here not of culture, but of civilization pure and simple—which grants men the right to share in the most common things of being. The taking away of telephones and radios; the ban on visiting cafés, movies, parks, on the practice of any sport, on going out after nine o'clock in the evening; the order to shop only between four and five o'clock in the afternoon—all this signifies the exclusion from the most elementary civilization, which lends added emphasis to the exclusion from culture as we represented it above.

The survival of Jews in Germany can only be described by the word "existence" in its barest sense, namely an existence to which a whole community is hounded and driven without means and without a chance to work, without any interest in today or hope for tomorrow. That after these seven years there is still a German Jewry at all to-day, that at its head stand men with unflinching determination and that, in spite of everything, there still are dignified divine services and, within modest limits, successful cultural arrangements, will one day form a very heroic chapter in the history of the Jewish people.

This is how they exist: with nostalgia for yesterday and with fear of tomorrow, in a religiously tinged mood, without work to fill out their empty days, waiting for letters which often do not come, lonely and growing ever more isolated, without hope. It is a sad carpe diem existence with a completely inverted import. It means here: enjoy the day as it is; it is always better than the next day.

II

So it was already when the war began: there were and are

no Jewish stores and no Jewish manufacturers. There are only a limited number of licensed Jewish physicians, known as sick-attendants (*Krankenbehandler*), distinguished by a large blue sign with a yellow Magen David on the door, and with a prescribed seal on every prescription: "Licensed exclusively for the treatment of Jews." The number of these doctors, who are always busy, has even somewhat increased in the course of the war, when new licenses were again granted to previously excluded physicians. There were and are also a limited number of lawyers, called solicitors (*Konsulenten*), who are authorized to represent only Jews in court. Aryan lawyers are forbidden to appear in court for Jews. There are furthermore an insignificant number in liberal callings, for example, sport instructors, which, however, have for some weeks now been absolutely forbidden to practice their calling. Finally, there is a numerically large but relatively small class of Jews who work for Jewish organizations, communities, schools, the bureaus of the *Reichsvertretung der Juden in Deutschland* (National Organization of Jews in Germany), the *Hilfsverein,* and the Palestine Agency. A large percentage of the employees of all these organizations which, under the leadership of the *Reichsvertretung,* were rigidly centralized by order of the German authorities have, during the last few months, been given notice and discharged. All who were not positively and absolutely needed, had to leave their posts—a measure taken by the German authorities partly for reasons of economy and partly for reasons that I shall discuss more fully.

The great mass of German Jewry is thus divided into those who had sufficient savings to be able to live on them even now after the deduction of all the taxes levied on Jews, and those who live on relief. As regards the first—and naturally small and dwindling—class, it is for the most part subject to the "security regulation"; that is, aside from the fact that the emigration tax is attached, they are permitted to withdraw from the bank only a small part of their money monthly. The amount was fixed in recent months at about 200 RM (*Reichsmark*) for single persons, and about 500 RM for families. For all larger expenditures, for example, medical care, special applications must be submitted to the Finance Office, which then, after a searching investigation, releases the required sum at the bank concerned. As for the second and by far larger class of relief recipients, the picture varies in the various cities of Germany, and has also changed materially during the war. In Berlin—to single out this example—there exists an agreement between the municipality and the Jewish Welfare Board whereby the city itself investigates all cases and gives its own aid, while the Jewish Welfare Board has to help only those cases which are rejected by the Municipal Welfare Department. The dole is very slight in the case of both the city of Berlin and the Jewish Welfare Board. Fortunately, the Jewish community, at least in the case of single, non-recurring subsidies (such as aid for household needs, rent allowances, and grants for vocational retraining, and emigration), as well as in assisting the respectable poor who are ashamed to ask for help, is allowed a freer hand. In addition, a large number of Jewish soup-kitchens operate in all sections of the city, in which every one, after investigation by the proper welfare district, may get one warm meal a day, free or for a few pennies—upon delivery of the appropriate food stamps—and from which, too, warm food is sent to the homes of sick or aged persons. By order of the German authorities, extremely high taxes and emigration imposts must be paid not only to the city, but also to the Jewish community. Compulsory winter relief contributions and perennial house-to-house collections are conducted each week by volunteer helpers under a different slogan ("For Feeding and Clothing," "For the Aging and the Ailing," etc.), and every one contributes in a truly self-sacrificing manner according to his ability. Owing to all this, the Jewish charitable organizations are still able to carry on and to save a large number of our most pitiable persons from total collapse.

Such was the picture until the war and in part also during the war. But only in part. For very soon after the outbreak of the war, the Labor Office began, in ever increasing measure, to deprive relief recipients of relief and to send them to any job instead—in the winter mostly to shovel coal or snow, for which they were paid by the hour according to the rates customary in Germany. At first this was done without general compulsion and effective organization, but one could surmise where it would lead to. The winter was a severe one; the losses at the front could be inferred from the crepe worn by gentile women and from the death notices permitted in the newspapers; more and more men were called to the colors, and the labor shortage grew ever greater. Our people, however, had no work; one saw them on the streets and in the stores; the sentiment of the press gave ground for fear of an impending measure against the "enemies from within."

The evacuation of the Jews from Stettin, which created a panic among the Jews of Germany, was taken to be the beginning of such a measure. [*Note: This was the first deportation of an entire Jewish community. The Jews of Stettin were taken to Lublin early in 1940 as a trial balloon by the Nazis to see if there would be a world protest. There was none. Editors*] In order to give the threatening calamity a somewhat bearable direction, the *Reichsvertretung*—of its own accord—worked out a plan whereby the Jews might again be drawn into certain types of work; one thus forestalled, so to speak, in order to steal the wind from the sails and thereby avert the worst. A miracle occurred: the plan was approved by the Labor Office and the *Reichsvertretung* was authorized at first to investigate thirteen thousand persons and send them to the Labor Office. The Jewish communities thereupon established their own investigation and registration bureaus from which men and women were sent to the municipal labor offices. At first this was obligatory only on relief recipients, that is to say, everyone up to the age of sixty had to work unless it was attested by a Jewish medical attendant and certified by a trusted Aryan physician of the Labor Office that the person in question was unable to work. Of those still living on their own means only those had to work whom the Jewish community itself, after a careful investigation of individual cases, sent to the Labor Office—to wit, men up to fifty-five years and women up to forty-five. Of course, the community had to send as many people as possible in order to fill the prescribed quota.

Suddenly, however, the investigation and registration of prospective workers was taken out of the hands of the Jewish community, and the city itself, with the aid of the *Volkskartei* (Census of the German People) which includes the Jews, issued the summonses to our Jewish men and women to report at the Labor Office. As a result, what at first was semivoluntary, has developed into general forced labor which per-

211

mits only few exemptions, namely, mothers with small children, or children who have very old parents to support, as well as the seriously ill, the sick-attendants, and the law solicitors. All others—insofar as they do not hold permanent positions with a Jewish organization—and this also explains the above mentioned compulsory notices of dismissal—are subject to forced labor, including even children from sixteen years on, if they no longer attend school. At first there were 13,000 Jews in the labor service, next there were 25,000, which presently grew to 33,000, while to-day there are 50,000. If one remembers that the total number of Jews in Germany proper is 160,000, half of whom are more than fifty-five years old, it is evident that this number includes nearly all able-bodied Jews.

What does this work consist of? It must be divided into two categories; viz., (1) the work of women, who for the most part work in factories like Siemens and the AEG (General Electric Company), where already hundreds of Jewish women are employed day and night in solid groups in a department of their own and receiving comparatively decent treatment; (2) the work of men, so-called heaviest labor (*Schwerstarbeit*), consisting of hauling iron, laying railroad tracks, underground construction, logging, as well as railroad and road construction work. Naturally, many of our people cannot endure such work. As a rule, in every gang of laborers there are only about three who can really perform the work and who then shoulder the entire burden. The number of accidents is unfortunately quite large, since, owing to the inexperience of these men, sprains and hemorrhages occur almost daily. Some of the firms insist on an outer distinguishing badge for Jews; thus one may encounter in the streets of Berlin's suburbs gangs of laborers with yellow and lilac armbands. The use of the canteens, as well as of the light railways leading to the places of work, is naturally forbidden to Jews. The treatment varies according to the whim of the Aryan foreman who supervises each gang. This absorption of the Jews into certain labor-processes, it must be acknowledged here, was wholly accomplished by the Municipal Labor Office, and that, too, over the outspoken opposition of Party circles, who inveighed bitterly against it in the columns of the SS paper, *Das Schwarze Corps*. However, the labor shortage in Germany is so acute that one cannot spare these 50,000 men.

As for us, it must be stated in this connection that, however humiliating the conditions are and however hard to bear the work, this wartime development nevertheless spells a certain advantage for the Jews of Germany collectively and for many of them individually. To the Jews collectively it means perhaps a momentary release from the fear of a decisive war measure against them, while for many individuals it is the first opportunity in years to work, to be able once more to fill out the long hours of the day with something and—to earn something; for the *Reichsvertretung* has brought it about that Jewish workers are paid the same scale as the Aryan. Heavy laborers receive, accordingly, seventy-two pfennigs an hour, which means that, after all deductions, their net monthly earnings amount to about 100 to 120 RM and that is already a large sum for many of them. However, food constitutes a serious problem, for the increased food ration cards which are issued to heavy laborers, and which at first were granted to some Jewish workers, have since been taken away from nearly all Jewish heavy laborers.

III

This article must not close without some reference to the positive phases which, despite the enormous gravity of the times, are being preserved in Germany. There is the *hachshara* (training) work of the Palestine Office, embracing approximately twelve hundred persons, who are being trained at various *hachshara* points in Germany, and who are waiting for their emigration to Palestine; then there are the vocational retraining camps of the *Reichsvertretung* with its important center at Bielefeld; then again the vocational retraining courses of the Jewish communities, where persons of all callings are taught different, mostly manual, trades. In this connection special attention must be called to the importance of the ORT school, which is admirably conducted. There some two hundred students are instructed in highly skilled mechanical trades, such as electro mechanics, optical mechanics and so on, in order to render them welcome immigrants in every place in the world. Together with the Jewish communities, ORT is just now making renewed efforts toward a more intensive cultural endeavor on behalf of its students.

All in all, this life is like a last meal out of the substance which German Jewry once so deservedly possessed. Things cannot long go on like this. For this reason, thousands of Jews are waiting and hoping that out of this *existence* there will again come *being,* and out of being, *life.*

MINISTRY UNDER STRESS:

A Rabbi's recollections of Nazi Berlin, *1935-1940*

From *Gegenwart im Rückblick,* (1970)

It was a strange life we led, those last years in Germany: a very poor life in many ways, poor in material blessings, restricted in all activities other than Jewish, deprived of basic rights and freedoms—a life of fear and trepidation, surrounded by a terror that grew more intense every day. And yet, there was a redeeming feature: we lived a fox-hole existence, and like among soldiers in the trenches there arose in us a feeling of mutual responsibility as it had never existed within German Jewry before this time. Nourished by an ever deepening Jewish consciousness, human relations became warmer, friendships deeper, and our impoverished lives richer.

Now that the events of those years have become statistics, and millions of Jews have been reduced to numbers on an arithmetic table, neatly dividing those who got out from those who did not, we are callously getting used to thinking of them as clear-cut cases, faits accomplis. We are even listening with interested detachment to some brilliant analysts who, from the safety of their couches or their lecterns, prove with faultless logic that those who were caught, regrettable as it was, had actually behaved like a flock of sheep, trotting willingly to their slaughter, instead of putting up a fight.

How easy it is to analyze, and how shallow the analysis! True, the Jews of Berlin and Frankfurt, and even those of Paris and Amsterdam, did not have the opportunity to fight like the heroic defenders of the Warsaw Ghetto. But then they—or rather we—were not in a ghetto and were besieged in a different manner, in a hundred different manners, and therefore we fought back in a hundred different manners. One thing is sure:

fight back we did, every day, every night, in any way possible to us, deliberately and defiantly, and any report to the contrary is a distortion of facts and a posthumous desecration of those who perished.

Until well into 1942, when the war engulfed a large part of the world, and all communication was cut off, the main target of our battle for survival was *emigration.*

In view of the constantly repeated question in America— "How did you get out?"—it might bear restating that the Free World did not realize then and likes to forget even now: until Hitler embarked on his program of total annihilation—the Final Solution as the documents call it—the Nazis were quite often willing to let Jews leave, in fact they wanted us to go. They were very much interested in our possessions which the emigrants had to leave behind, but otherwise they wanted to get rid of as many of us as possible in this "lucrative," "inexpensive," and "expedient" manner.

That this procedure was in itself criminal, unethical, and barbaric goes without saying, but is in this connection irrelevant. True, at first we, the trapped ones, waited for an outcry of protest from the world around us. We hoped the great nations of the Western World would at least try, through reprisals or blockades, through threats or diplomatic negotiations, to stop Hitler's inhuman program of expulsion. When this did not happen we expected they would choose the only remaining alternative, namely: to open the gates of their countries to our people.

It was the ironic tragedy of that period that this simple logic did not occur to the free, rich, and powerful nations of the world. Now that the question of "guilt" is being raised, in courts of law and on the stage of the modern theatre, and accusing fingers are pointed at this or that head of state or at the great international agencies of law and religion, it is important to remember that there is hardly a government, secular or ecclesiastic, that would be entitled to throw the proverbial first stone.

The struggle for a visa to a foreign country, any country, regardless what kind or how far away it was ("how far from what?" we used to ask as a joke), became the main preoccupation of every single Jew and of our Jewish organizations.

Sometimes there were flurries of hope: Bolivia is opening up! Or: San Domingo is selling visas against a guarantee of $1000 to $2000 apiece. Rumors spread like wildfire, and our people would leap on any opportunity that offered itself if it promised escape from Germany.

My study used to look like a travel office in those years. Many foreign consulates requested character references given by a clergyman before they would consider issuing a visa, so my visiting hours, which I held every afternoon at my home, were largely taken up by throngs of people in need of such a letter of recommendation. Sometimes there were so many that the living room would not hold them, they spilled over into the hall, on the stairs, or even all the way down the street to the corner, waiting for their interview after which I would give them the required reference—a formality at best and often a futile effort because in many cases the rumor was false and there were no visas, or so few that only those applicants waiting virtually on the doorsteps of the consulate had a chance.

However slight the hope, Ruth and I spent many of our afternoons taking down "case histories" and writing "to-whom-it-may concern" letters. We could not take this job lightly because in many cases we had to recommend families for financial help, either out of private or out of community funds, not to speak of the special attention we had to give those who were applying for emigration to Palestine, be it for one of those precious, almost unobtainable regular quota visas, or for *aliyah bet,* the so-called illegal aliyah, to which only the strongest, youngest and most idealistic applicants could be admitted—another, and a truly heroic, chapter in our fight for survival.

Never before or since have I felt that so many lives have touched mine as in those years, during these afternoons that stretched into evenings and even into nights. I emphasize this point because so many American students of the Jewish scene in Germany have criticized the impersonal character of its rabbinate. The difference, I believe, lies not so much in the ministry, as in the structure of the community.

The Jewish Community of Berlin (*Jüdische Gemeinde*) owned and operated all synagogues of all denominations except those of the ultra-Orthodox and separatist *Adass Israel.*

216

Each one of us was therefore not the rabbi of a specific temple but the rabbi of the entire Jewish Community. In a congregation of 170,000 members [1925], as it were, the relationship between rabbi and congregants differed in many ways from the personal, pastoral relationship we find in the smaller closely knit congregations in the United States. In the large metropolis of Berlin over which the thousands of member families were spread, the rabbi could not possibly attempt to visit all the sick or even call on the mourners after each funeral, unless they were personal friends.

The rabbi received his *Turnus*—a schedule indicating time and place of the worship services he was to conduct—at the beginning of each month from the Central Office of the Community. I preached each Friday night and each Shabbat morning at a different temple, in the East–West–North–and–South sections of the city. The Central Office also processed and authorized each wedding and funeral for which the rabbi was requested; they paid his salary, and he was responsible only to them.

In addition to these functions and to a certain amount of teaching at public and at Jewish schools, a rabbi could—and was expected to—devote his time to studying and writing, and his time was his own. His office was in his home, and the Jewish press carried weekly notices as to when and where people could visit the rabbi of their choice, very much like office hours of a doctor.

If this sounds rather stern and Prussian, it might indeed have been so, in some cases, prior to 1933, but during my rabbinate in Berlin which began only in 1934, things were quite different. Never at any other period in my professional life did I feel so strongly that my ministry or even a single sermon could be, and had to be, of such vital, practical value as it had to be then, for one of the most important arenas in our fight for survival was the synagogue, the spiritual rallying point for a shocked and bewildered Jewish community.

Yes, this well-integrated, placid Jewish community, the majority of whose members had been "German" for more centuries than any comparable American Jewish community can boast to have existed—this community was in a state of shock, and as always in times of terror, turned to the synagogue

217

where alone Jews could find a semblance of sanity and stability. No longer just a place to worship a "distant" God, the temple became an intimate haven, an extraterritorial asylum, even if only for the spirit.

Our services were overcrowded. Often we had standing room only, with children and teenagers sitting on the steps leading to the pulpit, and it was up to us, the few rabbis still there at that time, to give these bewildered masses of Jews at least a small measure of hope and encouragement, of direction and self-respect and, quite often, some factual information which could no longer be conveyed by any other media of communication.

The burning of the synagogues on the ninth of November, 1938, was therefore even more than the atrocious destruction of our houses of worship—it was the severance of the very lifeline of Jewish existence.

It was thus with deep relief—in addition to deep wonderment—that one day in early spring of 1939 we received the strange order from the German government to reopen as many synagogues as possible as quickly as possible. No official reason was given, but it was quite in keeping with the typically German tradition to throw a cloak of legality over their most unlawful and inhuman acts. In this particular case, no doubt, their motivation was also an attempt to counteract what they called *Greuel-Propaganda,* i.e., the "mendacious reporting of their atrocities abroad." This is why the Foreign Press and the Consular Corps were invited to see for themselves that religious services were conducted in synagogues that supposedly had been burned down.

I learned afterwards that my name also had been involved in one of the little tricks of the Third Reich: on one of the Passover morning services in 1939 I was on the newly reopened pulpit of the synagogue Oranienburger Straße preaching in the presence of the Foreign Press. One of their representatives told me later that the same morning an English newspaper had carried the news of my arrest, followed up by a detailed report of how I was dragged to a Concentration Camp and then shot. There they saw me, very much alive—another proof, so they were asked to believe, that this and similar reports all over the world were lies! This at least was what

Dr. Goebbels and his Ministry of Propaganda hoped to achieve by planting such an item and then making it appear as if it "leaked" out by mistake.

Another possible reason for the order to reopen the synagogues was that the Nazis found it easier to control large gatherings of Jews than to rely entirely on the surveillance of each individual. Another motivating factor might have been that within the Nazi machine entire departments had been set up for the sole purpose of dealing with the cultural and religious activities of the Jews, providing scores of deliciously soft and lucrative jobs for many a brownshirted, power happy German bureaucrat who disliked the idea of seeing his nice, safe little position go up in smoke, together with the synagogue—the smoke, coincidentally, of the very fire he and his friends had so carefully ignited.

Whatever the reasons, the fact remains that we were once more able to hold services and to preach, although preaching in those days required a technique all its own. In order to convey a meaningful message to my congregation without endangering their lives or mine, I used the time-honored homiletic device, to choose a "midrash," a legend, an allegory, or a biblical event as a camouflage for an up-to-date event. Instead of mentioning the specific, you used the closest but more general term: when you meant "Germany" you said "World." When you meant the Nazis you spoke of the Philistines, and it was not difficult to find synonyms for Hitler and Goebbels in our Pharaohs and Hamans. I had to be more subtle than this, of course, because the plaincloth-Gestapo men selected for this type of "intelligence" job were already wise to the more primitive aspects of this device which not only I, but probably most ministers, even the liberal Christians, practiced.

The sermons of those years might not have been remarkable in normal times but—full of innuendoes and rendered in a kind of spiritual code language—they were highly meaningful to the Jewish audiences in Berlin of 1938 or thereafter, and it was a source of deep satisfaction to me that sometimes a sermon seemed capable of giving a sense of perspective and a measure of élan vital to those who were on the brink of being engulfed by the night of despair and hopelessness. It was not enough for a sermon to be "uplifting" in the usual sense,

219

which would have meant to escape into the lofty realm of the spirit and make your audience forget reality. On the contrary: a people that was constantly told by newspapers, radio, and government pronouncements, that it was lower than the scum of the earth, had to be reassured from the pulpit that it was not only not bad, but good, better, the best, in order to keep up its self-respect and its sense of values.

It might not be without interest to a new generation "who knew not Hitler" to read one or two samples of what one could say, or rather how one spoke to a group of Jews under the eyes of the Gestapo, because this also belongs to the category of our fight for survival.

Leafing through my sermons of those years—which a faithful secretary of mine took down in shorthand while I spoke—I find one from November 4, 1938—the Sabbath prior to the Burning—and one dated April 5, 1939—the first or one of the first after that fateful date.

Our people has had the habit to chronologize historic events in their relationship to the destruction of the two Temples in Jerusalem. Our history books still say: this or that event took place before the destruction of the First or after the destruction of the Second Temple in Jerusalem. In keeping with this tradition, it may well be justified if future generations will calendarize our modern history by saying: this or that happened before or after the burning of the synagogues in Germany, before or after the tenth of November 1938.

It is therefore only for the sake of this symbolism that I selected some paragraphs of these two sermons to illustrate how one preached, before—and after.

The sermon of November 4, 1938—the last one to be delivered in my beloved *Friedenstempel*—was called "Slaves of Space," dealing with the idea that the life of man moves within two dimensions, one of Time and one of Space. Historically man has always been the slave of Time, but the master of Space—only in our age have we become slaves of Space also:

> How else is it possible that this great world of ours does not seem to be able to cope with such a tiny problem, comparatively speaking, of a few hundred thousand people desperately in need of a little space where they could live in peace and security? The

220

world has become the slave of space, the slave of border-lines, of frontiers, and human beings are shipped back and forth between these sacred borders as if the humans were lifeless objects. It is as if this magnificent and advanced world of ours has never been told not to shed human blood, has never heard of families torn asunder, has forgotten how a father loves his child—in short, it acts, this world of ours, as if all elements of humanity, of humaneness, do not exist any longer.

Having to live in this world, we Jews, a timeless as well as a spaceless people, take out our old book, the Bible, lift it up like a mirror to the world and say: "Look, World, this is the image in which you were made. What have you done with it? Are you still the descendants of Abraham, Isaac and Jacob, of Moses, Isaiah and Amos—or even of Jesus? They were just. They loved mankind. They loved peace. And they had compassion. We Jews have not always lived up to their image, but whenever we strayed, the prophets came and reproached us and reminded us of our responsibility toward humanity and toward the ideals of our heritage. Who preaches this responsibility to the world of today? Kant and Nietzsche? Rousseau and Voltaire? Do they impose any ethical commitment on the world?"

We modern men are able to sit at a radio and listen to Beethoven and Brahms, to Chopin and to Wagner, serenely being broadcast through the space of the universe and totally unaware of tens of thousands of homeless people down below. Art, music, even the great thinkers and philosophers of the world have no longer any influence on its morals and ethics. The cord is cut, and no radio, however precise and sensitive, is able to receive or to transmit the cries of children, the souls without compass, the moaning of men between frontiers.

There is a legend in the Midrash that when Abraham was born, a star appeared in the sky. "Star of Justice" the angels above called it. At that moment God said: "World, this is your blessing!" And to Abraham he said: "I will make you into a great nation, and I will bless you. I will make your name grow. And may you be a blessing (Genesis 12:2)!"—Never in our history have we been so desperately in need of the fulfill-

221

ment of both these prophecies: *we,* to become a strong people—the *world,* to be a blessing.

Here we stand, a small and tortured people, look at this tremendous world that could so easily ease our pain. Taking out an old message, we repeat prayerfully and fervently once more the same few words: world, may you indeed become a blessing!

When my secretary sent me the transcript of this sermon, she added a short letter, dated November 8, 1938, which reads in part:

Until last night's newspapers came out, I still felt some of the harmony your last sermon had created in my soul, too. "World, become a blessing!"—Don't these words sound different today than they did Friday night? Probably because we know that what we can expect from the world in the next few days will be anything but a blessing [*Possibly referring to the shooting in the German Embassy in Paris. Editor*].

The number of "souls without compass," hoping that you will comfort them and waiting for you to show them the way, will increase more and more. I hope you will have the strength to fulfill this arduous task. In any case thanks for the hour of devotion in the *Friedenstempel.* I hope we will hear you soon again. What else have we left but this.

Two days later this turned out to have been the somewhat ironical overture to a Wagnerian cacophony of sights and sounds: a red flaming *Feuerzauber,* accompanied by the rhythm of marching boots and the din of splintering glass, and then the most shocking sound of all, lending an effect that even Wagner would not have been bold enough to dream of: the complete and utter silence of an unblessed world.

On the fifth of April 1939, I was standing again on a pulpit. It was the second morning of the Passover, and I was preaching in the Levetzowstraße Synagogue of Berlin, which, if I remember correctly, had just been reopened. My topic was "Nation and God," and in this sermon I tried to explain to a crushed and shaken audience what had happened. I said that we as Jews have always believed that

Life, the life of individuals and of peoples—has a deep and sacred meaning: to put into effect on earth

222

God's demands upon man. We have not always achieved it, but since the time of the prophets, our tradition has requested it from us again and again. This demand is written down in the Bible. The Bible, thus, is heaven challenging earth. This is, basically, the reason for the century-old tension between Jews and the world.

One has to understand: the Bible demands the utmost, almost the impossible, from the nations of the earth, and all through history people have opposed it. But against their will God forces them from time to time to be confronted with his precepts, and usually it is we, the Jews as authors of this uncomfortable book, who remind them of its challenge. Maybe this is where roots of anti-Semitism can be found. Yet our obligation remains unchanged, and as long as we believe in the righteousness of this our mission, there is hope for our deliverance.

There is a story in Jewish folklore which tells of a strange custom among our brethren in Far Eastern countries: for the seder, the Passover meal, they sit down dressed in travel clothes, as if ready for the Exodus. At a certain point in the seder, there is a knock at the door; a wanderer from the outside comes in and tells of the forthcoming redemption. When asked how he knows of it he replies: "For three things the Hebrew language uses the word *chayim*—Life: for God—the God of Life; for the Torah—the Book of Life; and for the Jewish People—the people of eternal life. Has anybody seen God die? Again and again one feels his power. Has the Bible vanished? Again and again it becomes the fountainhead of our existence. As long as those two are alive, are eternal, so long will the Jews remain an *am olam*—"an Eternal People.""

Before closing the chapter on Berlin, I want to share two episodes closely related to the content of these pages—episodes very fresh in my mind, as if they happened yesterday. It was the first time I re-entered the main sanctuary of the Jewish Community, the Oranienburger Straße Synagogue in downtown Berlin—the first time after the burning, yet prior to the official opening. I was alone with Heinrich Stahl, the president of the Jewish Community, as he solemnly and tremblingly broke the seal which the Nazis had put on the doors of the temple on November 10, and opened the heavy doors. My heart was beating: I was not only entering a desecrated house of God in a modern European city, but I was entering upon the scene of two thousand years of pogroms and fires, and a storm of emotions ranging from utter misery to fervent defiance, almost overwhelmed me.

Heinrich Stahl, this great and dedicated old gentleman, must have felt like I did, for neither of us was able to speak. Stale air and semi-darkness surrounded us. We found the pews scorched, the walls blackened by fire and soot—a dead sanctuary.

So we thought, until we walked further, walked toward the pulpit, lifted our eyes to the ark and perceived—above the ark—our own, twentieth century miracle: the eternal light was burning, had been burning through the ninth and tenth of November, during all these months—a small, dim light outlasting all the fires of the Third Reich. It was an unforgettable sight—a symbol and a message.

In a similar trend of thought, I remember our last Passover in Germany, in spring 1940. We were sure it would be our last one there, but not quite so sure where the next one was to be—or if there would be a next one.

Our guests came early to the first seder that year. The price of admission was one egg which each one had been told, well in advance, to save from the bi-weekly ration, so we could all enjoy the customary hard-boiled egg at the outset of the seder meal. I remember our daughter's delighted outcry when Dr. Seligsohn, then head of the *Hilfsverein* and her special friend, produced not one but two eggs, one out of each of his coat pockets, just like a magician.

This was not a light-hearted seder, on April 22, 1940, in our apartment in Berlin, but it was an authentic one, closely akin to the first, the original seder of our forefathers in Egypt. If ever it was easy to follow the commandment of the Haggadah to feel as if we ourselves had been part of that Exodus, it was then. Each of us had an invisible "bundle on our backs" and a "staff in our hands," not to speak of the anxiety in the hearts and the tension of the nerves—the insignia of a Jew marked for the Exodus, that tragically recurring scourge of a homeless people.

224

When Hanneli, the youngest at the table, chanted shyly and sweetly the *mah nishtana,* the Four Questions, to the old melody which I had taught her, I was tempted to answer—not "What makes this night different?" as the traditional first question goes, but rather: "What makes this night similar, so terribly similar to previous nights in our history?"

My heart was heavy when I pronounced the ancient prayer which is more a sigh than a prayer: *l'shanah ha-ba-ah birushalayim*—"Next Year in Jerusalem," to which each one, I am sure, added silently his own prayer: "...or in America," "...or anywhere in the world, only away from Germany!"

The candles flickered low. The fourth cup of wine was blessed and drained. Hanneli was suddenly very drowsy, and we carried her off to bed. Our friends left, slowly, one by one. Good night, Paul Eppstein and Hedwig! Good night. Otto Hirsch. Good night, Julius Seligsohn. Good night, Michalowitz, and good friends Kurt and Eva Rosenberg! We were so glad to have you.

It was *our* last Passover in Germany. *For most of you it was the last Passover.*

NACHMAN KROCHMAL: THE PHILOSOPHER OF ISRAEL'S ETERNITY

From *The American Jewish Yearbook,* Vol. 44 (1942)
And I will put My spirit in you, and ye shall live. (Ezekiel 37:14)

The year 1648, the date of the Peace of Westphalia, marks the beginning of a new era in European history. It represents the setting of an old and the dawn of a new world, on whose horizon the sun of the Enlightenment was soon to rise.

In Jewish history, the year 1648 denotes a date both important and fateful: important for the West, fateful for the East. For the Jewry of Western Europe, this year marks the beginning of a period of transition which came to a close in the revolutionary year of 1789, which in turn inaugurates the era of Jewish emancipation. While Western Jewry is thus moving forward on the road to a broader culture, Eastern Jewry is driven backward. While the West progresses toward modern

225

humanism, the East retreats toward medieval barbarism. While Mendelssohn and his friends, Lessing and Dohm, are cementing a mutual cultural understanding as the first step toward enlightenment and emancipation, the East passes through a period of political conflicts, accompanied by pogroms and bloody persecution.

This discrepancy between the fate of Western and Eastern European Jewry found its counterpart in the spiritual expressions that Judaism gave to this period of transition. The hegemony of German-Polish Jewry that had been prevailing for many years was broken for the first time, and each partner took another course. The West started out toward the Enlightenment—the East toward Hasidism. Both movements had one thing in common: the yearning for a spiritual renaissance. But liberalism and enlightenment made Jews strive for a cultural revival and for a life in freedom, proclaiming the spiritual emancipation as the indispensable presupposition for civic emancipation. It was a centrifugal movement, directed toward the outer world of Europe. Hasidism, on the other hand, proclaimed the immanence of God and sought a religion not of reason but of the heart, which would afford the individual the feeling of God's presence in every phase of daily life and solace in times of tribulation. It was a centripetal movement, directed toward the more intimate values of Judaism. Thus, at the end of the eighteenth century, European Jewry had two faces, looking into opposite directions: the one toward Europe, the other toward the ghetto; the one toward assimilation, the other toward segregation. One face looked at the world with the eyes of Moses Mendelssohn (1729-1786), the other with the eyes of Israel Baal Shem Tov (1700-1760).

The decades following the French Revolution, up to 1848, again displayed two diverging trends of development in the West and in the East of Europe. In spite of setbacks and hostile attacks on the part of a disillusioned and dissatisfied populace, equality of rights—that trophy of the gallant fight for emancipation—was eventually raised to the status of an enacted law. Western Jewry, in its turn, was willing to pay the price for the gift of emancipation and civic rights. The price was assimilation—a movement that, nourished by the element of humanism on the one side and by practical utility on the other, character-

226

ized the nineteenth century in Western Europe. But before these ideas had a chance to be transplanted and to become effective in the East, the Russian pogroms started at the end of the nineteenth century, and what vital spirit there was within Eastern Jewry exerted itself in the new movement of a national renaissance. Once more European Jewry showed two opposite faces. While Western Jewry pursued the course of assimilation, Eastern Jewry emphasized its identity as a national group. As the cultural sediment of enlightened assimilation in the West, we have the *Wissenschaft des Judentums,* with the Reform movement as its religious accompaniment. Its counterpart in the East was the Russian Haskalah with its distinctly national character, reviving the Hebrew language and literature. Their "founding fathers" were Leopold Zunz (1794-1886) in the West and Isaac Ber Levinsohn (1788-1860) in the East; the one, the spiritual descendant of Moses Mendelssohn, the other, despite all, still virtually related to the Baal Shem Tov.

There was one country, however, where East and West met, and this was Austria. Here emancipation had come late, and when it finally came, it appeared as "tolerance" rather than as liberalism. This country lacked the intensity of both Western progressiveness and Eastern barbarism. Its device was the compromise of the *Toleranz Patent,* issued by Joseph II in 1782, which, though proclaimed as a document of emancipation, retained many disabilities.

The Jewry of Austria responded in a like spirit. Emancipation did not captivate Jewish souls here as it did in Germany, nor did the Haskalah inaugurate a national movement as in Russia. What we had there was a renaissance of Hebrew literature and letters. This Austrian movement was not removed from the world like Hasidism; it was cognizant of the world and took advantage of its progressive tools. On the other hand, it was unlike the Western assimilatory Enlightenment inasmuch as its main concern was Judaism as a whole. The goal of this literary movement was not to adjust Judaism to the surrounding culture. To analyze Judaism, to discover its substance and demonstrate its eternity with the help of the tools forged by Western Civilization and European philosophy, was its supreme purpose. The center and symbol of this literary renaissance is Nachman Krochmal. In his personality East and

227

West seem to have a rendezvous. He has been called the Mendelssohn of the East; and, significantly enough, it is claimed that he was of the family of the Baal Shem. Krochmal was an intimate friend of Isaac Ber Levinsohn, father of the Haskalah in Russia, whose first book he helped to publish; while Leopold Zunz, founder of the *Wissenschaft des Judentums*, edited Krochmal's principal work, *Guide for the Perplexed of the Time*. For the first time after long centuries, at least in one corner of Europe, Judaism is not Janus-faced, but is represented by a personality whose eyes, though trained to look through European glasses, view Judaism with the scholarly precision of a Zunz and the national instinct of a Levinsohn, with the intellectual penetration of a Mendelssohn and the pious depth of a Baal Shem.

II

Brody was a beautiful and flourishing town near the Russian border. Under Austrian government, in the latter part of the eighteenth century, it enjoyed the privileges of a "Free City" and, as such, was a center of prosperous merchants who used to travel to the West and bring home with them a breath of the new spirit of liberalism. It was a city of writers and thinkers, touched by the new rays of the Enlightenment.

Here Nachman Krochmal was born in 1785, the scion of a wealthy family. His father was a prosperous merchant who would often go to Berlin and Leipzig and, on those occasions, meet Moses Mendelssohn and David Friedländer. From his mother's side Nachman was—if our sources are reliable—a descendant of the Baal Shem Tov and the grandson of Rabbi Nachman of Horodenko, for whom he was named. His father was already a *Maskil* (enlightened) and gave his son a modern Jewish education with no radical leanings to any side. Though Nachman had to pass through all the customary stages of Jewish education—cheder, bet hamidrash, Torah, and Talmud—he was trained to think freely, justly, and independently, guided by his father's moderateness and intelligence.

Nachman Krochmal's life was uneventful and might have been peaceful but for annoying financial reverses. As customary at that time, he married very young, at the age of fifteen, and went to Zolkiew, an attractive little town near Lemberg,

228

where he spent ten years with his wife and his parents-in-law. It was here that he began seriously to learn, to study and to search: to search for truth. He read Maimonides, Abraham Ibn Ezra, and Nahmanides, as well as the Scholastics and Spinoza. He also read Lessing, Kant, Fichte, Schelling, Hegel, Mendelssohn, Maimon, and the French literature. These studies later on provided the background for his philosophical and historical conceptions.

After the ten quiet and fruitful years, the tide turned, and his life became harried by illness and poverty. In spite of all reverses, he continued his studies, and disciples, among them Rapoport and Letteris, gathered around him. With them he discussed historical, philosophical, and general Jewish problems. They urged him to publish his ideas, to put his philosophy into a book which would make him the leader of his generation. But Krochmal refused. The time was not yet ripe. Only years later, after the death of his wife, when he returned to Brody in order to earn a livelihood for himself and his little son, did he begin, despite his very depressed mood, to write the first part of his *Guide for the Perplexed of the Time.* His last years, however, he spent in Tarnopol with his daughter and son-in-law, where at last he found the peace and tranquillity needed for the continuation of his work. Before he died, on July 31, 1840, he asked that the manuscript be sent to Leopold Zunz in Berlin in order to be published. Zunz first issued the book in 1851, eleven years after Krochmal's death.

Many factors have shaped Krochmal's personality—his father's guidance and the modern Jewish education in his home; the free spirit of his native town and of Austria of that time; the revolutionary atmosphere of Europe, and his friendship with many leading Maskilim, among them the already mentioned Isaac Ber Levinsohn of Kremenez, and Dov Ber Ginsburg (1776-1809), the first writer of the Haskalah in Galicia, who lived in Brody. All these influences made him hospitable to all the modern currents of his time and prevented him from becoming prejudiced, narrow, or radical. The characteristic trait of his personality was moderation, the avoidance of extremes, and choice of the golden mean. As motto of the second chapter of the *Guide,* Krochmal quotes the famous parable of our rabbis: "The Torah has been compared to two paths, one of fire and one of snow. If a man takes the first path, he will die by the flames; if he takes the other one, he will perish in the snow. What then must he do? He must walk in the middle."

As a scholar, the aim of his life was to discover the truth. But how? Krochmal gave the answer: in every generation there are those who blindly believe in everything, "the fools among the believers," and those who, afraid of making the same mistake, go into the opposite camp of complete denial, "the frivolous scoffers." Where, then, is the truth? In the middle road that lies between both extremes and leads to the underlying principle common to both of them. The truth of this principle can be revealed through the methods of historical criticism.

This leads us to Krochmal's methodology. If we examine his way of thinking, we find that he has a threefold approach to the objectives of his research: a historical, a critical, and a philosophical.

Krochmal was a historian who under Hegel's influence introduced the historical method into Jewish thinking, maintaining that every fact of history had to be considered in relation to its surroundings, its time and place. This was a complete innovation in intellectual Jewish life, for even the highly advanced Jewish philosophy of the Middle Ages was not cognizant of the importance of "time and space" in the development of Judaism. Maimonides lacked the historical conception, and so did Mendelssohn. Krochmal was the first of the Jewish thinkers to employ the concepts of "time and space" as principal elements of his historical method. To appreciate the greatness of Krochmal's historical approach, we have to realize that at his time all the important books on Jewish history and tradition (those by Frankel, Geiger, Rappoport, and Graetz) had yet to be written, and that he had to start his work from the very beginning and all by himself. He had to do his own spade work; he had to gather facts and to confront them with the realities of time and space and the laws of development.

The second methodological tool that Krochmal used in examining the phenomena of Jewish history and tradition was that of criticism, that is the arrangement and microscopic analysis of individual items of history, and the determination of their value by the judgment of the intellect. This was not entirely new. Krochmal had a predecessor in the famous Italian Jewish scholar Azariah de Rossi (1513-1578); but Krochmal made criticism one of the main pillars of his ideological construction.

The third element in Krochmal's methodology was the philosophical. On the basis of his historical and critical research, he attempted to erect a towering structure of philosophy. Since Maimonides, generations of Jews had been without a comprehensive philosophical system of Judaism, and Krochmal felt the urge to provide a guide to his contemporaries. Hence he tried to rise above history and criticism toward the more elevated sphere of philosophy—metaphysics, philosophy of religion, and philosophy of history—and bring the results of his studies into one unified system. From the height of this structure, he was able to comprehend the universe as a whole and within it Judaism in its entirety, disclosing the eternal laws which govern the common events of life and history.

As historian, Krochmal was a synthesist; as critic, an analyst; as philosopher, a systematizer. All his endeavors, however, served but one purpose: to define Judaism as a unified whole of one spiritual process which, like a mighty stream, though often torrential, leads Israel securely through the ages from its eternal source to its eternal destination.

III

It is not the task of this essay to deal with Krochmal's entire system of thought as formulated in his *Guide*. I shall but single out one important topic from his discussion which may well stand as *pars pro toto*—namely, Krochmal's philosophy of history.

Its starting point is the idea of the sociability of the individual. Pursuing the line of ancient Greek philosophy, that of Plato and Aristotle, and influenced by Giambattista Vico and Hegel, Krochmal holds that, in contrast to the solitude of animals, man is a sociable creature by nature. Through divine predestination, sociability is an impulse innate in our souls, which inspires men to think in categories of society. Sociability is the cause and foundation of human development, that is, of

231

history. According to Krochmal, the development of society is effected by a natural process brought about by the necessity of living together and "by the help of God's guidance." When society first comes into existence, it establishes a social order of work, with habits of justice and righteousness, which later become stabilized in a code of laws, developing slowly the notions of mercy, love and honor in family, community and nation. Then society is no longer concerned with what is necessary, but with what is pleasant and sublime; it is creating art, music, poetry, and with these proceeds the religious knowledge of God which is "planted in the depths of the human soul." This is the stage that Krochmal calls the period of budding and growth of society.

At the next stage, society reaches a point of peaceful activity, putting all its social, ethical, cultural, and religious principles of the first period into realization, developing its language and science, spreading the knowledge of history, fixing its system of youth and adult education, and acquiring all the qualities which serve to identify a nation. At the same time the spirit is elevated, the cognition of God becomes a common heritage, and the worship of God attains to a most sublime ceremony "in sincerity of thought and in purity of worship." This is, according to Krochmal, the second period of human development. It is that of maturity and completion.

Finally, the nations enter into their third and last period of the cycle, that of decay and destruction. At a certain point, the material civilization of nations begins to spoil their character. Different symptoms: diversion, pride, domination, and superstition—like natural diseases attacking the body of society—indicate a moral decline; the spirit of justice and goodness vanishes; the knowledge and the worship of God perish; the members of the community are no longer united; influences of foreign powers begin to spread and weaken the heart of nations, so that everyone believes in everything. The consequence of all this is a spiritual decline which, in its turn, destroys the foundation of the state and leads to the death of the nation. The destruction is completed.

Such is the order of growth, consolidation, and destruction prevalent in history. However, Krochmal is not satisfied with stating the fact of this triple process but tries to discern the principle which is behind history, permeating all development, and governing the law of growth and decay. Here he introduces an idea which has played a most important part in German Idealism: that of "Spirit" and "Absolute Spirit."

Following Fichte—and unlike Hegel—the world to Krochmal is not the source but the creation of the Spirit, which is identical with God, who is the source of all being, the only true reality, the Absolute or Total Spirit. As God is immanent and indwelling in the universe, the God-Spirit reveals himself everywhere, in nature and history. In history, however, he reveals himself to the nations not totally, but partially, not in his entirety, but through one or another of his attributes only. Thus, each nation in history receives a spark of the divine light. This spark is the fountainhead of all the creative forces within the nation; it molds her civilization and her culture, it shapes her particular characteristics and individual features. This is what Krochmal calls *ruah ha-uma* (the National Spirit) or *ruah prati* (the Individual Spirit), which indeed he considers as being identical with the nation. For, says he: "The substance of the nation is nothing but the substance of the Spirit within her."

The revelation of this Individual Spirit is common to all nations; but in contrast to the Total Spirit which alone is eternal and infinite, the Individual Spirit is time bound and finite. Therefore, the nations being identical with their Individual Spirit are time bound and finite too; they are mortal and do not survive. The nations pass through the three periods of growth, maturity, and decay, because the Individual Spirit within them grows, flourishes, and degenerates.

This is one of the main ideas of Krochmal's philosophy of history, taken from the philosophy of nationalism of the German Idealism. But to Krochmal it serves only as an introduction to a conclusion of more vital importance—to wit, the uniqueness of Israel's place among the nations. The question which arises here, of course, is that of the miraculous survival of the Jewish people. If the triple process of growth, maturity, and destruction is a law of universal validity, how then have the Jews succeeded to exist until this very day? It is in this connection that Krochmal gives his famous answer.

The Jewish nation is subject to the same genetic laws of history as the rest of the nations and passes through the same process of growth and decay. This process, however, has occurred not only once in Jewish history but has repeated itself several times. Krochmal, in fact, distinguishes three such cycles in our history: the first reaching from Abraham to Gedalia, the second from the exile in Babylon to Bar Kochba, and the third from Rabbi Judah ha-Nasi to the expulsion from Spain, each of them being a triad of growth, maturity, and destruction. That is to say that at the end of the third period of each cycle, Israel always overcomes the deadly destruction and starts out for the opening of a new cycle. To explain this unique phenomenon in history, Krochmal, inclined toward mysticism, assumes that God—or the Absolute Spirit—revealed himself to mankind in a double way: to the nations of the world, partially; but to Israel—and to Israel only—totally. It is through an unseparable attachment between God and Israel, revealed on Mount Sinai, that the Jewish nation was privileged to receive the Total Spirit instead of the Partial one. Unlike Judah ha-Levi, Krochmal does not claim for the Jewish nation to be above the natural powers of development; he does not ascribe the fact of the Jewish survival to a miracle, but to the Absolute Spirit which, by the will of God, has become Israel's spirit throughout the ages. Because this spirit is timeless, always rejuvenating itself, and never called off from the sphere of humanity, Israel, its bearer, is also everlasting, always regenerating, and never leaving the scene of history. Israel is eternal.

It should be remarked that there is no metaphysical necessity for the special relationship between Israel and the Absolute Spirit, and, indeed, Krochmal does not attempt to prove it metaphysically. To him this relationship is a self-evident fact, the very pillar of his inmost belief, the axiom of his entire religious-philosophical structure. The idea, in this form, came to him from the Kabbalah, especially from Nahmanides who influenced him strongly. But, I think, we should not judge Krochmal too severely for being mystical on this point. After all, the representatives of the so-called "Hegel-Renaissance"— Nicolai Hartmann, Siegfried Marck, and Richard Kroner—have pointed out that even Hegel's Absolute Spirit is of mystic character and that Hegel himself was the greatest "Philosopher of Irrationalism," while Krochmal never strove to be as great a logist as Hegel. He may therefore be excused for taking refuge in mysticism in the explanation of Israel's eternity.

IV

With his *Guide for the Perplexed of the Time* Krochmal starts a new epoch in Jewish thinking. From Maimonides until his time, philosophy of Judaism was founded on *ratio*. Krochmal came and based it on historical criticism. The *Guide* indeed marks the beginning of an epoch of criticism and free searching in Israel.

Nachman Krochmal did not create a school. But Solomon Schechter says correctly "that there is scarcely a single page in Krochmal's book that did not afterwards give birth to some essay or monograph or even elaborate treatise, though their authors were not always very careful about mentioning the source of their inspiration" (*Studies in Judaism,* First Series, p. 67). Krochmal, in fact, exerted a strong influence upon the entire philosophy of Jewish Nationalism, though his name is very seldom mentioned. Most of his ideas have come down to our generation not in his own but in the name of his interpreters.

There is, for instance, J. M. Pines (1842-1913), one of the leading personalities of the national-religious romanticism who turned against the Haskalah, with his conception of Judaism as *dat ruhanit* (spiritual religion), serving as basis for Israel's eternity. There is further Perez Smolenskin (1842-1885) who was beating the way from the Haskalah toward Nationalism, explaining the eternity of the Jewish nation *(am olam)* by the spirituality of her substance *(am ha-ruah).* Even more evident than in the case of Pines and Smolenskin was Krochmal's influence upon Isaac Hirsch Weiss (1815-1905). In his famous book, *Dor dor v'Dorshav (Each Generation and its Interpreters),* which is a history of Jewish tradition, Weiss follows Krochmal's idea of development, especially with reference to the halachah.

It was Krochmal, moreover, who laid the foundation to Ahad Ha-am's philosophy of Zionism. Ahad Ha-am's doctrine of *uma* (nation) and *ruah leumi* (national spirit) that creates and permeates every development in a nation's history, emanates from Krochmal. Ahad Ha-am's statement that the

235

Jewish nation is eternal because *"zedek muhlat"* (absolute justice) is her mission, is, with but a slight change of the phrase only, a complete adaptation of Krochmal's *ruhani ha-muhlat.* Ahad Ha-am's philosophy of the development of the National Ego *(ha-ani ha-leumi)* which like the individual ego passes through three stages of childhood, prime, and old age, plainly shows the traces of Krochmal's *Guide.* The same influence becomes evident in one of the most prominent figures of Ahad Ha-am's school of thinking, David Neumark (1866-1924), who took from Krochmal the entire idea of the *ruhani,* the Absolute Spirit prevailing within Israel, and of the Partial Spirit prevailing within the other nations. Indeed, even one of the most ardent antagonists to the Krochmal-Ahad Ha-am ideology, Micha Joseph Berdyczewsky (1865-1921), could not escape Krochmal's world-outlook, especially in his irrational phase when Berdyczewsky became strongly inclined toward Kabbalah and mysticism.

Such, then, was Krochmal. Such were his life and personality, his method and ideology, seen against the background of his time, standing between a great past from which he learned, and a great future to which he handed down his spiritual message. It is for the student to decide whether our philosopher really was the Mendelssohn of the East or rather the Baal Shem of the West; whether he deserves to be called the Zunz of the Haskalah or the Levinsohn of the Jewish Science. We venture to say that, whatever he may be called, for us he will always remain—what he in reality was—the great unifier of East and West, the perfect blending of Enlightenment and Hasidism, of Jewish Science and Haskala. It was this rare synthesis which entitled him to be the true philosopher of Israel's eternity.

ZIONISM UNDER HITLER

From *Congress Weekly, IX:27* (September 11, 1942)

People in the United States are well informed about the fate of the Jews in the Third Reich. Every day, for nine consecutive years, the papers have been telling us of the agonizing destruction which has spread over the Jewry of Germany. Very little, however, is known of the highly constructive role that Zionism played during eight years of Hitlerism. The development and the achievements of the Palestine Office during that time are practically unknown to the Jewish public of America. On account of personal experiences in the Zionist work in Berlin, I shall attempt to give a short record of that period.

A comprehensive chapter of German Zionism has yet to be written. Only a man like Kurt Blumenfeld, president for many years of the Zionist Organization of Germany and the educator of my generation to Zionism, would perhaps be able to fulfill this task adequately. It ought to be remembered that Zionism was the only Jewish organization in Germany to foresee Hitler's rise to power. It hinted at the imminent danger already in the years 1930-31. It discussed a program based on the conception of a national minority with cultural autonomy, reiterated on several occasions by Robert Weltsch in the *Jüdische Rundschau* in 1933-34. I do not say that this program would have been carried through under Nazism, but if Jews had taken it seriously it would have helped to prepare them psychologically for the revolution to which their lives were to be subjected. Unfortunately, the attempt failed. The assimilatory groups did not recognize the danger and refused, besides, to be involved in a program of "cultural autonomy," because this, allegedly, would isolate the Jews from the German people. Instead, they stubbornly persisted in making war against Hitler merely as Germans, scrupulously sticking to their German democratic argumentations and also carefully omitting any Jewish viewpoint. The *Jüdische Rundschau* was the only Jewish paper to take seriously the ever-growing National Socialist power in Germany's political life, but its warning went unheeded. Thus, when on January 31, 1933, Hitler actually came to power, German Jewry suffered a heavy shock, because the majority was internally as well as externally unprepared; and all the efforts made in the last minutes failed because, even after that fateful day, many Jewish assimilationists, together with other democratic groups, still believed in a very brief existence of the Hitler government.

However, it turned out the other way; and German Jewry suffered greatly from the lack of a constructive program. The only unanimous resolution accepted later on was to unite all Jewish organizations into one purely defensive representation of all Jewish interests, which plan was consolidated in the following years as the *Reichsvertretung der Juden in Deutschland.*

The attitude of the Third Reich toward Zionism is difficult to define, complicated on account of contradictions, and liable to be misunderstood. The analysis would be much easier if, in accordance with their dogmatic anti-Jewishness, all the leaders of the Third Reich would have been straight anti-Zionists as well. But some of them apparently were not, and it requires some knowledge of National Socialism, its "spirit" and its technics, to understand this rather paradoxical issue. To sketch it roughly, it will suffice to say that the complete extermination of German Jewry was the final goal common to all groups within the National Socialist party. They differed only in the methods of achieving their goal. Some of the leaders (Goebbels, Rosenberg, and Ribbentrop) believed in the "liquidation" of German Jewry through ghettos, concentration camps and execution. Therefore they were against emigration, and particularly against a Jewish homeland in Palestine. The more "reasonable" elements (Goering and *Wirtschaftsministerium*) recognized that this would not be the quickest nor the most lucrative way to get rid of the Jews; this is why they recommended emigration as a more effective solution. For a few years, the official attitude of the government was a mixture of both propositions. They exterminated Jewish life by concentration camps on the one hand, and liquidated Jewry through regulated emigration on the other. As long as this policy prevailed, the Third Reich, of course, was interested in mass emigration. Since the Zionist Organization was the only one to plan an organized emigration, instead of an individual one to various countries, its activities were permitted to be carried on. This explains why the Gestapo tolerated at all the continuation of Zionist work after 1933.

I may be allowed to put a personal episode on record which may help to illustrate the paradoxical attitude of the Third Reich. The Gestapo had a special department for Jewish affairs which was headed by a *Judenkommissar.* For many years, one Mr. Kuchmann, who worked under the ill-famed Mr. Eichmann, was in charge of the "Jewish problem." Mr.

238

Kuchmann was more on the jovial side; he was simple and only rudely educated; but with German thoroughness he began to adjust himself to his new position—formerly he had been a small employee of the Criminal Police—by studying Jewish history and the terminology of Zionism, and by reading every available book on modern Jewish problems. As a result of his diligence, he suddenly fell in love with Revisionism, asserting to each of us who had the misfortune to be summoned to his office, that this was the only solution of the Palestine problem and constantly blaming official Zionism for being "red" and "left." One day in the spring of 1937, he called me to his office and told me bluntly that I had to take over the leadership of the Revisionist group, to make Revisionism more popular with German Jewry, to drop my propaganda work for the "Meineckestrasse-Zionism" (Meineckestrasse was the famous seat of the official German Zionism), and to concentrate, instead, on propagating Revisionism. When I refused for reasons of my conception of Zionism—he "punished" me by a speaking and writing prohibition for one year. [*This "prohibition" did not prohibit preaching. The "prohibition" was lifted on the Nussbaums' wedding day, as a gift from the Gestapo! R.N.*]. It was only after great and tedious efforts of the Zionist Organization that this order was revoked in July, 1938.

While the German authorities persisted in their queer but not entirely unfavorable attitude, the German Zionist Organization had a chance to grow; and actually the movement rose from a proportionally small figure to an organization counting many thousands. Jews from all parts of the country, having lost every foothold and finding themselves without leadership on account of the shortcomings of the assimilationist groups, were flocking to Zionism. The number of employees in our Palestine offices was trebled and quadrupled, our *Hachshara* centers increased, the *Hechalutz* expanded—there was something like a powerful wave of return to national Judaism. Many of these new adherents came to us for opportunistic reasons, namely to obtain an emigration certificate for Palestine. Nevertheless it remains true that, with the admittedly strong pressure from outside, a spark buried long ago came to life in thousands of Jews, so that they gathered under the flag of Zionism. As a result, the Palestine idea penetrated every Jewish home as well as the congregations and the Liberal synagogues, which until that time had kept aloof from any Zionist thought. Zionism grew to be the most prominent factor in public Jewish life, taking part in the work of the congregations and becoming the leading element in the *Reichsvertretung der Juden in Deutschland.*

The strength of Zionism at that time is easily demonstrated with a few figures: on August 1, 1938, we still had thirty-two *Hachshara* centers, sustained by Zionist groups alone or in cooperation with the *Reichsvertretung.* Out of these thirty-two, twelve belonged to the *Hechalutz,* three to the *Makkabi Hatza-ir,* four to the *Mizrachi* Youth, one to the *Betar,* one to the *Aguda,* one to the *Werkleute,* and ten to various Zionist youth organizations. The statistics of emigration shows the same trend: by July 1, 1938, 107,350 Jews had left Germany. This figure is composed as follows: 800 Jews had emigrated to various small countries, 9,400 had gone to the British Empire, 26,150 to South America, 27,000 to North America, and 44,000 had gone to Palestine, which means that Palestine had outranked all other countries, including the United States, taking in almost twice as many Jews as the United States in the same length of time.

A new chapter of Zionism under Hitler started with November 9, 1938, the day when not only the synagogues were burnt, Jewish homes destroyed, and almost 70,000 Jewish men brought into concentration camps, but also when all Jewish parties were dissolved, including the Zionist Organization of Germany. The offices of the organization were sealed, and for many weeks no entrance was permitted. (The furniture of most of the rooms with typewriters and other valuable implements had been shattered.) Gradually, some of the rooms were released to us, and half a year later, the Palestine Office was permitted to resume its functions on a much restricted scale and with the exclusive purpose of organizing the emigration to Palestine. The prohibition of the Zionist Organization as a political party continued. Later, the Jewish National Fund and Keren Hayesod were allowed to resume some of their activities. On account of a special agreement with the Ministry of Economics, we even had the possibility to transfer the collected money to the Jewish Agency, naturally at an exchange

240

rate very favorable to the German Reichsbank. This permission, of course, served the same purpose of encouraging emigration, as a way to liquidating the Jewish problem.

Again an enormous rush to the Palestine offices all over the country set in. We had never enough certificates to give to the applicants, although we could carry out many a Palestinian settlement and industrial project with the help of well-to-do Jews who, in return for their money, received a so-called Capitalist Certificate from the British Government. During that period, unity and harmony prevailed in German Zionism and in the whole of German Jewry to an extent that was unparalleled in earlier years even in Germany, not to speak of other countries. Representatives of all the former parties were united into one great Palestine Committee; all differences had vanished; nothing mattered except the common Zionist work and the effort to save as many lives by emigration as possible. The certificates that we had were delivered, in addition to workers, mostly to inmates of concentration camps or to otherwise endangered people. Nevertheless, we still adhered to the Zionist principle of testing the applicants' attitude to and aptitude for Palestine, so as to carry out our aliyah principles. All this was an immensely difficult task, enervating in endless night sessions, during which we had to struggle with the German authorities on one side and our Zionist conscience on the other. Our humanity often said save, while the Zionist responsibility ordered select. We had to assume this responsibility and did it to the very best of our judgment and abilities. Those were the conditions until the war broke out.

It was like a last climax of that period that, in August 1939, we had the privilege to represent German Jewry at the Zionist Congress at Geneva, which, in the memory of the German delegates, gleams like a last flare-up before ultimate darkness. Why the Gestapo granted us permission to leave Germany and to go to Switzerland for this purpose, is one of those miracles on which our lives more or less depended in all those years. Perhaps they had the vague idea that the Congress might bring about mass emigration of German Jewry to Palestine, costly to Great Britain and inexpensive to them. Whatever their reasons may have been we, the delegates, received special exit visas. Of course, each of us had to sign that he would come back, and the leading members of the *Reischvertretung* had to serve as guarantors for our return [*Family members also served as guarantors. R.N.*]. Knowing that Geneva was full of German spies, we did not participate in the open discussions of the Congress, with the exception of an official statement which one of our members read to the assembly.

A few days later war broke out, changing and shattering nearly everything and with it the fate of Zionism in Germany. The Goebbels-Rosenberg group grew much stronger, underscoring their antagonism against Zionism with political arguments against England. As a result, the Gestapo one day declared not to be interested any longer in emigration on such a small scale, because Germany would solve the whole Jewish problem in Europe by a settlement in Madagascar. In May, 1940, the word Palestine was banned from the pages of the only tiny Jewish newspaper, the *Jüdische Nachrichtenblatt.* Palestine, so they said, was going to belong to the "Italian sphere of influence" and was therefore not to be mentioned in relation to Jewish affairs. Our protests resulted only in the arrest of one of our best men and his deportation to a concentration camp.

Aliyah from Germany to Palestine was no longer feasible. But even then the attitude of the Third Reich toward Zionism was not altogether uniform. In spite of the official opposition against any further emigration to Palestine, unofficially it was still tolerated in order to get rid of a few more Jews. Thus, when at the beginning of the war, we attempted to organize *aliyah bet* boats, we did not encounter many obstacles.

Only those who have seen the rooms of the Palestine Office during the preparations for an *aliyah bet* ship, can fully realize the desperate situation of Jews in Germany at that time. The offices were crammed with people of all ages and sexes, imploring the officials to accept their application. Rich and poor, old and young, Zionists and former anti-Zionists—they all seemed to know but one road to salvation: the ride on a miserable, wretched boat to the shores of Eretz Israel, with less than fifty percent chances of arriving safely. Only those who have seen thousands of Jews clinging desperately to this last grain of hope, can fully understand what the news of the Patria incident did to that Jewry. [*The Patria was a ship bearing "illegal" immigrants to Palestine which sank in Haifa Bay.*

242

Over two hundred lives were lost. Ed.] An eyewitness told me—for by that time I had left Germany—that the scenes which took place in the Palestine Office after the announcement of the disaster were beyond words. In April, 1941, the complete list of the dead, wounded, and missing of the catastrophe was released to the Palestine Office in Berlin. The Gestapo did not allow an official statement to be issued for circulation by the Office. Therefore, our leading officials called personally on the relatives of most victims to inform them of what had happened, always accompanied by the physician of the Zionist Organization, because it was evident that the health and nervous condition of most Jews in that time could not stand such a blow. In some particularly cruel cases the officials preferred not to inform the family so that, with the lack of foreign newspapers, radio, and foreign mail, there might still be some who have not heard yet, and I know of such cases.

A last word may be devoted to the gradual strangulation of the Palestine Office and, in fact, of the whole Zionist work in Germany, in the first two war years. At the beginning of 1941, our Zionist workers still held on to their posts. Although there were only six of the leading staff left, the *Berufsvorbereitung* and the *Jugendhilfe* were carried on according to the educational principles of the *Hachshara*. Even the cultural work including Hebraization went on, to a certain extent, within the framework of the *Hachshara*. Gradually, however, our *Hachshara* centers, with the exception of those at Schnebinchen, Eichau, Paderborn, and Ellguth, were dissolved.

On May 5, 1941, the Palestine Office got the official order to stop its activities. The Funds had to be delivered to the *Reichsvertretung*. The few *Hachshara* centers then still functioning got word that they were not entitled to receive any further subvention from our Jewish organizations but that they had to live exclusively on outside labor and on their own agricultural products. Since this was impossible, their fate also was sealed. The Compulsory Labor Service murdered the rest of our *Hachshara* work by summoning boys and girls from fifteen years on to the service. The same fate was awaiting the faithful employees of all our offices.

This, as I said, is but an outline of a yet unrecorded chapter in our European Jewish history. Some of our men remained on their perilous posts until the very last moment; many of them are now starving in Polish Ghettos; others, among them the last president of the Palestine Office, "died" in concentration camps. They all ought to be remembered as heroes in the first battlefront against Hitler. Zionism, of course, could not save the totality of German Jewry, but it saved the lives of more than 60,000 Jews who are now in Palestine. More than that: it touched into flame the concealed spark of Jewish national dignity within the hearts of thousands of German Jews who are now scattered all over the world. As always in Jewish history, one remnant finds a home, physically or spiritually. This is what Zionism achieved in that period of agony: *sh'ar yashuv*— "the Remnant shall return (Isaiah 10:21)."

ERETZ YISRAEL, GALUT AND *CHUTZ LA-ARETZ,* IN THEIR HISTORICAL SETTINGS

From *CCAR Yearbook,* LXII (1952)

The whole of Jewish existence throughout the centuries can be summed up in the two terms of *eretz yisrael* on the one hand, and *galut* on the other. The pendulum of Jewish history has always swung between these two extreme positions. It pointed toward the first in our ancient history, and it turned toward the latter after the year 70 C.E. With the establishment of the State of Israel on May 14, 1948, the historic pendulum has recovered its old position. As we are privileged to live in this age when history has turned a full circle, the present is an opportune time to re-examine the conceptions of *eretz yisrael* and *galut* against the background of their historic settings. From such analysis one might learn many a lesson for our own generation, and receive many an answer to our present-day controversies. It might help us to a deeper evaluation of the historic significance of the State of Israel, to a more thorough understanding of our own position here, and to a greater insight into the relationship that ought to exist between the two hemispheres of Jewish life in our own time.

I am commencing this paper with an analysis of the term *eretz yisrael*. This audience of learned colleagues does not need an elaborate treatment of this aspect of our discussion. It is merely a restatement of known facts, in order to clarify its meaning.

From the early dawn of our history, when God commanded Abraham to get out of his country into the land of Canaan (Genesis 12:1-5), the Bible lavishly bestows upon that Mediterranean strip of land an almost interminable number of titles of honor: Genesis calls it *eretz ha-ivrim*, "the land of the Hebrews (40:15)," but Samuel knows it already by the name of *eretz yisrael* (I Samuel 13:19). As far back as the initial period of the prophetic movement, Hosea awards it the highest epithet of *eretz adonai* (Hosea 9:3), and as a result, to Jeremiah, Palestine is *eretz chemdah, nachalat tzvi, tzivot goyim*, "a pleasant land, the goodliest heritage of the nations (Jeremiah 3:19)," just before the exile; it is *admat yisrael*, and *eretz ha-chaim*, to Ezekiel (Ezekiel 7:2 and 26:20), early in the exile; and *admat ha-kodesh* to Zechariah, at the end of the exile (Zechariah 2:16). Much later in Joel, God himself, as it were, refers to Palestine as *artzi*, "My land (Joel 4:2)."

These biblical names in themselves already indicate the uniqueness of Palestine. It is a land with a special character: not only promised to a people, but wedded to God. The Land of Canaan is called the "Land of the Hebrews" in order to become the "Land of Israel"; in turn, this land, which is "a pleasant and goodly heritage," develops into the "Land of the Lord," and achieves the distinction of holiness. The uniqueness of Palestine consists then of the fact that it is simultaneously both the "Land of Israel" and "the Land of God." No wonder then that very often the Bible (Leviticus 19:23; 23:10, et al.), not to speak of the Midrashic and Talmudic literature, considers this exceptional character of the land so self-evident, that it hardly goes to the trouble of attaching the word *yisrael* to its name. The Torah calls it *ha-aretz*, "the Land" par excellence, knowing full well that this is the best way to underscore its particular character and distinguish it from all other countries.

The fact that Palestine is both the "Land of God" and the "Land of Israel" leads in our tradition to the two-fold principle of *kedushat ha-aretz*, the special holiness with which the land is imbued and which derives its essence from 1) the Shekinah that dwells *in* the land, and 2) Israel that dwells on it. As far as the first is concerned, namely, *kedushat ha-shekinah*, Palestine, which the Bible calls *nachlat adonai* (I Samuel 26:19) is, according to the Midrash, so beloved by God that he chose it for himself when he distributed the earth, in the same way as he selected Israel for himself when he created the nations. Having done so, God added, "May Israel which is my possession, inherit the land which is my portion (Tanchuma Re'ei 8)." So holy indeed is this land, that the Shekinah reveals itself there exclusively (Rashi to Jonah 1:3; Rashi to bMo'ed Katan 25a; *Kusari* 2:15). When some of the Sages wondered how Ezekiel could have become a prophet though living in Babylon, the answer was, that this only happened because God revealed himself to Ezekiel already in Palestine prior to the time of the exile (mMoed Katan, *ibid*). In addition, says our Jewish tradition, Ezekiel's book was not written by the prophet in exile, but by the Great Assembly in Palestine (Rashi to bBaba Bathra 15a).

Yes, so deep-rooted was the conception of the "holiness of the land" in the minds of the Rabbis, that they were motivated to make the provocative statement that "whosoever lives in the Land of Israel is considered as having God, and whosoever lives outside, is considered as if he has no God (bKethuboth 110b)."

There is no more touching description of *kedushat ha-shekinah,* and none that sums it up better, than the image projected in Deuteronomy 11:12: "A land which the Lord thy God careth for; the eyes of the Lord are always on it from the beginning of the year to the end of the year." Because of all that has been said, "the Land of Israel is holier than all other lands (mKelim 1:6)"; it is a place of Torah, because even "the air of *eretz yisrael* makes people wise (bBaba Bathra 158b)"; and it is a place of wisdom, because "ten measures of wisdom descended upon the earth; nine went to Palestine and one to the rest of the world (bKiddushin 49b)."

Occupying this lofty position, it is not astonishing to see our tradition put so much emphasis upon the commandment of *yeshivat eretz yisrael,* "the settling on the land." This was, of course, done for reasons of security. Thus, when the Bible says, "Ye shall dwell in this land safely (Leviticus 26:5)," says the Midrash, "In this land you will live in safety; you will not live in safety outside the land (Sifra, Bechukotai, Parasha 1, Perek 1)." But more than that, and overshadowing the reasons of security, is the conception of holiness: it is the settling on the land by the People of Israel from which the country derives its second holiness, called *kedushat yisrael*. Taking the cue from the Bible, "Ye shall possess the land and dwell therein (Deuteronomy 11:31)," the Rabbis not only elevated the idea of *yeshivat eretz yisrael* to a commandment, but one which outweighs all others. Says the Midrash, "Living in the land of Israel outweighs all other commandments in the Torah (Sifrei, Re'ei 80)."

The Rabbis meant every word of it. They first made unprecedented concessions in the execution of the law. Thus, "Whoever buys a house in Palestine may write his contract even on Shabbat (bGittin 8b)." This apparently was not too difficult to conceive, for they declared that if one lived in Palestine one could not commit any sins. As the Talmud says, "Whosoever lives in *eretz yisrael* finds himself without sin (bKethuboth 111a)," because it is written, "The people that dwell therein have been forgiven their iniquities (Isaiah 33:24)." Not alone is one free from sin, which is only a negative achievement, but the simple fact of spending one's life in the Holy Land guarantees one a place in the World to Come. More than that, it is not even a matter of living there permanently, but "whosoever walks four yards in the land of Israel is assured of the World to Come *(Ibid.)*."

The picture is now clearly discernible. The principle of *kedushat yisrael* brings with it remarkable advantages: concessions in the observance of the law, forgiveness for sins, the fulfillment of all the commandments, and the assurance of a place in the World to Come. The Rabbis apparently had some difficulty with these sweeping statements when they encountered the words of Ezekiel, "When the House of Israel dwelt in their own land, they defiled it by their ways and their own doings (Ezekiel 36:17)." They solved the problem by interpreting the prophetic words in the opposite direction: "The Holy One, Blessed be He, says, 'I wish my children were with me in the Land of Israel, even if they defile it' (Echah Rabbathi 3)."

247

The influence of this two-fold holiness of the land, *kedushat ha-shekinah* and *kedushat yisrael,* goes beyond the boundaries of race and creed. Says the Talmud, "Even a Canaanite maid who lives in the Land of Israel is assured of a place in the world to come (bKethuboth 111a)." And this is not all. For even the people who did not live in Palestine, but only came there to die, enjoyed the privilege of forgiveness for their sins. Interpreting the Bible, "And he makes expiation for the land of his people (Deuteronomy 32:43)," the Rabbis say, "because they are buried in the Land of Israel, and a plot of soil covers them, their sins are forgiven (yKilayim 32d)." The reason for this challenging statement is given in another place, "Whosoever is buried in the Land of Israel, is as if he were buried under the altar (bKethuboth 111a)." If one is mindful of the importance our tradition attaches to one's birth in Palestine—attributing, for instance, the presence of the Shekinah in Jerusalem to the fact that Benjamin was native born (Mechilta, d'b'Chodesh, Yitro 4)—one fully comprehends that the two-fold principle of holiness actually covers the whole of human existence, from the cradle to the grave.

To sum it up, *eretz yisrael* is not only a geographical name for the territory of an ancient people, but a title of honor that spells uniqueness and conveys the idea of holiness which, in turn, derives its essence from the immanence of the Shekinah *in* the land, and the settlement by the people of Israel on the land. More than that, *eretz yisrael* is a conception of bliss standing for all the high ideals that make for happiness in national life, and justice for society as a whole. There is a spiritual quality about the image of our Rabbis' projecting the "Jerusalem of below" into a "Jerusalem of above." There is something deeply touching in the interpretation which the Jerusalem Talmud gives to the words of the psalmist, "Jerusalem, that art builded as a city that is compact together (Psalm 122:3)," by saying that the psalmist had in mind, "A city that fosters the companionship of all of Israel (yHagigah 78b)." It does not happen by chance that, throughout the centuries of our dispersion, the name Jerusalem was bestowed upon great centers of Jewish learning—Vilna, for instance, was called the "Jerusalem of Lithuania"—in order to indicate that every place from which the Word of God comes forth is a replica of the ancient City of David. All the dreams of prophets and kings, all the aspirations of sages and teachers, and all the hopes of untold generations of Jews for the future of our people as it ought to be, can easily be summed up in the two words of *eretz yisrael*.

This is not only an ancient conception, but one that has remained prevalent in the minds of our people throughout the centuries to this very day. In a discussion of this subject in the recently published *Talmudic Encyclopedia* which quotes from dozens of authorities including the Ramban, the Chatam Sofer, and the late Rabbi Kook—the author gives his summary in the following words: "The holiness of the land...and its superior qualities both for the living and dead has not changed in any direction, neither in the time of the Babylonian Exile nor in the Diaspora of our own days—it is an eternal holiness till the end of days. It hasn't changed and will never change (*Talmudic Encyclopedia*, II, p. 214)."

II

The extreme opposite of *eretz yisrael* is the term *galut*. As if to parallel the commandment of *yeshivat eretz yisrael* which "outweighs all other commandments in the Torah" quoted above, the Midrash sums up the conception of *galut* by saying, "Heavy is the *galut*, for it outweighs everything else (Sifrei, Ekev 43)," meaning it is heavier than all the curses of the *tochachah* ["Admonition," *word of rebuke found in Deuteronomy 28-29. Editors*]. Under this heading, the word *galut* is used in different ways. To the author of the Book of Judges, the words *ad yom gelot ha-aretz* (Judges 18:30) mean that the land became bare of its inhabitants. Jeremiah uses it in the same vein, when he employs the words of *ad gelot yerushalayim* (Jeremiah 1:3). More frequently, however, *galut* means the compulsory banishment from the original homeland to a strange territory and the suffering which this tragedy entailed. The examples for this conception are literally innumerable, and they can be found even throughout the Bible (II Kings 17:23; Amos 7:17; Ezekiel 33:21; Ezra 2:1).

It is interesting to note that already our ancient literature went beyond the conception of *galut* merely as desolation of the land and the captivity of the people. It knew already of the *spiritual* suffering of the Jew who lived among Gentiles, in addition to the physical persecution. Thus, the Midrash, in commenting on the words of the Book of Lamentations 1:3, *galta yehuda*, "Judah was driven into exile," asks the obvious question whether non-Jewish nations were not from time to time driven into captivity. To this, the Midrash gives the following answer: "Even if they go into exile, their exile is not *galut;* Gentiles who eat each other's bread and drink each other's wine, cannot be considered as living in *galut;* but for Israel, which does not break bread with the non-Jewish world, and does not drink from its wine—dispersion is *galut* (Echah Rabbathi 1:29)." This shows that our Rabbis were very well aware of all the psychological implications in the minority-majority relationships, which we have begun to understand only in our generation with the help of the social sciences.

Again, no ancient, or for this matter no modern source, surpasses the description of *galut* in the *tochacha* of Deuteronomy. Here one finds all the real horrors of Jewish history which we usually associate with *galut*, formulated in words of awful power. One will have to look far and wide for a parallel to the following biblical words: "And the Lord will scatter thee among all peoples from the one end of the earth even unto the other end of the earth.... There, among these nations thou shalt have no repose, and there shall be no rest for the sole of thy foot; for the Lord will give thee there a trembling heart and a failing of eyes and languishing of soul. And thy life shall hang in doubt before thee; and thou shalt fear night and day, and thou shalt have no assurance of thy life. In the morning, thou shalt say, 'Would it were even!'; and at even thou wilt say 'Would it were morning!'; for the fear of thy heart that thou shalt fear and for the sight of thine eyes which thou shalt see (Deuteronomy 28:64-67)." Those of us who have come through Hitler's holocaust, cannot read these words without shuddering. The psychological image of *galut* which the Bible projects in these few lines, is unsurpassed in the literature of Western Civilization.

The Rabbis considered the *galut* such a heavy and crushing burden that they found only one way of explaining it: punishment for sins. The idea found in our ancient prayerbook, "Because of our sins, we were exiled from our land," pervades the whole of Midrashic and Talmudic literature. "The Rabbis say that *galut* only comes into the world because of the violation of commandments, principally, on account of idolatry, immorality, and bloodshed (mAboth 5:11; bShabbath 33a)." This interpretation of *galut* apparently left an indelible imprint upon the memory of our people, because, throughout the centuries of Jewish life, we find the rather strange and fascinating institution of *tikun ha-galut,* or in its Yiddish expression, *"Goles Oprichten":* in order to expiate one's sins and do penitence, one takes upon one's self the curse of personal exile. The Talmud already knows of that when it tells the story of Rabba who goes for this purpose to Rome (bBerakoth 56a). In subsequent centuries, we find the Gaon of Vilna practicing *tikun ha-galut,* by going incognito through the villages and towns in Poland, in order to inflict suffering upon himself. All this has to do with the principle stated above. In the same way as *galut* is punishment for sins, it also makes for expiation of sins (*ibid.*).

In citing the three definitions of *galut*—desolation of the land, captivity of the people, and spiritual and psychological suffering—we have by far not exhausted the variety of its meanings in our ancient tradition. Frequently, the Talmud uses the word *galut* only in the sense of dispersion without the corollary stigma of depravity. For example, the Talmud tells the story of Rabban Gamaliel who sat on the steps of the Temple mount, and next to him stood the scribe Johanan, the secretary of the Sanhedrin. Rabban Gamaliel dictated three letters in the form of three circulars, one to our brothers in the Galilee, the second to our brethren in the south, and the third to our brothers in the dispersion of Babylon and all other *galuyot* of Israel. In these letters he announced to all parts of the Jewish People wherever they lived, that that particular year was a leap year (bSanhedrin 11b). In this story, as in many others, *galut* simply means Jewish communities in other countries. Similarly, whenever the Talmud uses the word *galut* in connection with legislation, it simply means communities living outside *eretz yisrael.* For instance, when the Talmud speaks of *shenei yamim tovim shel galuyot,* it merely refers to the second holiday observed by Jews outside of Palestine (bBezah 4b).

There is even more to it. In spite of the general leitmotif that *galut* outweighs all other curses in the *tochacha,* there are state-

251

ments by the Rabbis, which indicate that sometimes they looked upon the *galut* even as an advantage in the battle for Jewish survival. Commenting on the words of the Book of Judges, *tzidkot pirzono b'yisrael,* (Judges 5:11) the Talmud says, "God bestowed a favor upon Israel in spreading them among the nations (bPesachim 87b)." Rashi adds significantly that this is so "because the nations cannot destroy them all together simultaneously." The same page of the Talmud has the famous statement "that the Holy One, Blessed be He, would not have forced Israel into exile among the nations, were it not for the purpose of attaching converts to them." There are many similar statements, but the ones quoted above will suffice for our discussion.

The question arises: how are these contradictory definitions of *galut* explainable? What is the motivating idea behind this shifting from one extreme to the other?

In order to answer these questions, one has to remember first that the word *galut* covered a very large territory. It referred originally to the forcible ejection from Palestine into strange lands. Later on when our people lived spread all over the world, *galut* did not mean exile, but as stated above, simply dispersion. It is in this vein that the political head of the community in Babylon was called *resh galuta* [Exilarch]. After the destruction of the first Temple, Jews in Babylon were living in "exile," because they were driven there by Nebuchadnezzar. But, after the destruction of the second Temple, they chose to settle there on their own volition, because of the critical situation in Palestine. The same thing happened after the revolt of Bar Kochba, when Babylon became the new home of the Jews because they fled from Roman persecution. *Resh galuta* was not then the name for the leader of Jews in a land of misery, but the head of an autonomous *kehillah* in Babylon. All this means that the word *galut* was used, rather ambiguously, to cover two types of Diaspora: one for *forced exile,* and the other for *voluntary dispersion.* The Rabbis felt the distinction between the two, though they used the same word; and although *galut* is always *galut,* there is a difference in shading, in degree though not in principle, and this might explain some of the friendlier statements of the Rabbis toward the same phenomenon of *galut,* which basically they considered the worst tragedy in the existence of our people.

252

There is a second and maybe even more important reason for this discrepancy of opinion, as far as the *galut* is concerned. It has to do with the *character of the dispersion,* and the *quality of the exiles,* as measured by the *climate of freedom* on the one hand, and by the *religious and cultural productivity* of their respective Jewish communities on the other. Under this aspect too, it is interesting to look upon the *galut* of Babylon.

Already from some indirect remarks of the Bible, one can assume that the ancient community lived a rich and full life in Babylon, otherwise Ezra and Nehemiah could not have been products of that generation. From the sixth chapter in Zechariah, we learn that even before the time of Ezra, namely in the period of Zerubabel, Jews in Babylon used to send gold and silver to Jerusalem for the building of the Temple. From Zechariah, we learn of a delegation from Babylon that came to Jerusalem bringing gifts to enhance the Temple. The prophet hoped that many more would come and do the same: "And they that are far off shall come and build in the Temple of the Lord (Zechariah 6:15)." This impression of Jewish life in Babylon was verified in 1897, through the archeological discovery, by the expedition of the University of Pennsylvania, of the Murashu Texts, excavated at the ancient city of Nippur in central Babylonia. From these cuneiform tablets we learn that the economic situation of the Jews in Babylon was favorable, that they owned land and possessed capital, and that many, not only Nehemiah, were in the service of the government. We also learn that there were no barriers between Babylonians, Persians, and Jews; that under Persian rule Jews were free citizens, occupying high social and economic positions, and that this was probably the reason why many of them stayed in Babylon in spite of the permission to return. But with that, Jerusalem still remained the Holy City, and Palestine the Holy Land. They sent money and gifts in order to maintain the Temple, were deeply interested in the welfare of the land, and wanted to see religion grow and develop.

Obviously then, this positive character of *galut* differed substantially in the minds of the Rabbis from the persecutions in their own times. *Galut* was still a curse and a tragedy for the nation, but the fact that the Jewish community in Babylon developed freely, made the Rabbis look upon it with friendlier eyes. The same is true with regard to the quality of the exiles. If they remembered their Bible well, the Rabbis knew that they were not creating any precedents. Similar sentiments were expressed by prophets prior to their time.

When Jehoiachin, the King of Judah, was exiled in 597 B.C.E. with the royal court and officers of the State, a new middle class group in Jerusalem inherited their power. The new lords began to look down upon the exiles, saying that, because of their sins, was the *galut* imposed upon the entire people. Jeremiah protests against this accusation in his famous vision of the two baskets of figs, in which he says that God himself, as it were, is on the side of the exiles against those who stayed on the land. "Thus saith the Lord, the God of Israel, 'Like these good figs, so will I regard the captives of Judah, whom I have sent out of this place into the land of the Chaldeans for good. And I will set Mine eyes upon them for good, and I will bring them back to this land; and I will build them, and not pull them down; and I will plant them, and not pluck them up. And I will give them a heart to know Me, that I am the Lord; and they shall be My people, and I will be their God; for they shall return unto Me with their whole heart' (Jeremiah 24:5-7)."

On the other hand, Jeremiah turns to the Judeans who remained in the Holy Land, and says in the name of God, "I will even make them a horror among all the kingdoms of the earth for evil; a reproach and a proverb, a taunt and a curse, in all places whither I shall drive them (Jeremiah 24:9)." The prophet here acknowledges that the quality of the people in exile was higher than that of the population that stayed on in the Holy Land but remained obdurate and spiritually deaf. Ezekiel speaks in the same vein and considers the exiled Jews in Babylon of a higher human type than those who stayed on in Judea. He, too, protests against the attitude of the Judeans who say "Unto us is this land given as a possession (Ezekiel 11:15)." And he says in the name of God about the exiles, "Although I have removed them far off among the nations, and although I have scattered them among the countries, yet have I been to them as a little sanctuary in the countries where they are come (Ezekiel 11:16)." Both Jeremiah and Ezekiel, then, were here of the same opinion and, contrary to what might be expected, considered the *galut* superior to the Judean population. It is because of this, that Jeremiah went even as far as to prepare the Jewish community in Babylon for their ultimate adjustment to their new homeland. Thus, in his famous message which he sent to Babylon, he admonished them, saying, "Build ye houses, and dwell in them, and plant gardens and eat the fruit of them; take ye wives, and beget sons and daughters; and take wives for your sons, and give your daughters to husbands, that they may bear sons and daughters; and multiply ye there, and be not diminished. And seek the peace of the city whither I have caused you to be carried away captive and pray unto the Lord for it; for in the peace thereof shall ye have peace (Jeremiah 29:5-7)."

It is clear that the prophets looked upon *galut* with as much disfavor as did the Rabbis in subsequent centuries. But the quality of the exiles motivated them to treat the Babylonian Jewish community as an exception to the rule.

History repeats itself after the destruction of Jerusalem when, again, the rich were exiled and only the poor population was left on the soil of Palestine. Again, those who remained said, "Unto us is this land given as a possession (Ezekiel 33:24)," and again Ezekiel protests against that attitude and threatens them with destruction. Ezekiel analyzed the situation correctly. He saw that in the rebuilding of Palestine the Jews of Babylon would play the major role, and that they would be brought back to the land for the very purpose of rebuilding it (Ezekiel 36:24).

Subsequent history proved his point. The spiritual hegemony, not only during the exile, but in the later period of reconstruction, belonged to the Jews of Babylon. The Rabbis of course, needless to say, were aware both of the attitude of the prophets and of the unique quality of the *galut* of Babylon. From a historic viewpoint they were right, because the *galut* of Babylon, though lasting no more than half a century, made the deepest impact upon the development of Judaism. It not only raised our people to a higher spiritual level, but caused a basic change in its outlook on life.

Chaim Schauss, in three remarkable articles on the subject of *"Galut and Eretz Yisrael"* in the magazine, *Die Zukunft* (October, 1948, Vol. 53, No. 8; July-August, 1950, Vol. 55, No. 6; July-August, 1951, Vol. 56, No. 6), rightly calls our attention to

*With Teddy Kollek, Mayor of Jerusalem,
and Ruth Nussbaum*

the magnificent contribution that the *galut* of Babylon made to the survival of Judaism. One has to compare, he says, the Jews and Judeans at the time of the First Kingdom to the time of the second Temple, in order to understand what the *galut* of Babylon did for us. In II Kings (Chapter 16), we learn that King Ahaz ordered the building of an Assyrian altar in the Sanctuary, a replica of an altar that he had seen in Damascus, and that his order was carried out without protest. Nobody was shocked. Compare this to a similar order for a Greek altar by Antiochus Epiphanes, and observe that the Book of Daniel calls it *shikutz meshomem,* the "detestable thing that causes appallment (Daniel 11:31; 12:11)." A guerrilla war was started, and it ended in the struggle of the Maccabees. One has to remember also the resistance of the Jews when Pontius Pilate ordered the raising of an image of Caesar in the Sanctuary. Jews offered their lives in resistance. The contrast is evident, and Ezekiel was right in saying that "the Jews who returned from Babylon will have a new spirit and a new heart (Ezekiel 36:26)."

Yes, the *galut* of Babylon is rather unique in the history of mankind. With all other nations, exile is doom, but in our history Babylon reinforced the national strength of our people and rejuvenated its creative power. The most amazing feature is the fact that this was not even a voluntary *galut,* like the one in the time of the Talmud, but one in which a people was forcibly ejected from its land and driven to another. It was in Babylon that Jews freed themselves from all the heathen elements in their religious observance. It was, of all places, in Babylon, that some of our most important commandments grew in their religious significance, as for instance the *berit mila* and the Shabbat, which became a day of prayer and of learning and a Holy Day. (Not only this, but apparently some of the important laws were kept only in Babylon and not in Palestine. The Shabbat was the market day in Jerusalem and we remember from the Book of Nehemiah, that he, Nehemiah, had to impose upon the Jews of Judea the conception of the Shabbat that had, in the meantime, been developed in Babylon (Nehemiah 13:15,22). It was in Babylon that the synagogue was born, and the prayerbook, and the prayer system. Finally, it was in Babylon that universalism and ethical monotheism

257

were proclaimed in the religious philosophy of Isaiah II (Isaiah 49:6—and almost every other chapter of the Book).

To sum it up, a *galut* like the one of Babylon—in spite of the fact that living in exile was considered a national catastrophe—had a rather high rating in the minds of both prophets and rabbis, because of the two reasons analyzed above: first, the Jews in Babylon enjoyed almost complete freedom of action; secondly, the Jewish community was of high human quality and was exceedingly productive in culture and religion. This is why one will, again and again, find statements in midrashic and talmudic literature which consider the *galut* of Babylon in a most friendly light.

III

We have spoken up to now of the two terms prevalent in our tradition, namely *eretz yisrael* and *galut.* Our midrashic and talmudic literature knows however of a third term, namely *chutz la-aretz.* It is sometimes used interchangeably with the word *galut,* yet in many places it has only a territorial connotation, meaning neither exile nor dispersion, but simply lands and communities outside the geographical boundaries of Palestine. Thus, when the Mishna speaks of *peirot chutz la-aretz* (mChalah 2:1) that were brought to *eretz yisrael* and were subject to the law of *chalah*—it is obvious that the Mishna refers here simply to fruits imported from foreign countries.

The term *chutz la-aretz* is similar to the one of *medinat ha-yam,* referring to all lands neighboring on Palestine which can be reached by boat only. In commenting on the discussion in the Talmud with reference to a *get* that is brought from *medinat ha-yam,* Rashi adds significantly that "the whole of *chutz la-aretz* is called *medinat ha-yam,* with the exception of Babylon (bGittin 1a)," which is *chutz la-aretz* only. The Rabbis then were aware of the distinction between the *chutz la-aretz* of the Babylon of their time and the *galut* of other lands. This high opinion of Babylon apparently reached its unexpected climax when the Talmud itself stated, in simple and candid words, that it was forbidden to emigrate from Babylon to other lands because "whoever lives in Babylon is as if he would live in *eretz yisrael* (bKethuboth 111a)."

I believe that in the whole history of our tradition, this has never been said of any other place on the entire globe. Babylon—even in its first, but surely in its second Diaspora—apparently deserved this accolade, because it gave to its Jewish citizens freedom and peace of mind and allowed for their cultural growth and religious creativity. Though the Rabbis used the word *galut* interchangeably with *chutz la-aretz,* even with reference to the Babylon of the talmudic period, we know today that it was only a *façon de parler,* and that the difference between Babylon on the one hand, and a real *galut* on the other, was very much in their minds. Says the Talmud, "The Holy One, Blessed be He, knew very well that Israel could not bear cruel decrees—this is why He exiled them to Babylon; and even to Babylon he sent them only because its language was close to the tongue of the Torah." Rashi comments on this statement, "So that the Torah should not be forgotten in Israel (bPesachim 87b)." We do not go astray by assuming then that our ancient tradition knew well how to operate with the term *chutz la-aretz* as a middle line between the two extremes of *eretz yisrael* and *galut.*

IV

If against the historical setting of these three terms——*eretz yisrael, galut,* and *chutz la-aretz*—the question would be asked, "What is America?" I would answer unhesitatingly, "America is *chutz la-aretz.*"

There is a story told of Shmaryahu Levin in connection with his visit to California on behalf of the Zionist movement. He delivered one of his famous addresses in one of the largest halls in Los Angeles, pounding away at the inferior position of the *galut* in Jewish life. After the meeting, a reception was held for the speaker of the evening in one of the loveliest estates in the Hollywood hills overlooking the city. Shmaryahu Levin stood on the balcony enjoying the view, when the host approached him with the question, "Dr. Levin, how do you like California?" To which, Shmaryahu Levin replied, without a moment's hesitation, in fluent Yiddish, *"Es is take a Goles—ober a gebenchter Goles."* Shmaryahu Levin's definition of California as a *"gebenchter Goles"* comes very close to my conception of *chutz la-aretz* applied to the United States of America.

259

I have, as do all of you, a deep affection for this beloved land of ours, but in historical terms it is obviously not *eretz yisrael*. I do not believe that one acquires faith in God simply by living here, or that one achieves *olam ha-ba* when one walks four inches on the boulevards of our cities or on the dusty roads of our prairies. It does not have the *kedusha* that comes from God's calling it *artzi*, or from Israel's calling it *eretz yisrael*. In short, I do not believe that living on this soil by itself "outweighs all the commandments of the Torah."

On the other hand, it is not *galut* in the sense of exile, because none of our parents were forced to come here. They were forced to flee other continents and assembled here in what one might call a voluntary dispersion. Here they built their homes, and all of us consider America our home to this very day. It would be unfair to call this settlement *galut*, because then you would have to test it against all the statements made about this term in the course of centuries. Would anyone seriously say that America is a *galut* that "outweighs in its burden all the curses of the *tochacha*?" Could it compare to the physical persecution and spiritual suffering, or even to the psychological difficulties of the Jewish communities in Russia, Poland and Rumania in the time of the pogroms? Is life here such that it could be considered "punishment for sins?" If so, sinning has paid off rather handsomely.

No, America is neither *eretz yisrael* nor *galut*, but it has all the characteristics of *chutz la-aretz*, so nobly exemplified by the second voluntary dispersion of Babylon. Here there is freedom, high economic and social position, intellectual leadership, and to a large degree, peace of mind. There is surely the opportunity of participating in the upbuilding of the Land of Israel, and of furthering its development and its growth, and it augurs well for making this America of ours into a cultural center. If we could develop this republic into a center of Torah, one could indeed speak with Jeremiah's words and say to American Jewry, "Build ye houses, and dwell in them, and plant gardens and eat the fruit of them...And multiply ye there, and be not diminished. And seek the peace of the city...and pray unto the Lord for it; for in the peace thereof shall ye have peace (Jeremiah 29:5-7)."

We are living in a time in which *galut*, in the real sense of the word, will soon come to an end. When the *galut* is liquidated, what will remain for us in future generations is *eretz yisrael* on the one hand, and *chutz la-aretz* on the other. There is no reason why there should not be a two-way passage between the two centers of Jewish existence. By saying "two-way passage" I do not mean the sending of money from the one end, and the receiving of spiritual values from the other, but also an exchange in the eternal verities of Judaism, with as many American Ezras and Hillels, and with as many Israeli Rabs and Shemuels as is feasible, in order "to return the Torah to its ancient place of dignity." There is no reason why this great American Jewry of ours should not leave as deep an imprint on our people, as did Babylon with its religious and cultural productivity in centuries gone by. If Jewish history should in any way serve as a model for our children's future—Israeli and American Jewry will have to function in a complementary relationship to each other, as the only way of translating the spiritual conception of Klal Yisrael into a tangible reality.

There is a remarkable speech by Dr. Leo Baeck, delivered in the form of a Presidential Address at the Eighth International Conference of the World Union for Progressive Judaism, which was held in London during July of 1949. Discussing the role of the new State of Israel, Dr. Baeck had this to say:

> The old soil has today become a center. Jewish life in its totality, the *klal yisrael,* has very rarely been a circle, that is to say a formation with only one center, only one focus of strength; it has mostly been an ellipse, a formation determined by two focuses, two centers. Nearly always it has been like that.... In the old days there were the Northern and Southern realms in Palestine, later Palestine and Babylon, later the Sephardic and Ashkenazic phases of culture, later Western Europe and Eastern Europe, and nowadays the Western world and the State of Israel.... Today the two centers are: the Jewish life in the land of Israel and the Jewish life in the Western world. Or to make it distinct in another way also: the weights on the scales are different today and differently distributed from what they were before. The weight of Europe has become slighter in the scales of total Jewish life; the two big weights are now America and Palestine, and a new equilibrium must be obtained, a clear, just, reasonable balance is to be kept in view...The joint task of this

261

generation and of the following, the task which may be the great opportunity given to our movement, is to bring about and to safeguard the right and clear connection, *the living and healthy relationship between these two spheres,* decisively to bear both in mind, to help *that they may give one another and receive one from the other their best,* that they may *both together, neither of them without the other,* bring it about in our world which has passed through revolutions, that our *Judaism shows its religious strength, its moral force* and *proves having its place within mankind,* its place among the religious, doing its part that the earth be prepared for God's Kingdom.

This statement by the great leader of our Reform Movement should serve as a Shulchan Aruch for all of us. Israel today is a State, and we are not. They are politically independent, and we are citizens of another land. But above the new State in the Middle East and the Jewish people here, towers the immortal name of Israel which has always meant to our people much more than the ethnic connotation of *yehudim,* because the term *yisrael* has consistently proclaimed the spiritual quality of our people in its attachment to God, as indicated by the *"El"* in its name. This alone is the essence of the stuff of which we are made. While we are not a political part of Israel, the Israelis are a part of our Jewish people, a section of which lives here on this soil. All of us together, then, are bound to each other by the historic name of Israel. It is the name of the young Jewish State, and simultaneously the title of honor of American Jewry. Taking the name seriously, we, the State of Israel and American Israel, can create a new future, erect a structure for Jewish survival, and become again a blessing to mankind.

ISRAEL: THE CAREER OF A NAME

From *Congress Weekly,* XIX:18 (May 19,1952)

The fourth anniversary of the establishment of the Jewish State has just been celebrated. Israel—the name which the young state bears—is frequently in the headlines and the title of countless speeches and articles. There is not a Jew in the United States who has not, at one time or another, used or heard the word Israel. Even if his knowledge of Hebrew is scanty, he has heard or recited the *sh'ma yisrael.* Each one of us has often come across the phrases "the people of Israel," "the land of Israel" "the children of Israel," and—here and there—even "American Israel."

Throughout the centuries of Jewish life, Israel has been a highly esteemed proper name to be given to newly born Jewish sons, and many distinguished families in our history have borne this name with great and justifiable pride. This being the case, it may be of value to attempt to answer the familiar Shakespearean question, "What's in a name?"

In biblical literature, the word Israel appears first as the name bestowed upon our forefather, Jacob. Subsequently, the word Israel is used in the Bible to designate all twelve tribes as one entity, and later on to signify the kingdom of Saul, David, and Solomon, which lasted for about a century. After the partition of the land into the northern and southern kingdoms, the word Israel is first employed to describe the northern part of the country to the exclusion of Judah in the south, but after the fall of Samaria, the word came to mean the southern kingdom of Judah also. Finally, in the period following the Babylonian captivity, the word Israel commences to be applied to the whole people wherever they lived.

For this discussion, it is not of importance whether the usage of the word Israel in biblical genealogy is historically correct or not. Whether the name of the father of the twelve tribes was really Israel, or whether the author of Genesis projected this name into the distant past, is of no consequence. It is quite plausible that originally Israel was the name of a tribe—of a single tribe—apparently the most important and most vital of the Hebrew tribes; that later the name was transferred to a group of tribes, and still later to the whole people living in the land, and at the end to the whole nation wherever it resided.

What is, however, of utmost significance is the fact that, beginning with the prophetic movement in the history of our people, the word Israel rose spectacularly to a most brilliant career. It came to mean excellency of character, religious

263

devotion, and the quality of spiritual values. The Book of Genesis explains the new name given to Jacob in the famous words: "Thou hast striven with God and with men and hast prevailed (Genesis 32:28)." The prophet Hosea takes his cue from this definition of the word Israel and elaborates on it: "By his strength he strove with a Godlike being; so he strove with an angel and prevailed; he wept and made supplication unto Him (Hosea 12:5)."

This conception of Israel as a spiritual aristocracy became the accepted platform of the whole of prophecy and reached its unsurpassable height in Deutero-Isaiah, who lived near the end of the Babylonian exile. It was this prophet who poured into the mold of the word Israel the sublime pattern of his religious philosophy: Israel is the people whom God has chosen to be a witness before the nations of the world; it thus undertakes the role of "the servant in whom God is being glorified (Isaiah 49:3)," and God himself, as it were, becomes therefore "the Holy One of Israel (Isaiah 49:7)" and the "Mighty One of Israel (Isaiah 1:24)." Says the prophet: "I, the Lord, have called thee in righteousness, and will hold thine hand, and will keep thee, and give thee for a covenant to mankind, for a light unto the nations; to open the blind eyes, to bring out the prisoners from the dungeon, and them that sit in darkness out of the prison-house (Isaiah 42:6-8)." In order to enable Israel to fulfill its divinely appointed task, it will be restored to the Holy Land, and God will remain its protector throughout all its historical experiences: "When thou passest through the waters, I will be with thee, and the rivers, they shall not overflow thee; when thou walkest through the fire, thou wilt not be burned; and the fire shall not kindle on thee; for I am the Lord, thy God, the Holy One of Israel, thy Saviour (Isaiah 43:2-3)." Thus Israel will be given the opportunity of realizing its high vocation and of remaining for all eternity "My witnesses and My servant whom I have chosen (Isaiah 43:10)."

This, then, is the way in which, at the climax of Jewish prophecy, the word Israel achieved the position of a *titre d'honneur*, a title of honor, which denotes both the spiritual, ethical, and religious values for which Judaism stands, as well as the idea of *noblesse oblige*, the nobility that obliges, to give an example of ethical conduct to the whole of mankind.

264

How deeply the prophetic interpretation of the word Israel influenced biblical literature can be gathered from a study of the Book of Esther. Throughout this book, the Jews are called *yehudim* and not *yisrael,* because the Jewishness of the Jews at the time consisted only in their defense against a surrounding gentile world which wanted to destroy them. There is no trace of any spiritual quality of the Jewish community of that period, and therefore the Book of Esther wisely refrains from using the word *yisrael*—a name reserved to express *religious* significance.

The momentous impact that Deutero-Isaiah's definition of Israel had upon subsequent Jewish history can be seen in the fact that Philo, living in the first century C.E., when speaking of the eternal spiritual verities of our people, formulates his thoughts in the following words: "Its high position is indicated by its name Israel, which means 'one who sees God,' an endowment which represents the highest gift of the mind. Possessing this gift of vision, Israel must serve as a means by which other peoples may be led to the light."

The purely spiritual and religious interpretation of the word Israel has also put its stamp on the whole of the Rabbinic period. In the literature of the Talmud and the Midrash, the word *yisrael* is consistently used to designate the distinctively religious inheritance of our people, in contrast to the name *yehudim* which is only employed when signifying the group without any spiritual specifications. Thus the people of Israel, according to Talmud and Midrash, are "compassionate, chaste, and gracious in the service of their fellow man"; they are the "children of the covenant" and "believers and descendants of believers," and "their whole heart belongs to the Father in Heaven"; they are *banim la-makom,* children of God, and even "more beloved by God than are the angels." It is because of this special affection that God himself calls them by the name, "my first-born son, Israel."

As a result of Israel's special relationship to God, he accompanies them from one exile to another in order to protect them, and he will also return with their captivity and be redeemed with their redemption. Literally hundreds of similar passages could be quoted from the talmudic and midrashic literature. In a concise and felicitous formulation in the Jerusalem Talmud, the whole interpretation of the name Israel is summed up in an allegory. Say the Rabbis: "The Holy One, Blessed be He, attached his great name to Israel," (*yisra-el,* and *El* means God), like the king who had once a key to his treasure house and had the key attached to a chain to make sure that he would not lose it. Similarly, God said, "If I leave the people of Israel as they are, they may be swallowed up among the nations—so I will attach my name to them and they will live forever (yTaanit 64b)."

All these examples show that whenever the sages of Talmud and Midrash wanted to express the idea of worthiness, it is conveyed by the term *yisrael.* Only when the Jewish group is referred to in its purely ethnic character, or when non-Jews utter a sentence about Jews, the word *yehudim* is frequently to be found.

This explanation holds good throughout the whole subsequent history of our people. More and more the word Israel expresses both the humane quality of our people as well as its relationship to God, whereas the name *yehudim,* already in the period of the Second Temple, came to express the political and national connotation of our group. This is why in the whole Greco-Roman sphere of culture the word *Jew* is consistently employed, and from there it enters the sphere of Western Civilization. Only in designating Israel as a religious entity was the name maintained, and this is the way it remained throughout the Middle Ages. It is not surprising, therefore, that to Judah ha-Levi, Israel symbolizes the national genius of our people for the "light of the spirit," and that in the *Kusari* even Moses derives his preeminence from Israel, because without it there would have been no Torah. This historical interpretation of Israel has been steadfastly upheld not only in traditional Judaism but even in the Reform movement.

This is also the reason why in modern times, beginning with the epoch of Emancipation, the word Israel came to the fore in order to emphasize the religious community as against the conception of the Jews as a national entity. This was in keeping with the times, when the Jewish community in Germany and in France was officially recognized as a religious body only. As the name *Jew* was again and again used by the anti-Semitic movement of the time as a word of contempt, the

266

name Israel was raised as a shield of protection. By calling themselves *Israelites,* the Jews of the Emancipation period were saying to the world that they were only a religious group without any national aspirations. As late as 1921, even in this country, Isaac Bernheim proposed that American Jews should call themselves "the Reformed Church of American Israelites," apparently in order to emphasize the religious character of American Jewry, in reply to the charges of anti-Semites that they formed a "state within a state."

There is, of course, a long road from Deutero-Isaiah's interpretation of the name Israel to the twisted usage of this word by the assimilationist fighters for Emancipation. But it is obvious that they used a historical argument in order to turn an exaltedly spiritual conception of our people into a weapon that came in handy at a time of need. If this should seem strange to the casual reader, or even to the diligent student of our history, it is not by far as appalling as the edict of the Nazis that forced every Jew in Germany and in the conquered territories to attach the name Israel to his signature in order to identify him as a Jew. In the spectacular career of the word Israel, in its manifold ups and downs, Hitler caused it to reach its lowest ebb.

But within one decade it not only recovered but reached the apex in the establishment of the new Jewish State. It is interesting to compare the historical beginnings of Zionism with the events of our own time. When Herzl wrote his famous book on Zionism, he called it *Judenstaat* and the Hebrew translator rendered it *Medinat ha-Yehudim*—obviously because Herzl wanted to restore the name *Jew* to a place of dignity and because he was thinking mostly in national and ethnic terms. However, the founders of the new Jewish State, after much consideration and lengthy discussion on the selection of a proper name, came up unanimously with the choice of Israel, thus again emphasizing the spiritual quality of our people, its conception of humanity and its relationship to God. In historic terms it was a decision worthy of our tradition, for the young Jewish State of today is not only an aggregation of *yehudim* defending themselves against their enemies, as in the Book of Esther, but the Land of Israel from which will again come forth the Torah and the word of God, a new conception of humanity, and a new message to a troubled world.

With Elizabeth Taylor and Eddie Fisher, c. 1960

JEWS IN THE MOTION PICTURE INDUSTRY: HOW JEWISH ARE THEY?

From *The Reconstructionist,* November 28, 1952

Much has been written about Hollywood in recent years, dealing with the community from a social, political, moral or religious viewpoint. Most of the literature that has appeared on this subject has, for some unknown reason, always been negative in result and hostile in approach. It is time to change this unfavorable impression, because it has not conveyed the truth. Basically, the Hollywood community is neither better nor worse than the balance of the country. And this goes for politics and morals, for social responsibility and religious affiliation.

What is true about Hollywood in general terms of American life is also true under the specific aspect of Judaism. For quite some time I have gained the conviction that the Jewish members of the motion picture industry are as good or as bad as the rest of American Jewry, be it in regard to their affiliation with synagogue and Jewish organizations, or to their participation in charity work and fund-raising.

Participation in Jewish Communal Life

I have in mind a study of the Jewish population conducted by the Jewish Community Council of Los Angeles for the past two years. In that report, which was published in October 1951, the results indicate that one-third of all Jewish households in Los Angeles do not identify themselves in any way with the existing denominations of Orthodox, Conservative or Reform Judaism; and that of the two thirds of the Jewish households that do identify themselves with one of these categories, only one out of three claims membership in a synagogue. In other words, less than twenty percent of the Jewish population of the community is affiliated with a temple or a synagogue.

Consequently, when I received a letter from the Editor of the *Reconstructionist,* requesting that I write an article on Hollywood I decided to do some research, in order to make sure that my impression of the Hollywood Jewish community could stand the test of facts and figures. In this vein, I approached the major motion picture studios with the request for permission to ask their Jewish producers, executives, writers and directors the following two questions:

1. How many belong to a synagogue?

2. Regardless of whether they do or do not belong to a synagogue, are they members of any secular Jewish organizations?

I am glad to say that I have had the fullest cooperation of the studios I contacted. I am not at liberty to reveal either the names of the studios, or the persons polled, but in terms of figures, here is the result of the investigation:

Of the producers, executives, writers and directors of the motion picture industry who are Jewish, forty-four percent belong to synagogues; fifty percent belong to secular Jewish organizations; and only six percent are entirely non-affiliated. These figures clearly show that in respect to Jewish affiliation, religious or secular, the Jewish group within the motion picture industry can point to a better record than the Los Angeles Jewish community as a whole.

In fact, compared to the population study of the Los Angeles Jewish Community Council, the record of Hollywood, according to the survey I made within the major studios of the motion picture industry, is almost twice as good. Obviously, we are not very happy with the result of the population study of the community at large, but fairness demands of us to state that, by and large, the Jew in the motion picture industry has shown a larger sense of Jewish responsibility than the average Jew in the rest of the community.

One arrives at the same conclusion when one compares the number of pledges and the amounts of funds raised by the total Jewish community, with the pledges and the funds of the Motion Picture Division of the United Jewish Welfare Fund. From 1943 to 1951, the average number of pledges from the Jewish community as a whole, comprising about 105,500 families, was 48,261 per year, and from the industry, comprising approximately 3,800 Jews, 3,160 per year. The average yearly amount in this period, raised by the total Jewish community, was $4,421,647, and the average yearly sum raised by the motion picture industry, was $1,046,045. This, in turn, means that the comparatively smaller, though admittedly wealthier, group of the industry raised almost one-fourth in every UJA campaign fund.

Here too then, one must come to the conclusion that the rumors spread all over the country about the Jews in the motion picture industry, often accusing them of non-cooperation in matters of fund raising for national and overseas needs, is a distortion of the truth. It is high time to begin an objective study of the Hollywood community. One will easily find that the reality is better than the impression gained by occasional visitors.

Relation to the Synagogue

In discussing the subject of the attitude of Jews in the motion picture industry to Judaism, I happen to be in a good position to provide an excellent example in the history of my own temple. Twenty-seven years ago, seven Jewish citizens of Hollywood met one day in a private home and decided to initiate the founding of a congregation. They felt that a community with such a reputation in the field of motion picture production should have a religious institution with which Jewish members of the industry could affiliate and where they could find their spiritual home. Who were these seven people? Studying the records of our temple, I found that all of them were, in one way or another, connected with the making of motion pictures. The first man was the head of the Fox Film Studios; the second was the head of production at Universal; the third was the president and owner of the Chadwick Productions; the fourth was a writer at Fox Studios; the fifth was a Hollywood talent agent; the sixth was an independent producer; the seventh, finally, was an M.D., the doctor of the movie colony at the time, and thus a part of the social set of the industry.

This is a rather fascinating little piece of American Jewish history. There was no Gestapo in Hollywood twenty-seven years ago to separate Jews from the Gentile community and thus drive them into a synagogue. There was not even the religious climate to impel Jews in Hollywood to build a house of worship. What then motivated these seven men to start a congregation which, in the course of years, has grown to a membership of almost eight hundred families? As most of these seven founders are, fortunately, still alive, I inquired into it myself. The answer might surprise many a reader. "We felt," said one of the founders to me, "that Jews in the motion pic-

271

With Harry Belafonte, June 24, 1960

ture industry are not exempt from the responsibility of continuing the heritage of our fathers, which makes every Jew, wherever he lives, a part of the totality of Israel." It may be of interest, to add to this story, that of the five surviving members of the founding group, three are still members of this temple. Of these three, two have served twice as presidents of the temple, and they are still heavily engaged in the day by day work of my congregation. And of the remaining two, one is still active in another temple. All in all, not an unimposing record.

Temple Israel has a rather large number of Jews in the motion picture industry as its members, and so do several other congregations in the area. I cannot say that all of these Jewish members of the industry are regular worshipers, or active in religious and cultural undertakings. But there is a strong psychological bond between them and our religious institution that usually makes them respond wholeheartedly to our needs and our demands. When the nominating committee of our Board of Trustees drafted one of the best names in the industry for the presidency of the temple, he not only willingly accepted, but gave so much of his energy and devotion to the cause of our congregation that it astonished those who did not value the Jewishness of motion picture producers too highly. Many more examples of this kind could be added. But I believe that this one will suffice for the purpose of this discussion.

One last thought. The participation in Jewish life by Jews of the industry cannot always be weighed either in quantity or in numbers. Who of us could figure out the thousands of dollars that one man, Eddie Cantor, brought, single-handed, into the treasury of the United Jewish Appeal by his personal appearances at many of its functions? The same is true of George Jessel, Dore Schary, Edward G. Robinson, and many others, in all philanthropic and humanitarian endeavors. The campaign for the Bonds of Israel will derive, I think, the same benefit from the appearances of Jack Benny, if he continues, as I believe he will, to lend his services to this most important project of the American Jewish community.

Jewish Themes on the Screen

I have often been asked whether the Jewish attitude of the film producer has any influence in determining the choice of a story. To this, I would like to say, in all frankness, that in selecting a story for a film, the first consideration is given to its box-office value. The motion picture industry is, after all, a business enterprise, and like any other business, the studio wants to make sure that it will be investing money in a film which will bring large returns. Any responsible member of the motion picture industry will agree with this statement. But having said that, I must add that the adherence to Judaism, as well as the patriotism to America, always serve as controlling influences. Just as no responsible studio will produce a picture, even if it suggests a box office success, that would harm the United States, in the same manner, no Jewish producer I know of would select a story that would in any way be harmful to our people. There is, I believe, a Jewish consciousness in the hearts of most of these men which guides their obligations, both to our Jewish group and to the community at large. I know of instances where some of these oft maligned producers went out of their way to acquire a book or a script to be filmed, either in order to enhance the position of the Jewish community, or to stress a fundamental principle of liberty or justice on the American scene.

In the last several years, biblical stories have been made into pictures. People often inquire into the reason why one particular Bible story is preferred above dozens of others. The answer is simple: it must be a dramatic story, woven around the love theme between the opposite sexes. This is why stories like "David and Bathsheba" and "Samson and Delilah" suggest themselves to Jewish and non-Jewish producers alike. This is also the reason why the studios have recently bought the "Story of Ruth," the "Story of Esther," and a script on "Joseph and Potiphar," which will shortly be made into films. Whenever the industry wanted to tell a great love story complete with ancient flavor and biblical atmosphere, the film proved to be a tremendous drawing card to millions of people all over the world. Of course, the box office idea was not entirely disregarded in their decision.

Affirmative Attitudes to Judaism

In general, the positive attitude to Judaism, and the consciousness of Jewish values will always play an important role, either in the selection of the story at the outset, or in the imaginative creation of certain scenes within the picture once the story is selected.

This Jewishness of most of our producers—not always obvious and not always tangible, but nevertheless existing as an inner moral force—will also have its impact upon the problems of intermarriage and on the Jewish education of their children. It would be useless to deny that there are many cases of intermarriage in the motion picture colony, but here two things must be kept in mind. First, examined in the light of the statistics of the Jewish community at large, the Hollywood index compares favorably with the rest of American Jewry. Secondly, even intermarriage does not mean a complete loss of interest in things Jewish. There are in our Hollywood community several prominent examples of intermarried couples who attend Friday evening services with the regularity of a clock. In some instances, the producer's wife, though non-Jewish and an actress, is actually the motivating factor in their regular service attendance. Wherever Jewishness pervades the home of the people in the industry, you will find their children in regular attendance in Sunday Schools, through bar mitzvah to their final graduation in confirmation classes. In this connection, it might be interesting to recall a few words from a statement by Mr. Jack Benny, urging support for the Combined Campaign of the Union of American Hebrew Congregations and the Hebrew Union College-Jewish Institute of Religion. Said Mr. Benny,

> Without religious leaders and teachers, without a careful fostering of our cultural and religious heritage, the tradition of Judaism of which we are so proud would surely die. I do not think any of us are willing to allow that tradition to die. I think that all of us take pride in our past and have faith in our future.... We want to see our kids grow up understanding their background, and bringing the best ideals of our religion to their lives as Americans. If we can not pass this along to our youngsters, then nothing else we've accomplished really matters. I think of this campaign as a personal obligation—as much of a personal obligation as the one that made me send my little girl to Sunday School to learn what she knows about her religion.

275

One can easily see from this statement that all is not entirely dark in Hollywood, even as far as Jewish education and adherence to the values of our people are concerned. By and large, in this department too, as the rest of American Jewry goes, so goes Hollywood.

I do not want people who read this article to misunderstand me. Having been a rabbi in Hollywood for ten years, I am far from satisfied with the Jewishness of my community. (Which rabbi, in any community in the United States, can say that he is?) But the important fact to remember is that taken all in all, the Jewish members of the motion picture industry reflect the same attitude to Judaism as the Jewish community at large. Even more than that, measured against the background of American Jewry as a whole, they have given a slightly better account of themselves. There is no reason, either for them or for us, to be ashamed of the Hollywood record.

Essays, 1959-1971

With Bobby Kennedy, Presenting a Book of John Kennedy's Writings on Israel and Zionism, June 3, 1965

WHO IS A REFORM JEW?

From *Papers for the 45th General Assembly,* U.A.H.C.
(November 17, 1959)

In June 1958—as a result of a debate in Israel on how to register children of mixed marriages—there appeared in the Israeli press an exchange of letters between Rabbi Maimon and Prime Minister Ben-Gurion.

Said Rabbi Maimon: "This question (Who is a Jew?) is a halachic historic question of first magnitude, and it touches upon the very basis of Judaism and is strongly tied to the most fundamental laws of Judaism and its very roots. A Jew, according to the Torah and tradition, is one whose mother is Jewish, and no one can have either the permission or the privilege to change through legislation something which has been accepted and sanctified by countless generations."

This by now historic letter was then obviously the position of the halacha, the traditional law which has governed Orthodox Judaism through the centuries. It is based on many statements in the Talmud, specifically in Kiddushin. "Rabbi Johanan said on the authority of Rabbi Simeon Ben Yohai: because Scripture says 'For he will turn thy son from following me (Deuteronomy 7:4).' Thy son by an Israelite woman is called thy son, but thy son by a heathen is not called thy son (bKiddushin 68b)."

To Rabbi Maimon's position representing the halacha—the prime minister of Israel, not being an Orthodox Jew, replied from his non-halachic viewpoint. After stating that, on the one hand, the government has no intention of passing "halachic rulings" and that, on the other hand, the Declaration of Independence had announced freedom of religion and conscience and did not set up the Jewish State as a halachic state and that Israel has already acted in this vein by giving equal rights to women and to non-Jews—which is at variance with the halacha—the prime minister gives his own definition of "who is a Jew" by saying that in his opinion the essence of Judaism is to be found in Psalm XV. And so Mr. Ben-Gurion continues:

> It is a fact that in matters of religion in halacha there is no unity in the Jewish people, and in the United States there are Orthodox, Conservative, and

279

Reform rabbis, and there are many Jews who belong to neither of these nor to others. They are, in my opinion, Jews as long as they do not convert to another religion. Many individuals regard themselves as sons of the Jewish people although they do not maintain halachic rules.

What is Psalm XV? Here is the text:

"Lord, who shall sojourn in Thy tabernacle?
Who shall dwell upon Thy holy mountain?
He that walketh uprightly, and worketh righteousness,
And speaketh truth in his heart;
That hath no slander upon his tongue,
Nor doeth evil to his fellow,
Nor taketh up a reproach against his neighbor;
In whose eyes a vile person is despised,
But he honoureth them that fear the Lord;
He that sweareth to his own hurt, and changeth not;
He that putteth not out his money on interest,
Nor taketh a bribe against the innocent.
He that doeth these things shall never be moved.

The prime minister did not just cull this psalm out of thin air. For it is one of the great gems of biblical literature which describes the Jewish ideal of human conduct, enumerating the qualifications of the man worthy to worship at God's sanctuary and to have communion with him. It is a challenging psalm, the demands of which are the moral acts of integrity and faithfulness, of genuineness and sincerity, of honesty and straightforwardness, of truth and of righteousness. Indeed, Rabbinic literature considers this psalm an embodiment of the six hundred and thirteen commandments. It will, therefore, come as no surprise to anyone if I underscore the fact that Mr. Ben-Gurion, too, was on solid ground when he made his famous pronouncement.

Still—in spite of the fact that both definitions given in this correspondence are grounded in tradition—the two definitions of "Who is a Jew?" are not satisfactory. The halachic viewpoint, with all the understanding that we may have for it under the aspect of the survival of the Jewish people, is still purely ethnic, if not racial in character, and slightly repugnant to the taste of our generation. It is an extreme viewpoint which can lead to utter absurdity. The Israeli wit may be credited with finding the proper example for it: Ben-Gurion's son is married to a French girl. They live in Israel, are part of the new State, and the atmosphere of their home is quite religious; Khrushchev's son is married to a Jewish girl, and they are both part of the Communist party and quite vociferous in their fight for atheism. According to the halacha, the Israelis say, Ben-Gurion's grandchildren are gentile and Khrushchev's grandchildren are Jewish.

Fortunately for us there have been other voices within Jewish tradition, both in the Bible as well as in the Talmud, which manifest a more flexible philosophy. In enumerating those who returned from the Babylonian captivity unto Jerusalem and Judah, so the Book of Nehemiah informs us, "And these were they that went up from Tel-melah, Tel-harsha, Cherub, Addon, and Immer; *but they could not tell* their fathers' house, nor their seed, whether they were of Israel (Nehemiah 7:61)."

Similarly, Mishna Kiddushin 4:1, speaking of the distinctive classes that came with Ezra from Babylonian captivity to Palestine in 450 B.C.E., lists "priests, levites, israelites, *chalalim* (of impaired priestly descent), proselytes, the emancipated, illegitimates, Nethinin (descendants of the Gibeonites), *shetuki* (the silent ones), and *asufi* (foundlings)." The Mishna goes on to explain that a "silent one" is one who knows his mother, but not his father; a "foundling," the one who was gathered in from the streets and knows neither his father nor his mother. The Gemara, in discussing this rather colorful mixture of immigrants, says of them, in the name of Rabbi Abbahu, "The Lord said, 'Though they have made themselves like the leopard'—meaning an animal not known for caution in association with the other sex—'yet they are as precious to me as a cherub (bKiddushin 70a).'"

It seems from here that both the Bible and at least some sages of the Talmud were not as concerned with the racial purity of our people as was the later halacha and as is Rabbi Maimon, today.

Ben-Gurion's definition leaves us unsatisfied because the psalm is the presentation of the Jewish ideal of human conduct in purely humanistic terms with general religious overtones. It is an agenda that can be adhered to and has been by

281

many outstanding non-Jews. Francis of Assisi, of former years, or Albert Schweitzer, of today, are classic examples of how one can fulfill Psalm XV without being Jewish. Only when the demands of Psalm XV are channeled through Jewish forms can they serve as definition. Therefore to a Jew living in Israel, breathing Jewishness in his daily life, surrounded by a Hebrew atmosphere from morning to evening, expressing his Judaism in the multi-colored variety of Jewish customs and observances with the Shabbat and the holidays as national institutions at his disposal—to an Israeli, Psalm XV is a classic and challenging guide. But for Jews living in the Diaspora, Psalm XV may serve as the ideal for individual and social morality, but not as a definition of "what a Jew is," for the psalm is a guide to human conduct but not to Jewish fulfillment. As Maimon's viewpoint is the one of the halacha, Ben-Gurion's can be termed one of the aggada for it is content without specific Jewish form; it is poetry but not prose; it is a challenge but not an obligation. If Maimon is halacha, Ben-Gurion is aggada.

II

The great poet Chaim Nachman Bialik dealt once with this subject in a remarkable, rightly famous, and by now classic essay. It is called "Halacha and Aggada" or "Law and Legend." In it, he uses these two terms "halacha and aggada" as representing two different modes of living. Says he:

> Halacha wears an angry frown; aggada, a broad smile. The one is the embodiment of the attribute of justice, iron handed, rigorous and severe; the other is the embodiment of the quality of mercy, essentially lenient and indulgent, as mild as a dove. The one promulgates coercive decrees and knows no compromise, the other presumes only to suggest and is sympathetically cognizant of man's shortcomings; she is shilly-shally and weak-willed. Halacha represents the body, the actual deed; aggada represents the soul, the content, the fervent motive. Halacha enjoins a dogged adherence and imposes upon us stern obligations; aggada, on the other hand, holds out the prospect of continual rejuvenescence, liberty and freedom.

The two, halacha and aggada, express themselves, also, differently in literary forms:

In the former we find a dry prose, a stiff stereotyped style, a monotony of language, eloquent of the supremacy of reason; but in the latter, that is, in the literature of the aggada, we meet with a poetic buoyancy, a style fresh and fluent, seasoned with colorful language, qualities pointing unmistakably to the supremacy of the imagination.

And, yet, asks Bialik, do they constitute a complete and absolute antithesis? Those who take this position, in his opinion, may be:

compared to the person who considers the ice and the water of the river as forming two distinct elements. For, in fact, halacha and aggada are two elements that in reality are one; they are merely two phases of the same phenomenon.... They are to each other what the word is to the thought and the impulse; or what the deed, the plastic representation is to the concept. Halacha is the crystallization, the necessary and ultimate consummation of the aggada; whereas, aggada is the real content, as well as the soul, of halacha. The reverberations of the turbulent passions of a heart that yearns for the fulfillment of its desires and ambitions—that is aggada. The pause—the temporary gratification of this yearning and its quiescence—that is halacha. Dreams press on to reality, the thought to the spoken word, the will to the deed, the flower to the fruit—and aggada to halacha.

Based upon this approach Bialik makes the point that the six hundred and thirteen commandments are nothing else but the final quiescence of the living or oral law—he calls it "the law of the heart," which were afloat in the air for thousands of years and became eventually stabilized in the form of laws and observances. The halacha, then, fulfills the greatest of tasks in the world because it embraces the art of living and the conduct of life and through it ideas are materialized and thoughts become actualities. This is why a people that wants, not only to survive, but to be creative, needs both aggada and halacha.

Bialik asks, "Does that mean that we should return to the *Shulchan Aruch* as a directive for our generation?" He replies in the negative, saying that anyone who interpreted his words in this manner has not understood him at all:

283

The words "halacha" and "aggada," are of the Talmud and they have there a specific meaning; but in their essence and scope they are much wider and include all cognate phenomena, both of the epochs preceding the Talmud and of those following it. They are two distinctive forms, two style variations that accompany each other in life and literature. Every generation has its aggada and every aggada, its own halacha.

III

I have quoted at length from the essay of Bialik because at least some of the things he wrote therein could have been written yesterday. For almost a century in Reform Jewish life in the United States we have been living on the fluid and unstable elements of aggada and, in my opinion, the time is long overdue to take halacha—both words are used here in the light of Bialik's interpretation—into serious consideration. We in the Reform Movement have our own aggada, and the time is ripe for the creation of our own halacha.

Let me explain what I mean by it: as far as the synagogue goes, our movement has created a theology, to which it gave a popular interpretation in the Union Prayerbook, and allowed the spiritual content to manifest itself in a particularly distinguished and decorous form. By doing this we achieved a remarkable harmony of halacha and aggada, of theology and prayerbook, of content and form, but the same cannot be said of the Reform Jewish home or about the Reform Jewish individual. Here there has developed a type of Jew who belongs nominally to a synagogue, attends services on the High Holidays, or at its best on several Friday evenings a year, whose religious affiliation carries very little weight for his daily life, whose home is devoid of any custom or Jewish observance, and who is committed to absolutely nothing because we have offered him through the decades a non-exacting and non-demanding religious denomination. He too, has been living on the vagueness of aggada, with nice words, beautiful phrases accompanied by gay sociability and good fellowship. All these elements are important, but they do not make for a creative force in modern Jewish life. The time has arrived to add a

284

Reform halacha to the aggada on which the Reform Jew has been fed.

There ought to be certain standards for the definition of a Reform Jew. Speaking broadly, I would say that he is

1. One who, either by birth or conversion, believes in God who is One and manifests himself a) in the Universe which is his creation; b) in man who is his child; c) and in Israel who is his witness.

2. Is a member of a synagogue and attends its services.

3. Provides Jewish education for his children and improves his knowledge of Judaism through adult study.

4. Observes the Sabbath and the holidays in his home within the frame of reference of our Reform ideology.

5. Identifies himself with the Jewish people and participates in all causes that make for Jewish survival and the upbuilding of Israel.

6. Shares in the activities of the general community and works actively in behalf of all universal ideals that are intended to improve the character of our society.

Of the six ingredients that go into the making of a Reform Jew—and each one of great importance—three are of such immediate necessity that they ought to engage our fullest attention. One is education and specifically adult education, because though most of our members have an understanding for the Jewish education of their children, it has not dawned on them yet that Judaism is an adult religion and that, according to our rabbis, ignorant people cannot even be pious. We ought, therefore, to tell our delegates at this convention that a Reform Jew is one who learns and studies and sets aside hours for the Torah.

There is, secondly, the matter of participation in the causes of our people that make for Jewish survival. There has developed here a scandalous habit of some sectors of our Reform membership who do not participate and do not even contribute to the Welfare Funds and the United Jewish Appeal of their own communities. Here our living on the basis of

285

aggada has reached its most absurd point. It has always been a puzzle to me how some of our members could come to our services, listen to sermons explaining the situation of our people, be moved by the needs of the hour, pray to God for their own welfare, and the happiness of their children—and then have the effrontery of absenting themselves from the very causes when it comes to the slightest of personal sacrifices. We ought to say to our delegates at this convention, and ask them to interpret it to their congregations at home, that a Jew who so utterly fails to translate our religious concept of charity to his own people deserves neither the honor of being called a Jew nor the distinction of calling himself a Reform Jew.

As many private Jewish clubs have already grown up to the point of not admitting to membership people who do not contribute adequately to the United Jewish Welfare Fund, our Reform synagogue might as well mature to the point of making memberships in synagogues conditional upon the fulfillment of this elementary duty toward Jewish responsibility.

There is the problem of the home observance of the Sabbath for a Reform Jew. I suggest that we make at least a small beginning and concentrate on giving some concrete halachic form to the content or lack of content of the Sabbath in the life of our members. I have no interest whatsoever in all the "don'ts" of Orthodox Jewish law dominating the Sabbath, but I am interested in educating the members of our congregation to an understanding that the Sabbath is first of all a day which, by its very nature, differs in character from the other days of the week and that the Friday evening has no similarity, whatsoever, with the Monday or Tuesday evening. We ought to inform our members that *a conditio sine qua non* of being a Reform Jew is the family observance of the Friday evening at home, with the kindling of the lights and the reciting of the blessing over the wine and the bread; and that, secondly, the Sabbath day itself or at least a part of the day ought to be devoted exclusively to things Jewish and things of the spirit. This is the day to attend a synagogue, to study a chapter of the Bible, to read a Jewish book, or to listen to a recording of Jewish or classical music. Most of our members work hard during the week, and the celebration of the Sabbath in this vein will elevate their spirit and enhance their personalities. Being a part of a pressing economic machine all during the week, we may yet recapture the rabbinic idea of the *neshama y'teira,* the additional soul, which a Jew acquires through the observance of the Sabbath.

This I believe, is the crying need of the hour, and nowhere was it more beautifully and touchingly stated than in the deeply moving words of Chaim Nachman Bialik, in the concluding part of the essay quoted before:

> Today, we have lived to see a generation dominated exclusively by aggada.
>
> Behold a generation that is growing up in an atmosphere charged with phrase and popular refrains and fed on things that are mere breath and wind. A Judaism of convenience is being created. People talk of a renaissance, literature, creation, Jewish education and Hebrew thought—and all these depend upon the hairbreadth thread of some 'love': the love of the land, the love of literature, the love of the language. What is the value of such airy infatuations? Love, you say? But where is duty? Whence shall it come and whence derive its nourishment? From aggada? Ah, but is not convenience its very nature?
>
> A Judaism that is all aggada is like steel that has been in the furnace but has not been tempered in cold liquid. Ambition, good-will, enthusiasm and love are all good and admirable qualities when they are crowned by action; iron-strong, determined action and cruel duty.
>
> Come now, let us set up ordinances for ourselves! Give us molds wherein our soft, fluid will may be minted and given definite and enduring form. We are thirsting for actual deeds. Give us a stronger disposition for performance than for talk....We bend our neck: where is the iron yoke? The strong hand and the outstretched arm—why don't they come?

It is along such lines that our Reform Movement will inevitably have to develop. This has nothing to do with the Orthodox conception of the law which, according to traditional interpretation, is God-given and has, therefore, to be obeyed as a Divine commandment. What we are after is a man-made

287

halacha, a creation of our very own, in order to solidify the great ideological heritage of our movement and concretize it in such a manner that it may serve as a guide for daily living for the hundreds and thousands of our members here and abroad.

CHRISTIAN ADVOCATES OF ZIONISM: FRANCE AND ISRAEL—HOW DEEP ARE THE ROOTS?

From *Recall* (1960)

At the end of the Thirty Years' War in Europe, mystic movements began to appear in England, France, Germany, and Holland. Religious leaders, who went to the trouble of studying the bloody wars among the European nations, came to the conclusion that there must be a way out of this conflagration and a better way of living together. As a result thereof, organizations were born within the Christian community which envisioned a better future through the reforming of society: to live in accordance with a moral code, by a greater degree of social justice and by a more profound toleration of one another.

This mystic movement, being deeply religious, looked upon the wars of their time as forerunners of the Messianic Age. Its leaders came to this conclusion from the study of the Book of Daniel in which it is stated that preceding the salvation of mankind there will be horrible and destructive wars. The mystics applied this biblical prophecy to the wars of their own days. In the course of their activities they delved more and more into the study of the Bible, and as an indirect result thereof their attention was called to the problems of the Jews who wrote the book. Commencing by looking upon their own suffering as a forerunner to a Messianic Age they were quite startled by the discovery of the ten times more horrible sufferings of the Jewish people. The pogroms of the middle and second half of the seventeenth century convinced them that the people who authored the Bible, which includes Daniel, from which they themselves had gained their inspiration, were enduring hardships far beyond those of the Christian community; that the Jews, therefore, were suffering under a system which could only be called unchristian and barbaric; and final-ly, that this unique tragedy of the Jews must be viewed—again in mystic terms—as the forerunner of a brighter future. The more they delved into the sources of the Bible, the more they came to the conclusion that in the same way as Christians have a right to look upon their sufferings in time of war as a forerunner to a Messianic Age, so the Jews themselves ought to be entitled to look upon their misery as the last dark hour before the dawn. From this they drew the logical conclusion that it was the duty of the Christian community to see to it that the Jewish community was made a part of the general redemption of mankind.

It is in this context that the mystics of the seventeenth century made what was to them a startling discovery: that in order to bring about the Messianic Age and to have mankind live in toleration, mutual acceptance, and social morality—the Jews would have to be returned, as prophesied in the Scriptures, to their ancestral homeland. We will concentrate on the echoes of this movement in France only.

The first recorded voice to be found in France came as early as 1643 in the form of a book published in Paris by a famous Huguenot scholar. His name was Isaac de la Peyrere; and his book was a treatise on the recalling of the Jews. The name of the book is *Traité du Rappel des Juifs,* in which the author makes the point that the time for the fulfillment of the biblical prophecies is at hand; that if there should be any solution to the problems of society, it would never come about without the Christian community paying its heavy price for the maltreatment of the Jewish People; and as the Jews' Bible itself promised the land of Palestine to the Jews and their seed after-wards, it is upon the Christian community to execute the divine plan. The author insists that it ought to be done immediately, now that the wars are at an end; and that it is upon the kings of France—he is referring specifically to Louis XIII—to help in this undertaking by recalling the Jews from the Dispersion and leading them back to the Holy Land. Even more than that, it is the duty of the kings of France, says the author, to be the tem-porary kings of a newly established Jewish State, until the Jews can stand on their own feet and choose a king of their own. So much for the first voice raised in behalf of the Zionist ideal.

It was not, however, the only voice of the seventeenth century. In the last part of it, in 1686 to be exact, there appeared in France a book written by a leader of the Protestant Movement whose name, Pierre Jurieux, became a household word among religious families. He was a great biblical scholar and at the time was engaged in halting the persecutions of the Protestant Movement by the Catholic Church. Because of the atmosphere prevailing in the country the book had to be printed outside France, and it actually appeared in Rotterdam. It was called *L'Accomplissement des Prophéties ou de la Délivrance Prochaine de l'Eglise,* in which he too deals with a return of the Jews to Palestine as a symbol of prophetic fulfillment. The only way, the author believes, the Christian Church can free itself from the many sins it has committed, is by seeing to it that she, the Church herself, plays a leading role in returning the Jews to the land from which they were unjustly driven.

A remarkable feature of the book is an open letter addressed by the author to the "Jewish nation," asking the Jewish community of his time to get in touch with him and offering the services of the Protestant Movement, inside France, and the Protestant refugees, outside, for whatever purpose they might be needed. It is interesting to note that the rabbis of Amsterdam take Jurieux's book and letter so seriously that they enter upon a correspondence stretching over three years, explaining to him their attitude on the question of the return of the Jews to Palestine, counseling him on how it ought to be done and what movement has to be created to foster it, and enlightening him on the Jewish conception of the Messiah. Jurieux, like de la Peyrere before him, has to be looked upon as an important Christian advocate of Zionist philosophy which is necessarily related to the whole idea of the rebuilding of the state.

Out of the many voices of the seventeenth century these two, de la Peyrere and Jurieux, ought to suffice as examples of a school of thought that started with them and continued, without letup, throughout the eighteenth, nineteenth, and twentieth centuries. There was, for instance, one of the most spectacular and adventurous figures of the eighteenth century—a French General by the name of Marquis de Langallarie.

290

He was born at the end of the seventeenth century—and by the beginning of the eighteenth century his name was already the most popular name in the chancelleries of empires and states. A colorful, yes fantastic, figure, he served as general in the French army and afterwards with the Austrian, Russian, Lithuanian, and Polish armies. He married a refugee girl who fled from France because of the persecution of the Protestants. Apparently under her influence, he left the Catholic Church and made it the goal of his life not only to fight the Pope, but to destroy the Papacy and the Catholic Church.

He published a book called *Journal Chrétien* which is full of mysticisms, aphorisms, and sayings, and makes for very difficult reading. He was obsessed by the idea of creating a universal religion for the whole world. For this purpose, he was received by emperors and kings and received large sums of money from Protestant states. At one time he even played with the idea of organizing a Protestant army to fight the Pope, and of sending evangelists to France to destroy the Catholic Church from within. His biography reads like a fiction story upon which even a Hollywood movie could not improve.

What interests us here, in this connection, is one of his plans for the rebuilding of a Jewish State. In devoting his life to the destruction of the Catholic Church and the creation of a new world religion based upon the Bible, he went as far as actually making a contract with the Turkish Empire, promising the Turks an army of ten thousand soldiers to fight their cause against the Pope. As Turkey was as interested in destroying the Catholic Church as was the Marquis himself, the deal was even consummated. But—and this is our point of interest—as a part of this great scheming he developed a complete project for the rebuilding of a Jewish State, because, influenced by Jurieux's book, he was convinced that the Protestant Church would never be victorious over the Catholic Church, freedom of religion never exist, and happiness of society never come into being, unless the Christian Community undertook to become the instrument of divine providence and the prophetic vision to recall the Jews from the places of dispersions and to make Jerusalem the religious center of the universe. To Langallarie this philosophy was not idle talk. He spent years of his life visiting the Jewish communities of

Emden, Hamburg, Frankfurt, and specifically the one of Amsterdam. In all these cities he met the leaders of the synagogues, asking the Jewish leaders for financial help—which was actually given to him—on the assumption that he would bring about the redemption of Palestine. From there he proceeded to make his political deal with Turkey which called for the re-establishment of the State in the ancient homeland and the designation of Jerusalem as the religious center, from which would radiate again the law and social morality so necessary for the survival of society.

Personalities of this type, though not as spectacular as the one of the Marquis, continue to play their role throughout the eighteenth century. There is, for instance, a brochure, written during the last part of the same century—somewhere between 1775-1779—by a French Nobleman, Count De Ligne, in which the author undertakes a defense of the Jewish people, accusing parts of French society of persecuting the Jews, if not physically then surely psychologically, and coming to the conclusion that the Jews are a wonderful people. If, the count argued far ahead of his time, we find flaws in the character of the Jew, it is what Christians have made of him. In this booklet, De Ligne demands a complete reform of society and toleration and citizenship for the Jews, and urges the Christian community to return the Jews to Palestine so that they can take their place among the nations, and so that it may be evident to everyone that they are basically a decent, deeply religious, and highly spiritual people.

It is clear by now from all that has been said that when Napoleon conceived the idea of the re-establishment of a Jewish State—the best known story in Franco-Jewish relations—it did not come as a great surprise to the average Frenchman. Napoleon was not the discoverer of a new idea. He only followed an existing trend. I say the idea was not new—not only Jewishly speaking. The idea was not new—even in French literature. This is the important point to remember: Napoleon conceived the idea for his own purposes in connection with his expedition to Egypt. He wanted to occupy Egypt in order to cut the arteries of the British Empire. On the way to Egypt he began to study the Bible and held many a discussion with a Jewish Orientalist whose name was Moise Ventura. The more

292

he indulged in the reading of the Bible and the more he discussed the book with his Jewish friend, the more he came to the conclusion that it would be a historic gesture of great significance if he could offer the Jews the restoration of their ancient kingdom. He was later reinforced in this conviction when he ran into unexpected difficulties in the Middle East: the Turkish Empire sent a strong army, and Napoleon was held up at Akko, a Palestinian fort, which he was unable to capture though he besieged it for over three months. It was then that he made up his mind to put the project into operation. Napoleon believed that the best way to penetrate the Middle East and Asia, and to fight Turkey and Russia successfully, would be to win the Jews of that whole area over to his plans. So in April 1799, Napoleon issues his famous proclamation asking the Jews—wherever they live—to gather around his banner and to partake of the idealistic goals of the French army, promising them that he will accomplish the restoration of the Jewish kingdom, and Jerusalem will be returned to its ancient glory.

Such Zionist echoes, as those of the seventeenth and eighteenth centuries, have continued to play a major role in the political and religious thinking of France to this very day.

It is possible that all this is a result of the love of France for identification with the whole of humanity. A remark by Jean Jacques Rousseau in his famous book *Emile* is probably characteristic for the entire trend. "I do not think," Rousseau wrote, "I have ever heard...arguments as to why they (the Jews) should not have a free state, free schools, free universities where they can speak and argue in their own language without any danger. Then alone can we know what they have to say." This is a conception of a Zionist philosophy far ahead of modern developments. We used to argue, in days prior to the establishment of Israel, that until our people will have one place in which it is master of its own destiny, the world will actually never understand us and never know what we really are. For what we seem to be, in the places of dispersion, is mostly made by an unfriendly environment in its own image. The only place in which the genius of our people will be allowed to play its own role on its own terms is in a rebuilt Jewish State, to serve as a model of the soul of our people.

Rousseau understood that already in the second half of the eighteenth century.

THE JEWISH COMMUNITY TODAY AND TOMORROW: WHAT KIND OF LEADERSHIP DO WE NEED?

From *The Jewish Teacher*, XXX:4 (April, 1962)

If one studies the American Jewish community in depth, one will soon find that one of its unique characteristics is that it is a community of sentiment, largely motivated by emotion, nostalgia, and a vague "Jewishness." Our community will, therefore, always respond well to pressing needs and problems when they touch upon the strings of the heart.

Motivation by emotion expresses itself even in the religious field, where it is not so much conviction as nostalgia, not so much faith as sentimentality. I believe, by and large, this is the only Jewish community on earth where a Jew can absent himself from the house of worship and religious life the whole of the year, eat ham and eggs for breakfast, sea food for dinner, and then compress four thousand years of Judaism into three Holy Days, by davening in a traditional shul—and calling himself an Orthodox Jew, without even being aware of the conflict.

As the whole process is largely emotional, our Jew gives to the year what is secular, and to the three days what is religious. This is his way of emulating the life of his forefathers. A way of life which they practiced every day he practices for three days in the year, and then, neatly packaged, he labels it Orthodoxy.

As a result of this motivation by emotion, American Israel will give of its time and its energy, of its devotion and its substance, to further rescue work around the globe—for the genius of the American Jewish community plays most magnificently and most majestically upon the strings of the heart. It will always give sacrificially to solve deeply felt Jewish problems.

I attribute to this power of emotion the whole glorious chapter of philanthropic help our Jewish community has extended to Israel as well as to Jewish communities abroad. The question, however, is: is it enough as basis for the future? It is surely impressive in an age of crisis. No society is better equipped to deal with crises than an emotion-laden community that still has the power to think and act.

We Cannot Depend on Emotion Alone

Still the question remains: is this a solid basis on which to build a future? I believe it is not, even if Jewish emergencies should continue to stir our souls in the years that lie ahead. Whereas the heart of American Jewry is full, Jewishly speaking its mind is all too often empty; whereas the feeling is rich, the knowledge is poor; whereas the sentiment is appealing, the ignorance is appalling. The Bible has warned us against such a state of affairs by saying, "Without knowledge the soul is not good; and he that hasteth with his feet sinneth (Proverbs 19:2),"—meaning that without knowledge even the soul of a people is of no significance, for it projects the image of feet running hastily and aimlessly.

Assuming that this analysis of mine is correct, how does one build a future with this generation of Jews, the way we are now? My answer is that we must decide to ask ourselves what type of American Jewish community we would like to have; what we expect of it, in which direction we want it to develop, what the goals of our own movement are, and how we expect to realize them within the American Jewish community.

The Goals We Pursue

Every generation has to look upon itself with the perspective of history. If, on the American scene, so much has been published in recent years on the "goals" and the "mission" and the "national purpose" of the United States, if the most powerful nation on earth needs this type of literature to be guided by, how much more so the Jewish community, so much smaller, and at the very crossroads of history.

If I would formulate our goal in one short sentence, I would say that the philosophy we need for this day and age is "integration without assimilation."

Let me explain what I mean by these three words. For the first time in our nation's history, a member of a minority entered the White House, and we may say that fences were torn down to enable a non-Protestant to reach that high position. This election was accompanied by an interesting discussion in which some of the top leaders of the nation participated—such as Mrs. Roosevelt and President Truman—in debating as to when a Jew will live in the White House. They agreed that it will probably be in the lifetime of this generation, surely by the end of this century.

It is not important whether this prophecy will materialize or not. What is important is that the word "Jew" can be taken seriously when put next to the words "White House." This is entirely new and unprecedented in the history of the United States, as well as in the history of the American Jewish community. The chances are, therefore, good that the decades to come may show an expansion of our liberties and an even greater progress in the achievement of equality. This being the case, the question I am asking is: how will Judaism survive in this climate of greater freedom and more perfect equality?

This is not meant facetiously. One of the Chasidic rabbis, long ago, felt this problem. He referred to the biblical story of God addressing Moses, prior to his death, telling him what would happen to the Jewish people, if they would not follow in His ways. The Bible uses the words *ra'ot rabbot v'tzarot*, "manifold catastrophes and evils (Deuteronomy 31:17)." Asked this rabbi, "Isn't this a redundancy? Aren't all catastrophes evil?" To which he replied that in Jewish history there are two different types of catastrophes and evils. There is the one in which the Jewish community lives handicapped in the ghetto, without freedom of movement, without liberty, and without rights—but then the Torah flourishes and things of the spirit are taken seriously. That is one type of evil, one which has its advantages. There is another type where Jews are equal citizens and live in liberty, with freedom of movement and opportunity for careers—but the Torah is neglected, with none to study and none to learn. Here we have advantages that are, also, *tzarot.*

Integration Without Assimilation

It is in this latter situation that we find ourselves in the United States: we live in an atmosphere of freedom with very

296

little attention to the Jewish things of the spirit. The question, therefore, remains: how, in the midst of an attractive, glittering American Civilization, will our cherished heritage of Judaism advance or even survive? Again, I say, the only answer to that is *Integration Without Assimilation.*

This is an entirely new challenge. We have had Jewish communities in Eastern Europe which survived because they had neither integration nor assimilation. We had the opposite example of many historic phases in Western European Jewish communities where there was integration plus assimilation—with almost fatal results. What I believe we have to call for at this hour in the United States is a philosophy that says "yes" to America and to our full participation in its civilization, without yielding a single inch of the spiritual territory of our ancient heritage. This has not been accomplished by any generation in the history of our people, with the possible exception of British Jewry.

The challenge has, therefore, no precedents, and we are thus embarking upon a totally new experiment. For centuries we have been fighting the battle of equality, making it possible for the Jew to become a citizen equal with the majority. Now we have to begin the battle for the right—and the duty—of this equal Jewish citizen to be and remain "different" in the expression of his religious way of life, and with it to assure that this religious and cultural differentiation does not detract from his integration into the nation. In short, integration without assimilation.

I can best introduce what I have to suggest for the implementation of this program with a very simple question. When does an American Jew live his Judaism? A Jew in Israel, even if he is not religious, lives in a Hebraic atmosphere that revolves around the Hebrew morning paper, the Hebrew radio, the Hebrew book, the Hebrew school, and the Hebrew lecture. Not all of it is religion, but a good substitute for it. A Jew in Poland, even if he was not religious, expressed his Jewishness in the daily Yiddish newspaper, the Yiddish radio, the network of Yiddish schools, the Yiddish forum, and the Yiddish theater. But when does an American Jew live his Judaism and how does he express it? From the morning to the evening, he is surrounded by an American Civilization, with Christian overtones. What accompanies him is the English newspaper and the English magazine, the English radio and the English television, the English lecture and the English sermon. At what time of day does he manifest his Jewishness, even on a smaller scale than the Jew in Israel or the Jew in Poland?

Accent on Adult Education

There are, in my estimation, in addition to memberships in temples and attendance at services, five specific areas which I would like to suggest as proper steps in the direction of implementing integration without assimilation.

The first is the education of our adults. The curse of our generation is the appalling ignorance of our laity, and even of its top leadership, in things Jewish. The statement of the rabbis that "an ignorant person cannot be pious (mAboth 2:5)," ought to be relearned in all its implications. It is tragic that only the other day a leading Catholic spokesman, Cardinal Cushing of Boston, had to call our attention to what will happen to Jewish knowledge and Jewish learning if we continue in the process of what he called "Americanization without deepening of Jewish learning."

The noted cleric pointed out that the complete Americanization of the Jew in this country was "a new experience for the Jewish community," and it posed the threat that "the vast accumulation of Jewish learning and culture will now be dissipated into the wider community and in the process lose much of its strength in the generations that lie before us." The warning that, in the course of its integration into American life, Judaism may lose its very soul, should have come from us rather than to us.

It is ironic that we have already come to such a pass that a leader of the Church has to call American Jewry's attention to what some of us, I am sure, as rabbis and educators, have known for a long time, namely: the process of Americanization without the buttressing of our spiritual citadel can easily lead to the disappearance of the whole substance of our religious heritage.

It is then a matter of seeing to it that adult education projects are instituted in our congregations, even if it means a further taxing of both the educational staff and the rabbinate to the very limit of human possibilities. Our most alarming weakness is Jewish ignorance, and this illness can only be cured by a fresh and imaginative approach to adult education.

What I have just said about our adult congregation is doubly true for our younger generation. Our young people are now going, more and more, into American colleges, entering more and more the type of society that is academic, professional, and white collar. These young people may possess college-level knowledge in general civilization, but usually a kindergarten level in the sphere of Judaism. The relationship is one of inverse ratio: the farther they advance into the academic field, the more they are likely to retreat in the Jewish field. Theodor Herzl felt this problem keenly in his time and set, therefore, for himself the task to make *aus Judenjungen, Junge Juden*—out of Jewish youngsters, young Jews.

The time has come for us in the United States to emulate Herzl's example and concentrate all our efforts to make of intellectual Jews, Jewish intellectuals. We have not achieved it yet in America; there is a long way to go.

Survival Value of Observance

Secondly, in this process of integration without assimilation, one has to add to the knowledge of our heritage the area of observance. For some unknown reason, there has developed a theory in our congregations that anything that has to do with observance in the home is of no consequence to us, and that one is completely at liberty to shape one's Shabbat and one's holidays according to one's own wishes, and that one can, with good conscience, spend, for instance, the whole of the Shabbat on the golf course.

This *hefker* (state of anarchy) cannot be tolerated any longer. I am not interested in the "do's" and the "dont's" of the halacha. The point I am making, however, is that it has to be a Shabbat and a holiday according to our Reform ideology and our progressive philosophy. It ought to express itself in the forms which are our very own. We have a liberal viewpoint of the Sabbath, for in our conception the Sabbath day may be spent not only in the atmosphere of our religion, but also in that of art, literature, or music, all related to the things of the spirit.

299

This is obviously a position unacceptable to the Orthodox, yet there is a vast difference between this Reform interpretation of the Sabbath and the golf and card playing version practiced by too many. We have never sanctioned such promiscuousness. The founders of our movement never consented to it. The time has come to correct it—and the sooner the better.

I warn our movement, as I am warning educators, that both learning and observances will have to be taken seriously, because no Jewish community in our people's history has ever survived without knowledge and without observance, and surely not without some type of consecration of the Sabbath. It is here that we, as educators, have to initiate some fruitful and carefully planned work, because, in the years to come, the question of knowledge and observance will, in spiritual terms, become a problem of sheer survival for American Israel.

The Centrality of Hebrew

Thirdly, in addition to adult education in our synagogues and observances at home, there is need of a deepened and more Hebraized education of our children. I believe that our one-day-a-week schools have, for a long time, been outmoded. The instruction of our children for two or two-and-a-half hours a week simply does not suffice. I do not favor just an increase in hours of instruction or the mere changeover from a one-day to a two- or three-day-a-week school.

What I have in mind is a more Hebraized type of instruction, so as to be in touch with realities of contemporary Jewish life. A teenager growing up in the era of the reborn State of Israel and at a time in America when top American colleges are featuring Hebrew as a modern language, is not as well prepared for life as he should be either from an American or a Jewish viewpoint—if he emerges in blissful ignorance of the language which is the daily tongue of Israel, a language in which he can now earn his doctorate in many a major American university.

Recently, I came across some fascinating statistics reported by Trude Weiss Rosmarin, and based on the work of Professor Abraham I. Katsh:

> Over 20,000 students are at present pursuing courses in Hebrew language, culture, and Hebrew Bible

300

studies in 245 U.S.A. institutions of higher learning (61 colleges, 72 universities, and 112 seminaries), of which only three teachers' colleges and four seminaries are under Jewish auspices. Since the rise of Israel in 1948, the number of students taking college and university courses in Modern Hebrew has more than doubled. Also, non-Jews in these courses appreciably outnumber Jews. Even more spectacular is the gain in the academic recognition accorded the language of Israel. In 1945 less than one percent of U.S.A. colleges recognized Hebrew as a modern language for college entrance. Today, over ninety percent of colleges accord this recognition.

As many of our members, and even our lay leaders, suffer from a severe inferiority complex which causes them to be deeply impressed by every word non-Jews say about Judaism, maybe this *hechsher* stamp of American universities upon the ancient tongue of our people will finally kosherize a more positive approach to Hebrew in our Reform religious schools.

I would like to suggest to you to undertake one more step in the direction of integration without assimilation. I believe the time has come, and a resolution to this effect ought to come out of this convention of educators, to urge our Union to establish in each one of our large metropolitan areas one model All-Day Jewish School for our best children, the most talented and the most intelligent, for those who would like to delve deeper into the fountain of Jewish knowledge; for those who aspire to leadership in our National Federation of Temple Youth; for those who want to prepare themselves for educational positions; and finally, for all who consider themselves "called" to the cantorate, the rabbinate, or the profession of Jewish education.

If we do not take this step into courage, where will the future leadership of our Reform movement ever come from? Please, understand me correctly: I am not speaking of taking all our children out of public school and of establishing parochial schools. I am suggesting, however, for those of our children who are especially talented and have leadership qualities, a Reform atmosphere of intensive Jewish studies.

However we may differ on the type of Reform movement we would like to have—we are, I am persuaded, united on desiring a Jewishly literate leadership. If this is so, one must

301

find a new way of encouraging Jewish literacy in our ranks. The fruits of Jewish leadership will not grow on the trees of our Sunday Schools.

Importance of Jewish Peoplehood

The fourth area in this process of integration without assimilation is what I would like to call "identification with World Jewry." We have, for a long time, been rather vague on this issue, attempting to avoid the controversy, because it might hurt some people of the American Council variety or some of its allies. But I believe that a national organization of educators—and for this matter the whole Reform Movement—cannot, with good conscience, refuse any longer to define our Jewish group, honestly and truthfully, whether some of our members like it or not. It is important in our approach to Jewish life to state the facts clearly.

I believe one has to start with the *aleph bet,* by saying that we consider ourselves a people. A people, in sociological terms, is a group of human beings whose ancestors lived in one and the same place, and at one and the same time, and whose descendants succeeded in surviving by some mutual bond. We Jews are such a people. Our ancestors, long ago, lived in a land which had different names: Palestine, the Holy Land, *eretz yisrael, eretz adonoi,* etc., etc. That is where our people lived and established itself, and we, their descendants, managed to survive as Jews via the mutual bond of Judaism. This is the historic truth.

Our people, the Jews, lives today in varying political climates and on different social levels. One part of our people, the two million living in Israel, have regained the status of "nationhood." The three million Jews in Eastern Europe, according to the formal constitutions of the Communist countries, are considered a national minority and are called a "nationality," as in Russia, Bulgaria, Yugoslavia, Rumania, and the rest of the East. Where the name "nationality" is taken seriously (not in the Soviet Union, but, for instance, in Poland), Jews have a way, not a religious one to be sure, but at least a Yiddish secular way to express themselves.

This means that we have about two million of our people in a status of "nationhood" and three million of our brethren in a

302

status of "nationality." In between these two extremes, there is the large center of the Jewish community of the free world of today, anywhere from seven to seven-and-a-half million souls. This center, our largest group, is neither a "nation" nor a "nationality." It functions as a religio-cultural community only. From this viewpoint then, we have before us a people living on three stages of history, with different atmospheres, different levels, and different status. But all of them, whether belonging to the nation of Israel, to the Jewish minority nationality of Eastern Europe, or to the religious-cultural community of the free world, are members of the Jewish people, because Judaism, the historic experience, is the bond that holds them together.

Active Identification is a Must

This being the case, the American Jewish community of the Western world is an integral part of a larger grouping called the Jewish people. As such it is duty bound to take full responsibility for the protection and advancement of the two Jewish groups associated with it. This has nothing to do with any theory of nationalism. It has to do with the religious principle of Jewish responsibility called *Klal Yisrael.*

If the American Jewish community—the largest, richest, and most powerful segment of our people—would not manifest care for other Jewish communities which are not in the same fortunate position, we would violate not a law of nationalism, but a mitzvah of Judaism. For Jewish law demands that as soon as a minyan of ten Jews finds itself in one and the same place, its members have to collect enough money in order to build a school, a synagogue, and a cemetery. But, says the *Shulchan Aruch,* if there is another community in danger, and it involves the question of *pidyon shevuyim,* "redemption of captives"—then you do not build a school and you do not build a synagogue and you do not acquire a cemetery, but you send the money to redeem those in bondage.

From a religious viewpoint then, American Jewry has been living up to the injunction of our ancient heritage that "all Jews are responsible for one another." But the law of mutual responsibility has thus far been fulfilled largely in terms of philanthropy. What we need at this hour, however, is identification with world Jewry.

303

Identification is more than sympathy or friendship. It is empathy. Again, we are dealing here with a religious vocabulary, because the basis of the approach of Judaism to life, as far as great ideas are concerned, has always been identification, not sympathy. It is the key word to the understanding of Judaism. It is imperative then that we teach this philosophy of identification in our schoolrooms, on the pulpit, and from the forum to young and old alike.

This, of course, does not conflict with the loyalty of the Jewish community in the United States to the American flag and the institutions it represents. It means the inner participation of the Jew in the affairs of his people, motivated by religious principles out of his majestic legacy. Identifying with our people is so essential a religious principle that without it one cannot even begin to understand the "abc's" of Judaism.

We as educators have to see to it that Jews who give of their time, their energies, their devotion, and their substance to the survival of the Jewish people understand themselves in historic terms. They are not just giving philanthropy. They are fulfilling one of the greatest mitzvot of our religion—a mitzvah which is still binding upon our generation as it was upon generations past.

We Must Work Toward Social Action

Lastly, under the aspect of integration without assimilation, it is incumbent upon us, as educators and as rabbis, to develop a greater sensitivity on the part of our congregations and of the children in our religious schools and youth organizations to the whole area of social justice, with all its problems and ramifications. There ought not to be a single temple in our movement which does not sponsor a social action committee charged with studying the affairs of the city and the county, the state and the nation, from a strictly non-political, but religio-ethical point of view.

It is in this area that our members, and surely our leaders, can best express themselves as American Jews—with emphasis on both words—because the ideal toward which we strive is, in itself, a manifestation of both Judaism and Americanism at their very best. We are, then, reaching out for the great heights of both Judaism and Americanism when we lend a

304

helping hand to the cleansing of the nation's soul and to the removal of the barriers of hatred between races and religions, and when we fight the good battle for the brotherhood of man in practical terms.

Martin Buber, in his *Reden über das Judentum,* his first famous speeches on Judaism delivered in German, makes the point that the goal of Jews living in the Diaspora is *"Mensch sein–und es Jüdisch sein"*—meaning "to be human—and to be it Jewishly." Buber's friend Gustav Landauer, after reading this beautiful formulation, added to it a parallel of his own saying that the goal of Jews living in a Jewish State ought to be *"Jude sein–und es menschlich sein"*—meaning "to be Jewish—and to be it humanly."

If you combine the two quotations, we have the best summation of what this paper has attempted to convey. For when we suggest to the American Jew to enlarge his knowledge and to increase his observances, to deepen the Hebraic education of his children, to intensify his identification with the Jewish people, and to engage in activities on behalf of social justice—what else are we saying to him, but to "be a Jew and be it humanly," and to "be a human being, and be it Jewishly." No better slogan for what I call "Integration Without Assimilation" can possibly be found.

May this National Conference of Reform Educators be privileged, I pray, to serve as an instrument for the fulfillment of this vision—a vision that weaves Judaism and humanness into the colorful tapestry of American Israel.

THE NEED FOR AN ALTERNATIVE

Excerpt   From *Israel Magazine,* I:5 (1968)

I

Theodor Herzl enriched our Jewish vocabulary with two words, "peoplehood" and "statehood" which together spelled "Zionism"—the doctrine that anti-Semitism and social upheavals were bound to wreak havoc among the Jews scattered about the world and that salvation must be sought in the establishment of a Jewish State.

Underlying this ideology was the basic principle of the unity, the oneness of the Jewish People. No matter where Jews lived, what citizenship they possessed, whether they were believers or agnostics, committed or estranged Jews, they were all members of one and the same entity called the Jewish People. The philosophy of one Jewish people was reflected in the structure of the Zionist Movement with its religious "right," its neutral "center" and its secular "left."

The expectation was that when the Jewish State came into being, all its citizens regardless of their *Weltanschauung* would be equal before the law; the progressive Jew would feel as much at home as the Orthodox; there would be freedom of conscience and worship. It was inconceivable that religious observance would be enforced by legislation, imposing on the nation the straitjacket of one specific denomination. On the contrary, it was hoped that the State would stand for the common denominator of Jewry as a whole, namely, peoplehood, the prophetic heritage of justice and righteousness, decency and fair play, equality and liberty—in short, the moral values that make for individual freedom, social justice, human brotherhood.

Such was the vision, the prayer in the hearts of a whole generation, that this Torah would come forth from Zion.

II

At the end of March of this year, the Rabbinical Assembly of America—the organization of Conservative Rabbis—held its annual convention in the Catskills. In his report to the assembled delegates, the distinguished president, Rabbi Eli A. Bohnen, had this to say: "We had dared to hope that the Torah would really come forth from Zion and that, faced with the pressing needs of the day, the halachists of Israel would prove that they were using a living, vital, legal system. We have been greatly disappointed." Further along in his address, he added: "Religious Jews in Israel will rue the day when they decided to depend on politicians to help them achieve their goals. Political deals...are abhorrent to moral responsibilities."

For his part, the incoming president of the Conservative Movement, Rabbi Ralph Simon, announced in his acceptance

306

speech that he was soon going to Israel in order to arrange for closer cooperation between the Conservative and the Reform Movements there, and that he would be looking for promising young Israelis to study for the Rabbinate at the Jewish Theological Seminary in New York, because "there is a desperate need in Israel today for an alternative religious expression."

What has happened in the two decades of Israel's existence which makes outstanding leaders of the Conservative Rabbinate utter such challenging statements in open convention? What has occurred in the last twenty years that makes conservative rabbis, who accept the halacha as a guideline for action and who are observant Jews in their daily lives, confess to such keen disappointments? The answer is that hand in hand with the triumph of the Zionist vision in state-building, immigration and absorption, there went an utter failure in the area of human relations, religious liberty and respect for the individual conscience in matters of belief. (Ironically enough for a Jewish State, all these elements exist for Christian and Moslem citizens but not for Jews.)

The medieval concept of the union of church and state has been thrust upon Israel by the Orthodox Synagogue, which functions as a political party—a small party, but a powerful one, since it holds the balance of power in parliament and in the administration. For its participation in coalition governments it has exacted a heavy price. The Orthodox Synagogue is today virtually the "State Church" of Israel and forces on an unwilling majority of the population a way of life utterly alien to them—with halacha as the veritable constitution of the State.

In the entire history of Zionism, there was never any question of a Jewish State conducted according to the tenets of one branch of Judaism, namely, Orthodoxy. Any resolution to this effect would have split the movement, causing an exodus not only of the socialist parties, but also of the liberals, of rabbis of the stature of a Stephen S. Wise, an Abba Hillel Silver and many others. Nowhere does Israel's Declaration of Independence say or hint that the State should be ruled by halacha.

"We know that what has taken place is political blackmail," a left-of-center party leader said to me the other day, "but as long as we need the Orthodox politicians, we'll humor them along."

307

I have been in Israel now for over three months, traveling around from Galilee to Sinai, speaking to hundreds of people, to old-timers, sabras, kibbutzniks, soldiers. I was deeply disturbed by the hatred I heard expressed for the Rabbinate and—on account of the Rabbinate—for religion as such. The coercion exerted by the religious establishment with the backing of the laws of the State, is bitterly resented. Non-Orthodox groups and individuals are victims of constant chicanery. There are cases of liberal congregations that could not find a hall for worship because of the pressure of the Rabbinate, which threatened among other things to withdraw kashrut certificates; liberal congregations that could not get Torah scrolls from the Ministry for Religious Affairs, even though Rumanian Jewry recently shipped over a thousand such scrolls to Israel and many of them are still not in use; Progressive congregations that are treated as heretics and are therefore denied official subsidies; rabbis who are not allowed to perform marriages, though they are graduates of the most distinguished rabbinical seminaries in Europe and America. There are countless stories of lives of individuals and families, broken because of the halachic constitution.

I confess that it is sometimes difficult to believe that all this can indeed happen within a Jewish State: the non-recognition of marriages, divorces, and conversions solemnized by non-Orthodox rabbis, abroad or in Israel proper; the shameful procedure that members of Progressive congregations have to go through the meaningless perfunctory marriage ceremony with an Orthodox rabbi and then return to their own synagogue and to their own rabbi for a real wedding with decorum, dignity and personal character; the gruesome spectacle of refusing the bar-mitzvah to a boy because some of his relatives drove a car into town on the Sabbath; the cruelty toward children of mixed marriages, and especially toward women who had saved the lives of Jews in the darkest hours of the Hitler period and then got married to the Jewish survivors; the perpetration of barbarously outmoded customs on widows and abandoned wives; the meticulous investigation of the mother's background as to the purity of her Jewish origin when it comes to marriages in the Jewish State, sometimes involving concentration camp victims whose children have no certificates to prove their "racial" purity. All these and countless other tragedies in the name of the Jewish religion! Here is Orthodoxy without a heart. Whatever happened to that Judaism of which our Sages said that "God, the Compassionate One, demands the heart"?

What value is there to a religion that rests on the authority of a government and the power of the police? Religion is the most intimate form of man's relationship to God. It flows from the deepest source of his conscience and the deepest recesses of his heart. The glory of religion stems from the freedom of the soul, from the fact that every individual has a choice to select for himself the style of dialogue with God that best fits his personality, affording him the greatest happiness and fulfillment. Religion stands for the highest ideals of justice and human brotherhood. It stands for inner content, not for outer forms. Forms are time-bound, ideals are eternal.

It was Isaiah who proclaimed long ago one of the most majestic ideas in the whole of Judaism: "The Lord of Hosts is exalted through justice and the Holy One sanctified through righteousness (Isaiah 5:16)." There is very little left in Israel today of this sublime concept of religion.

When—in all the twenty years of Israel's existence—has the Rabbinate ever raised its voice on any issue of social significance? This is why the last thing that would ever occur to a sabra, would be to consider the rabbi as a spokesman for moral conscience, for social justice, for inter-faith and human relations, for individual freedom, for integration of the Sephardim or for friendship with the Arabs, or for a hundred causes which are relevant to modern-day life, and in which every rabbi in the United States—Orthodox, Conservative. and Reform—is constantly engaged. Instead, all that our young generation in Israel hears from the rabbis is a boring repetition of "dont's," usually referring to outdated formalities. Is it then at all astonishing to hear young Israelis derisively referring to the headquarters of the Chief Rabbinate in Jerusalem as the "Datican?" (Dat is Hebrew for religion).

IV

I am writing all this with an extremely heavy heart, because I am a religious Jew, and I want to see a religion-oriented Jewry

309

in Israel. But the fact of the matter is that the unholy alliance of halacha and State has already split the Israel nation into two separate camps—the minority who are Orthodox, and the others who, religiously speaking, are out of the picture. I fear religion will perish in Israel unless a radical change is wrought—soon.

One must first of all separate religion from politics, and the State from the Synagogue. Secondly, one must establish alternative expressions of our religious philosophy focused on challenging contents instead of meaningless forms. A religion that deals from morning to evening only with such "world shaking" problems as mikveh, Sabbath travel, or the selling of chametz to an Arab for the Pesach week, and so on, cannot hope to attract young people of the twentieth century to enter a synagogue. An establishment that refuses to permit a young man to be buried in a Jewish cemetery because his mother was not Jewish, though he lost his life fighting in the Israel army for the defense of Israel—such a religion will not induce the sabra in this troubled age to take Judaism seriously.

As we cannot expect the Orthodoxy to change, the crying need of the hour is to support existing and to establish new Conservative and Liberal congregations for the benefit of all those who cannot possibly feel at home in an Orthodox atmosphere, but who hunger for identification with the great spiritual values of our heritage which are relevant to our own time.

There is also another consideration relating to overseas Jewish communities that are vitally important to Israel. Take the American Jewish community. There are in the United States today some 5,500,000 Jews of whom roughly 1,250,000 are Reform, another million are Conservative plus 40,000 to 50,000 Reconstructionists, another half to three quarters of a million are organized in various secular Jewish organizations. The Orthodox group, split into three different sections, claims that it enjoys a total membership of close to a million—a figure which some sociologists doubt, but which I am ready to accept for argument's sake. This means that within a community of 5,500,000 Jews, there are to be found 1,000,000 of Orthodox persuasion, with the other 4,500,000 either organized in Conservative, Reform, or Reconstructionist congregations, or in secularist and nationalist bodies, or without any affiliation whatsoever.

One does not have to enter into deep speculation in order to

310

understand the implications of these figures. If it ever comes—as we hope it will—to a larger aliyah from the United States, the overwhelming majority of American Jews that will be settling in Israel will, of necessity, be non-Orthodox. Will they submit to this reign of coercion in the field of religion, after having grown up in a country of complete separation of Church and State? Will they accept halacha which rules that half of American Jews are the illegitimate fruit of illicit liaisons?

Conservative and Reform rabbis have already had a difficult time in recent years to explain Israel and to apologize for its religious dilemma to members of their temples who return perplexed to America after visiting the Jewish State.

Judaism, the religious bond that held our people together for so many centuries, has now in our time become a divisive force to such a point that the identification of the majority of Western Jewry with Israel is entirely on the secular level. Should the leadership of American Jewry today decide to settle in Israel they would not even be acceptable in the eyes of the halacha, because the overwhelming majority of them and their parents were married by Reform or Conservative rabbis, in many cases involving mixed marriages, solemnized, after due conversion, by Conservative or Reform rabbis.

A solution to this problem must be found, both for the sake of the unity of the Israeli nation and the oneness of the Jewish people. Only then will Israel gain for itself and in the eyes of the world—the distinction of personifying the universal ideals of our prophetic heritage. Let us hope that the government of Israel and the leaders of the nation in all walks of life will vigorously react to the crisis. Let us pray that they overcome it in good time.

REFORM JUDAISM APPRAISES
THE RELATIONSHIP OF AMERICAN JEWRY
TO THE STATE

Excerpt   From *CCAR Journal,* (June, 1971)

Some of our leaders in the Reform Movement have not agreed with certain phases of Israel's foreign policy, specifically with

Israel's attitude to peace negotiations with the Arabs. I sincerely hope that this chapter is now coming to a close, because all the "doves" in our midst must have surely been pleasantly surprised by recent moves of the Israeli government, testifying to Israel's readiness for huge territorial concessions, only short of endangering her own security—-and to her great flexibility in her sincere quest for genuine peace.

This problem, as of April 1971, centers around the question of territory versus security. Two statements are of crucial importance to the subject under discussion. The American position was summed up by the secretary of state at a press conference on the 16th of March. Said Mr. Rogers: "Some think of geography as best for security. We do not think geography is essential for security. In large measure political arrangements, agreements understood by the parties, and a willingness by the parties to maintain them, are an equal consideration.... Security aspects do not require territory."

Israel's position was formulated in the by now famous interview which Golda Meir gave to *The Times of London,* was published on Saturday, March 13, in which she outlines the minimal demands of Israel: the four security points of East Jerusalem, the Golan Heights, the Gaza Strip, and Sharm el–Sheikh—and stressed the point that "secure, negotiated and recognized frontiers were necessary to prevent another war. International guarantees could not replace them." In reference to Mr. Rogers' statement quoted above, she replied swiftly on Wednesday, March 17, that "we cannot trust what Rogers offers us, even if he does so with the best of intentions. Israel could not agree to borders which would lack a deterrent so that some future Sadat may try to attack us."

Thus the lines arc sharply drawn, and the basic argument between Israel and the United States over the future map of the Jewish State and the underlying problem of what constitutes security, came into sharp focus. To the State Department, guarantees by the Big Four, signed by the United Nations, are the best security available in this imperfect world; whereas to Israel, certain territorial strong points must be retained so as to deter Nasser's successors from adventurous attacks in the future, like the ones the Arabs have perpetrated so often in the past. I am convinced that Israel's position is solid, and from a logical, and even legal, viewpoint unbeatable.

Jacob Caroz, one of Israel's best experts on international law, recently published a fascinating study entitled "Why the Guarantee Idea Is Dangerous for Israel" (*Jerusalem Post*, February 21, 1971). In it he quotes from the authoritative work on international law by Oppenheim-Lauterpacht the following passage:

> The duty of the guarantors to render...the promised assistance to the guaranteed State depends upon many conditions and circumstances. Thus, first, the guaranteed State must request the guarantor to render assistance. Thus, secondly, the guarantor must at the critical time be able to render required assistance. When, for instance, its hands are tied through waging war against a third State, or when it is so weak through internal troubles or other factors, that its interference would expose it to a serious danger, it is not bound to fulfill the request for assistance. So too, when the guaranteed State has not complied with previous advice given by the guarantor as to the line of its behavior, it is not the guarantor's duty to render assistance afterwards.

One should read these lines, from the "bible" of international law, over and over again, and let the words sink in, so as to understand the ramifications—all the more that Israel has such vivid memories of the failure of the United States' Government to make good its guarantees of 1956-57 to keep the Straits of Tiran open for Israeli shipping. It means that the guarantor state has many possibilities of evading the fulfillment of its promises and, on the other hand, the guaranteed state often becomes "a sort of vassal of the guarantor." The author gives here some arresting examples showing that human history is an unbroken record of broken guarantees and this not only by European nations but even by the United States.

At the dawn of the history of our Republic in 1778, the United States signed a treaty with France to come to her aid in case of attack. The treaty obliged the United States to offer France help in defense of the French colonies on the American continent. In 1793, Britain launched an attack on Revolutionary France, and the French ambassador in Washington demanded that the United States fulfill its treaty obligations. America refused, and the French ambassador who protested was asked to leave the country. The United States did not refuse out of viciousness but because of a difficult situation in which she found herself at that particular moment. An offer of help to France would have drawn the United States into a war with Britain. The American Government published therefore a declaration of neutrality.

According to the international law quoted above, America even acted with a certain legitimacy. If one adds to this amazing example of the United States the better known facts of this century, one easily understands Israel's apprehension. To wit: Germany's guarantee of Belgium's neutrality which did not deter Germany from attacking Belgium in 1914; or Russia's repudiation of her treaty of alliance with Iran of 1942, by her attempt in 1945 to establish an independent state in the Persian region of Azerbaijan; and, finally, the tragedy of Czechoslovakia in our own lifetime, which had a treaty of alliance with France obligating the French to come to her immediate aid in case of an attack by Germany—a treaty later incorporated into the Locarno Pact of 1925, and of which Edouard Benes, then foreign minister of Czechoslovakia, reported to his Parliament in the words: "We must emphasize that the assistance in question would take effect automatically." This treaty was even strengthened when in 1938 after Hitler threatened Czechoslovakia, the British Prime Minister Neville Chamberlain declared in the House of Commons that Britain would stand by Czechoslovakia if France did the same. All these promises of guarantees, however, did not change the fact that France and Britain not only did not come to Czechoslovakia's defense, but even assumed the opposite role of pressuring that little state to succumb to Hitler's demands. More than that, after the Munich Pact of September 1938, France and England undertook again to guarantee the new borders of the truncated Czechoslovakia. When, however, in March 1939, Hitler took control of the so-called free part of Czechoslovakia. Britain and France issued verbal protests.

314

This is the type of world in which we live, and to all those among us who are advising Israel to accept the guarantees of our State Department instead of territorial deterrence, I would direct the following question: "who is to guarantee that the guarantor will carry out his guarantee?"

This, then, is the basic disagreement between the United States and Israel which has caused a sharp divergence of views between the two friendly nations. Israel finds herself at present beleaguered on all sides: by the Arabs, by Russia and the Communist East, by enemies in the West including leaders of the Protestant Church—and now by our own State Department. For the first time in Israel's history, the American Jewish community may have to challenge our own government with one united voice and galvanize public opinion on behalf of the struggle of the Jewish State for its very survival. This is not the same type of battle which English Jewry had to wage at the time of the Labor Government in London against Foreign Minister Bevin. The latter was an anti-Semite and a vicious antagonist to the whole idea of a Jewish State. Our present difficulty with Washington is not parallel to that chapter in Britain's history. We are not dealing here with enemies. The president of the United States is a sincere friend of Israel and has proven it in a hundred different ways. Even our secretary of state is, on the whole, well disposed to the idea of Israel's security. Nonetheless, our disagreements are deep, and unless we have the capacity to persuade our own administration to show a deeper understanding of Israel's genuine anxiety about its future in the Middle East, the peace talks will not progress and the danger of a renewal of hostilities on the Suez Canal will become very real.

The challenge of the hour, therefore, is to mobilize the American Jewish community, and to commence the battle on behalf of Zion—with tact, maturity, and persuasion, and by enlightening public opinion through presentation of solid facts until, with the help of our many friends in the House and in the Senate, we can change the atmosphere of this debate, alert America to the dangerous implications of her present stand, and achieve from Washington the necessary concessions which spell security for Israel, a state which has not known a single peaceful day in her twenty-three year old history.

With Ruth Nussbaum at a Zionist Convention, c. 1973

I hope that, on this subject, we can close our ranks within the Reform Movement, both in its rabbinic and lay constituencies. But even if some of our colleagues disagree with my analysis, this is not the time to say anything that weakens Israel's stand and strengthens the one of its opponents. The Jewish State is, at the moment, fighting for its very survival, and the least it has the right to expect of us is our identification with its problems and our commitments to its future. As partners in the most majestic undertaking in our people's history, we can do no less.

* * *

Actually, why shouldn't we give abundantly of our energies and devotion and all our empathy to the State of Israel? During the months of my sabbatical in 1968, I was particularly interested in one phase of Israel after the Six–Day War. I wanted to study and see for myself how a Jew behaves as a "conqueror." After all, this is a new phenomenon in our history, and we have not played this role since the days of the Maccabees. To my surprise, I learned that our biblical heritage of social justice and our prophetic concept of moral values motivate to this day the policies of the government as well as of the army, even in the areas of occupation.

A few examples will suffice to make this point—and I only wish that in some countries of our dispersion, in the far-flung corners of the earth, we would have been ruled by such "cruel" conquerors: the traffic which proceeded smoothly across the Allenby Bridge, taking Arabs in buses from Israel to Amman and returning them at the end of the day or by the end of the week; the import and export of goods, which moved in both directions in the midst of a war—a fact that would have aroused the envy of every Berliner, East or West; the twenty thousand students from Arab countries who were visiting their Arab relatives in the occupied areas and were taken on tours to see Israel proper; the Arabs from the West Bank who were being treated free and without charge at Hadassah and other hospitals in the Jewish State; the vocational guidance freely given to hundreds of El Fatah prisoners, so that they could learn a trade and earn some money. All these features are the deeply moving result of our Hebrew heritage and of the goodness of the Jewish heart, unparalleled anywhere in the world.

317

We have always felt, and rightly so, that Israel cannot just be a state like all others, but must be a Jewish state in spirit and in motivation. Seen in light of the incredible odds against its very survival, the small Jewish State has maintained a moral posture beyond our expectations, and is very much on the way of becoming a "Light unto the nations."

All this came to me dramatically when I was asked, one day, to visit an exhibition of paintings by Arab children in Gaza. These were paintings of Arab teenagers, found by the Israeli army when they occupied the city, and arranged in a makeshift exhibit in one of the classrooms. When I looked at the "art work" of the children, I could not help but feel the word "hatred" crying out at me from every painting: a giant Arab soldier putting his foot upon a cowering Jew and slicing his back with a long knife which he holds in his left hand, or a class of young Arab children setting fire to a kibbutz with whole families burned to ashes. This theme, in a hundred different variations, was the leitmotif of the exhibit.

Quite by chance, when I returned to Tel Aviv, I read in the Hebrew press that there was an exhibition of paintings by Jewish school children on the theme of "War and Peace." As I had just seen the Arab exhibition, I was interested to see how Israeli children interpret these words. The exhibit took place in the old Dizengoff Museum. There were hundreds of paintings. Some of them I still remember: war, to a nine-year-old boy, meant a grandmother saying kaddish over the dead members of her family; war, to an eleven year old girl, meant the sun, with a human face, shedding bitter tears when looking down upon the earth. So the theme went from wall to wall.

One entered the hall called "Shalom" to learn how a young sabra generation understands this popular word. Again, in hundreds of variations: peace, to a ten-year-old boy, meant Jewish and Arab children playing together on the playground of the school, or walking together down a street in Tel Aviv with arms around one another's shoulders; peace to a twelve-year-old girl, meant two tanks next to one another, with an Arab and an Israeli officer standing on the tanks and shaking hands with one another saying, "These we will not need anymore." In the whole exhibition, not a word of accusation, not a word of hatred—and this total absence of hatred of the Arabs is one of the most fascinating facets of Israel's society today, among the young and old alike. Reflecting upon this exhibition, one is reminded of Golda Meir's remark that the Israelis love to quote: "When peace finally comes as it must, it may be easier for us to forgive the Arabs for killing us than for the fact that they made us kill them." If this be the image of a conqueror, I am very proud to be his brother. More than that, the American Jewish community may consider itself privileged to have been singled out by Providence for the historic partnership with the Jewish State.

This topic was discussed once before. Centuries ago the prophet Jeremiah addressed the Jewish community of Babylon on the same subject. And so he admonished them:

> Ye that have escaped the sword,
> Go ye, stand not still;
> Remember the Lord from afar,
> And let Jerusalem enter your heart.
> (Jeremiah 51:50)

Indeed, we, the Auschwitz-Jerusalem generation, that escaped the Nazi sword and survived, we who made it from the fiery furnace of the concentration camp to the golden glow of the Holy City, let us not stand still but go on in the deepening of our identification with and our commitment to Israel. Let us remember the Lord who promised and fulfilled, and may Jerusalem enter our hearts.

Note on Transliteration and Citation

For transliteration of Hebrew I have chosen a consciously inconsistent procedure. The most common terms are spelled according to accepted American English practice (Torah and not Tora, *Yisrael* and not *Yisraeil*) following *Webster's Third New International Dictionary* (G. & C. Merriam: Springfield, Massachusetts, 1971). For less common words or phrases, I used—with some modification—the system found in recent liturgical publications of the Central Conference of American Rabbis. See *Gates of Prayer* (New York, 1975), p. 728.

Vowels and Consonants for Special Notice (see *Gates of Prayer*, p. 728):

a	as in 'papa' (short) or 'father' (long)
e	as in 'get' or 'the' (sheva)
eh	as in 'get' (used only at the end of a word)
i	as in 'bit' (short) or 'machine' (long)
o	as in 'often'
u	as in 'pull' (short) or 'rule' (long)
ai	as in 'aisle'
oi	as in 'boil'
ei	as in 'veil'
g	as in 'get' (hard)
ch	as in Scottish 'loch' or German 'ach'
ts ,*tz*	as in 'its'

Hebrew names which appear in transliteration in the original manuscripts or published works have been changed to reflect English practice; for example: Judah and not Yehudah. The spelling of the names of biblical books and biblical personalities follows *Holy Scriptures* (Jewish Publication Society: Philadelphia, 19171) or *TANAKH* (JPS: Philadelphia, 1985).

Similarly, the names of tractates of the Mishna and Talmud follow, with some modification, the spelling found in the translations published by the Soncino Press; see the *Index Volume to the Soncino Talmud* (London, 1952), pp. 1-2. References to tractates of the Mishna are preceded by a lower case "m" (mKiddushin), to tractates of the Babylonian Talmud *(Bavli)* with "b" (bKiddushin), and to the Jerusalem Talmud *(Yerushalmi)*—also known as the Talmud of the Land of Israel—with "y" (yKiddushin).

Quotations from the Bialik essay "Halacha and Aggada" follow, with some modifications by Max Nussbaum, the English translation of by Julius L. Siegel, (Bloch Publishing Company, 1923).

Select Bibliography

THE WRITINGS OF MAX NUSSBAUM

"How Jews Live in Germany Today." *ORT Economic Bulletin* 1:4-5 (July - October, 1940): 3-5.

"Untitled." *Why We Fight* 5 (no date): 37-40.

"Nachman Krochmal: The Philosopher of Jewish Eternity." *The Jewish Herald-Voice* 3:3 (April 10, 1941): 11, 36; and in *The American Jewish Year Book* 44 (1942): 81-92.

"Sinai-The Career of An Idea." *The Southwest Jewish Chronicle* 15:7 (July 1941): 3.

"Chosen and Called: A Sermon for Shovuos [Shavuot]." *A Set of Holiday Sermons:* 5702-1941 (UAHC): 72-78.

"Is This a Religious War?," *The National Jewish Monthly* 56:8 (April, 1942): 252, 270-271.

"*Der Veg tzu a Tzionistischer Masen-Bavegung* [The Path to a Zionist Mass-Movement]." *Dos Yiddishe Folk* (May, 1942): 5.

"Zionism Under Hitler." *Congress Weekly* 11:27 (September 11, 1942): 12-15.

"In Quest of Eternal Values." *The Reconstructionist* 12:5 (April 19, 1946): 9-17.

"Congress Ideology Re-Defined." *Congress Weekly* 13:1 (May 24, 1946): 5-6.

"'Israel'—The Career of a Name." *Congress Weekly* 19:18 (May 19,1952): 6-8; also appeared in *Jewish Affairs* 5:8 (August, 1952): 4-7.

"Jews in the Motion Picture Industry: How Jewish Are They?" *The Reconstructionist* 18:15 (November 28, 1952): 25-29.

"*Eretz Yisrael, Galut* and *Chutz La'Aretz,* in Their Historic Settings." *CCAR Yearbook 62* (1952): 489-509.

"Hail, The Marrano: A Sermon for Yom Kippur Eve." *A Set of Holiday Sermons:* 1955-56 - 5716 (UAHC): 16-24.

"Can Conservative and Reform Judaism Merge: a Symposium; Comments by Max Nussbaum." *The Reconstructionist* 22:14 (November 16, 1956): 11-12.

"Israel's Contributions to American Jewry." *The American Zionist* (November-December, 1958): 8.

"Charles Henry Churchill: A Christian Advocate of Zionism." *Recall* 1:3 (1960): 40-43.

"Address by Max Nussbaum." *The Dropsie College for Hebrew and Cognate Learning Addresses* (April 18, 1961): 5-10.

"The Zionist Movement in Search of an Image." *American Zionist* (June 29, 1960).

"The Need for a United Jewry." *Bnai Zion VOICE* 34:2 (December, 1960): 7, 9.

"The Jewish Community Today and Tomorrow: What Kind of Leadership Do We Need?" *The Jewish Teacher* 30:4 (April, 1962): 3-7.

"Integration Without Assimilation." *American Judaism* 12:1 (Fall, 1962): 12-13, 53.

"The Future of the Zionist Movement" (Hebrew). *Bitzaron: The Hebrew Monthly of America* 48: 5 (April, 1963): 11-14, 18.

"Bonn, Arabs and the State Department." *The American Zionist* 55:6 (March-April 1965): 9.

"What Does Zionism Mean To The Young American Jew?" *The American Zionist* 56:3 (November 1966): 13-14.

"Whither Germany?" *World Jewry* 2:10 (March/April 1967): 6-7.

"The Glory and the Challenge." *The American Zionist* 57:10 (June, 1967): 11-12.

"The Need for an Alternative." *Israel Magazine* 1:5 (1968): 38-41.

"Ministry Under Stress: A Rabbi's Recollections of Nazi Berlin." *Gegenwart im Rückblick.* Edited by Herbert A. Strauss and Kurt R. Grossmann. Heidelberg: Lothar Stiehm Verlag. 1970: 239-247.

"Reform Judaism Appraises the Relationship of American Jewry to the State." *CCAR Journal* (June, 1971): 9-21.

"Mein Leben in Amerika." *Emuna Horizonte* 6:5 (October, 1971): 353-356.

Index

Germany, xiv, 5, 9, 11-18, 20,
79, 89, 101, 114-115, 121-122,
173, 179, 187-188, 190, 192,
194-206, 208-214, 216, 219-
220, 224-225, 227, 237, 240-
243, 266-267, 288, 314, 323-
324
Goethe, Johann Wolfgang, 8,
15, 126-127
Goldmann, Nahum, 171
Goldwyn, Samuel, 16
Graetz, Heinrich, 230
Grass, Guenter, 202
Great Britain, 150, 176, 241,
314-315
Greenleigh, Arthur, 124
Grueber, Reverend Heinrich,
202

Habe, Hans, 142
Halacha, 279, 281-285, 288, 299,
307, 310-311, 322
Halprin, Rose, 171
ha-Levi, Judah, 1, 234, 266
Hanukkah, 1, 40, 49-51, 55-56
Harriman, Averell, 200
Hartmann, Nicolai, 234
Hebrew Union College, xiii, xv,
1, 18, 275
Hegel, Georg Wilhelm F., 68,
73, 229-231, 233-235
Herzl, Theodor, 1, 7, 69, 166,
168-171, 181, 267, 299, 305
Hitler, Adolf, 11, 22, 80, 93, 107,
109-110, 118-119, 121-122,
135, 150, 160, 188-192, 194,
197-198, 203, 206, 215, 219-
220, 236-237, 240, 244, 250,
267, 308, 314, 323
Hoelderlin, Friedrich, 65
Hollywood, California, x-xi, xiii-
xv, 2, 13, 15-17, 19, 22-23,
129, 259, 269-271, 275-276,
291
Holocaust, xvi, 97, 103, 135,
163, 204, 250
Horodenko, Nachman of, 228
Hussein, Rashid, 176
Hutchins, Robert Maynard, 39

Ibn Ezra, Abraham, 229
Inquisition, 33, 45

Iran, 20, 47, 314
Iraq, 79, 160, 174, 200
Israel, see State of Israel

Jacoby, Johann Georg, 126
Jeanne d'Arc, 69
Jerusalem, xiv, 20, 86, 96-98,
104-106, 118, 130, 152, 174,
206, 220, 225, 248, 253-257,
281, 291-293, 309, 312-313,
319, 322
Jessel, George, 273
Jesus of Nazereth, 57, 221
Jewish Theological Seminary,
Breslau, 9
Jewish Theological Seminary,
New York, 19, 307
Johnson, Lyndon Baines, 22, 59,
200
Jolson, Al, 5, 16
Jurieux, Pierre, 290, 291

Kant, Immanuel, 14, 221, 229
Kaplan, Mordechai, 18, 21, 83
Kennedy, John, 59
Khrushchev, Nikita S., 161, 194,
281
Kiesinger, Kurt, 201-202
King, Martin Luther, 17, 21, 46
Kissinger, Henry, 59-60
Klal Yisrael, 261, 303
Klatzkin, Yaacov (Jacob), 173,
178
Krochmal, Nachman, 225, 227-
236, 323
Kroner, Richard, 234
Landauer, Gustav, 305
Langallarie, Marquis de, 290-
291
Leibowitz, Isaiah, 186
Lessing, Gotthold Ephraim,
226-229
Letteris, Meir, 229
Levin, Shmaryahu, 259
Levinsohn, Isaac Ber, 227-229,
236
Leyte, 120
Liberalism, 11, 16, 81, 226-228
Little Rock, 41
Locarno, Pact of, 314
Louis XIII, 289
Lowell, James Russell, 46

Suez Campaign, 130, 198
Synagogue, xiii, xv, 8, 36-38, 40-
   43, 53, 56, 80, 88, 98-99, 101-
   102, 104-105, 118-119, 134,
   149, 153, 185, 190, 217-219,
   222-223, 257, 269-271, 284-
   286, 303, 307-308, 310
Synagogue Council of America,
   36

Taylor, Elizabeth, 16
Tel Aviv, 40, 318
Teller, Edward, 100
Temple Israel of Hollywood,
   xiii, xv, 2, 5, 13-15, 18-22, 60,
   271-273
Tessier (Teshow), Ernest, 89-90
Todd, Michael, 16
Toledano, Daniel ben Joseph, 50
Toledano, Samuel, 50
Truman, Harry, 296

U. S. Department of State, 18,
   160, 162, 179, 195, 198, 200,
   312, 315, 324
Union of American Hebrew
   Congregations, xv, 18-20, 275
United Jewish Welfare Fund,
   270, 286
United Nations, 35, 40, 43, 50,
   52, 57, 78, 94, 100, 120, 122,
   160, 174, 181, 185, 188, 193-
   194, 205, 312

United States, x, 3, 13, 18, 22,
   114, 118-126, 128, 141, 151,
   153-154, 156, 158-159, 161-
   165, 171, 174, 178-179, 183,
   188-189, 193-195, 197, 200,
   203-204, 217, 236, 240, 259,
   263, 274, 276, 279, 284, 295-
   297, 299, 304, 309-315
Universalism, 257
Urbach, Efrayim E., 186

Ventura, Moise, 292
Vico, Giambattista, 231
Voltaire, François M. de, 221

Wagner, Richard, 221-222
Weiss, Isaac Hirsch, 235
Weltsch, Robert, 237
Wilkie, Wendell, 120
Wise, Stephen S., xiv, 13-15, 21,
   307

Yiddish, 3, 8, 251, 259, 297, 302
Yom Kippur, 21, 42, 53, 67, 83,
   88-89, 91, 98-99, 103, 105, 323

Zionism, xiii-xiv, 3, 7-8, 10-11,
   13, 17-20, 32, 107-110, 140-
   143, 147-149, 151, 155-173,
   176-178, 180-184, 198, 235-
   244, 259, 267, 288-290, 293,
   305-307
Zunz, Leopold, 227-229, 236

328